Communications and
National Integration in
Communist China

MICHIGAN STUDIES ON CHINA

Published for the Center for Chinese Studies
of the University of Michigan

*The research on which this book is
based was supported by the*
CENTER FOR CHINESE STUDIES
*at the University of Michigan.
It is published as part of a series,
Michigan Studies on China.*

NUMBER 2

Communications and National Integration in Communist China

ALAN P. L. LIU

UNIVERSITY OF CALIFORNIA PRESS

BERKELEY, LOS ANGELES, LONDON 1971

University of California Press
Berkeley and Los Angeles, California
University of California Press, Ltd.
London, England
Copyright © 1971, by
The Center for Chinese Studies, University of Michigan
International Standard Book Number: 0-520-01882-6
Library of Congress Catalog Card Number: 79-142050
Printed in the United States of America

To
ITHIEL de SOLA POOL and LUCIAN W. PYE

Contents

Foreword by Ithiel de Sola Pool   *ix*

Preface   *xvii*

1. The Analytical Framework:
   Mass Communication and National Integration   *1*
2. Social Infrastructure   *12*
3. Ideology of Mass Persuasion   *25*
4. The Communication Process:
   The Formal Organization of Propaganda   *34*
5. Mass Campaigns   *87*
6. Radio Broadcasting   *118*
7. The Press   *130*
8. Book Publishing   *147*
9. The Film Industry   *157*
10. Patterns of Reception   *168*
11. Conclusions   *174*

Appendices   *183*

Notes   *203*

Bibliography   *215*

Index   *223*

Map of Railways and Highways Built in the Early Years
of the Communist Regime   *15*

Foreword

Seldom in human history, and never in as unmechanized a society as China's, has so much agitation reached as many people as during Mao's experiment at remolding man by mass persuasion.

For social scientists contemporary China offers something like a laboratory test of the limits of what propaganda can do. The question of the limits of persuasion has appeared in many guises. An early form—at least as early as the myth of the wolf children—was the issue of nature versus nurture: to what extent is man at birth frozen into a mold of what he will become, and to what extent does he take form according to what he is taught and told. A normative form of the same question is, how to teach; what can pedagogy do to develop a student's knowledge or skills?

In the West, since World War I, the same question appears regarding propaganda or advertising. In that war, leaflets by the millions, capitalizing on Wilsonian idealism, were dropped over German lines. When Germany lost, her nationalists claimed that she had not failed in battle, but had been "schwindeled" out of victory by propaganda promises. In support of this myth, there evolved in interwar Germany a large body of literature extolling the power of propaganda.

In the United States at the same period, a parallel literature emerged on behalf of advertising. Advertisers advertised their ability to influence a public that was said to have a mean intelligence no higher than that of a twelve-year-old.

But side by side with this myth of "The Hidden Persuaders," there emerged in American social criticism an opposite set of cliches expressing the frustrations of those who tried to educate for good causes. Effort after effort to inform the public failed despite the heroic efforts of true believers to dent the indifferences of the masses. A classic study of a public information campaign in Cincinnati, combined with a survey of public knowledge about the United Nations before and after, revealed essentially no learning, no change, despite massive propaganda inputs.[1]

Can it be that the much feared hidden persuaders are really paper tigers? Do they attract billions of dollars from hard-headed advertisers and persuade no one? Clearly not. Persuasion sometimes works, but when and under what circumstances?

Experimental psychologists have produced a substantial literature on the conditions of effective persuasion as they appear in the laboratory. Experiments deal with the effects of repetition, of one-sided versus two-sided presentations, of explicitness or implicitness, of source credibility. But as Carl Hovland, the creator of much of this experimental knowledge, has pointed out, what is found in the laboratory is not often found in the field.[2] In an address which compared his own work with that of the sociologist Paul Lazarsfeld, Hovland noted that in virtually every laboratory experiment, a persuasive stimulus has an effect, while in sociological studies in the field, the usual finding is no effect. In Paul Lazarsfeld's studies of American presidential campaigns on which tens of millions of dollars are spent, the main conclusion was that few voters are converted and most votes are predictable in June.[3] There are plausible explanations offered by Hovland for this conflict in findings. In the field, the free citizen chooses to expose himself mainly to propaganda with which he already agrees. Selective attention makes the audience in real life less amenable to persuasion.

Thus in various ways social scientists in the West have concerned themselves with the problem of the limits of mass persuasion.

Dr. Liu shows us that in a different guise that issue appears as central in Chinese Communist politics and ideology too. Hidden behind the party curtains, there has apparently raged a bitter debate about it between bureaucratic elements and the Maoist left-wing. The bureaucrats, as Dr. Liu tells us, had limited faith in mass persuasion. They believed that the political

consciousness of the masses could not be precipitated by agitation. "These leaders," we read in this book, "believed that a
long period of education was needed to cultivate a degree of
intellectual sophistication in the people." Mao and his disciples,
on the other hand, believed that "sheer political agitation can
bring forth a new world outlook in the constricted mind of the
peasantry." Maoists seem to believe that the mass media coupled
with grass roots oral participation could transform one-fourth
of the human race. They act on the assumption that incessant
meetings, discussion groups, little red books, and blaring loudspeakers can change men and society in fundamental ways.

The view of the bureaucratic wing was in agreement with
that of the Russian Communists, whose past experience in
propaganda and mass communication provided them with their
model. The Maoists were the innovators, or in communist
jargon, deviationists. In goals, the Chinese Communists of either
wing differed but little from their Bolshevik mentors. In both
Russia and China, the Marxist doctrine which said the workers
have no fatherland, had been transformed into a vehicle of
nationalism. Dr. Liu, in this volume, demonstrates how the
Party and its agencies helped China achieve a measure of national integration. In both Russia and China, the goal was to
modernize a peasant population for the sake of nation building.
In both countries, the Communists believed that to achieve this
goal they had to change the state of consciousness of hundreds
of millions of traditional peasants.

Beyond that shared goal, differences emerge. Lenin had no
use for the "idiocy" of rural life. While the Soviets like the
Chinese tried to keep people down on the farm when they had
no room for them in the cities, for the Soviets that was an ex-
pedient. But Mao's peasant orientation was more than that.
The moving of millions of Chinese from the city to rural communes expresses a populist, rural, anti-intellectual, anti-urban
doctrine. In the Bolshevik view the peasants can be more than
passive followers of a revolution made in the cities. In Maoist
doctrine they are the instrument of the revolution.

To a Bolshevik the Maoist conviction that backward peasants,
by believing the right thoughts (those of Mao), could change a
nation irrespective of the development of its productive forces

and social structure is the heresy of voluntarism, one of the various deviations in the Bolshevik canon. As Dr. Liu tells us, voluntarism was rejected by the Chinese Communist bureaucrats too. But the left wing, the Maoists, can be fairly described as voluntarists.

Dr. Liu traces for us the sequence of shifting postures as the political pendulum in China has swung between left and right. The years from 1948 to 1953 were years of revolution and of leftist attacks on what remained of the past society. From 1953 to 1957, on the other hand, were the years of consolidation and the growth of a new communist bureaucratic structure.

Mao's first major experiment in voluntarism was the Great Leap Forward in 1958, which sought to reverse China's course toward conventional bureaucratic methods of development. Backyard furnaces were to produce what factories produce elsewhere. Communes were to replace for the peasants the millennia-old links of family and village. With the failure of the Leap, Mao's opponents temporarily forced acceptance of a policy of economic reconstruction and bureaucratic regularization. But Chairman Mao did not take defeat for long. By 1963 his counter-attack had begun, and in 1966 he launched the Cultural Revolution, a second attempt to transform China by exhortation and to replace the routines of the bureaucracy by enthusiasm.

How can we understand the Maoist hysteria? As with any complex social phenomenon, explanations are numerous. Mao's repeated attempts to storm against reality and to deny the limits of politics can be explained at many levels, and validly so. Lucian Pye and Richard Solomon have examined the structure of the Chinese family and personality, and have noted both the wish-fear of disorder, and the prevalence of hatred in the culture, as well as the rebellion of sons against fathers that accompanies traditional notions of filial piety.[4] Maoist storming is the institutionalization of hatred and rebellion. Dr. Liu notes, at one point, that in contrast to the elite Confucian tradition, Chinese popular culture (which Mao extolled) has always emphasized conflict. Another interpretation presented by Paul Hiniker uses dissonance theory and views the Cultural Revolution as an attempt to prove by proselytizing the rightness of the first failed attempt, the Great Leap Forward. Proselytizing he argues, was necessary to prove that the first failure did not evidence foolishness. Dr. Liu in this volume finds in both Mao's personality and in ideology parts of the explanation, but he also sees in the Maoist reliance on propaganda a partly successful attempt to cope with a real problem under circumstances where other resources were lacking.

The real problem was the national integration of a backward country almost totally lacking the prerequisite conditions for the creation of a nation: a common language, adequate roads and railroads to tie the land surface together, literate people capable of communicating over distance, an effectively organized bureaucracy to govern the nation, and radios, newspapers, telephones, and telegraph to provide normal modern communication.

To an extraordinary extent, Chinese efforts surmounted these obstacles by creating a novel and innovative mass communication system at fantastically low capital costs, though very high labor costs. During mass campaigns, discussion meetings attended weekly or more often by hundreds of millions of people substituted for scarce newspapers, magazines, and books. A highly economical wired loudspeaker system that reached almost all Chinese villages substituted for radios that even in battery-transistor form would have been too expensive. The wired radio network also provided secure communication for military mobilization for much of the country, and did double duty as a telephone system for official business. Movies are shown in fantastic number by mobile projection teams who may move the equipment by bicycle. Newspapers are rented by the hour at the post office to people too poor to buy them. Confidential information bulletins brought by delivery boy and picked up again after being read tell the cadres what is going on in the world. During campaigns the walls are covered by *tatzpao*—posters with short, handwritten, large-character slogans—which everyone is asked to write.

In most respects both the Great Leap and the Cutural Revolution were failures. Dr. Liu leaves the reader with little doubt that the future, after Mao, lies with the bureaucratic wing whose propaganda strategy was far more conventional—a large structure of professionalized newspapers; a press service; the New

China News Agency; a Ministry of Culture; a Propaganda Department of the Central Committee with various sections; and a national radio structure based on Radio Peking. Yet transitory and unsuccessful as Mao's efforts to replace these structures with *ad hoc* mass campaigns may have been, the fact remains that they did reach virtually the entire Chinese population, and not once, but dinned repeatedly into their ears. To the extent that mass persuasion can work, it had the opportunity to do so. Despite the poverty of China the nation was successfully organized to listen. To Mao's disappointment, the power of repeated chanting of his thoughts proved insufficient. But it would be foolish to think it had no effect. We cannot as yet observe the consequences very well. The time has not yet come to draw final conclusions. But certainly whatever power mass persuasion has, it has been tested to its limits. To some degree at least, Dr. Liu tells us, it has served to create national consciousness.

Maoism represents an extreme form of a shared Communist propensity to try to shape man by agitation. What distinguishes the left from the right, the Chinese from the Soviets, the Maoist from the bureaucrats, is a matter of degree. Clearly, Mao got his thoughts from Lenin, and then embellished them.

Leninism rests on the conviction that human consciousness is politically manipulable. Certainly that is the point at which Lenin made his sharpest departure from Marx. Marx's doctrine was that the intellectual superstructure in any society is but a reflection of the state of development of the productive forces and class alignment. Persuasion plays but a minimal role in orthodox Marxism, and indeed, in the *Manifesto,* Marx relegates the Communist Party to the role of intelligent interpreter of a process that it can influence but little:

The Communists . . . do not set up any sectarian principles of their own, by which to shape and mould the proletarian movement.

The Communists are distinguished from the other working-class parties by this only: 1. In the national struggles of the proletarians of the different countries, they point out and bring to the front the common interests of the entire proletariat independently of all nationality. 2. In the various stages of development which the struggle of the working class against the bourgeoisie has to pass through, they always and everywhere represent the interest of the movement as a whole.

The theoretical conclusions of the Communists are in no way based on ideas or principles that have been invented, or discovered, by this or that would-be universal reformer.

They merely express, in general terms, actual relations springing from an existing class struggle.[5]

Lenin in *What Is to Be Done* and in *State and Revolution* turned Marx on his head. While denying any deviation from orthodoxy, Lenin argued for the crucial role of the Party in bringing the workers to socialist consciousness; all that their life experience would bring them to, Lenin believed, was trade union consciousness. It was the Party that had to lead them to the Communist revelation.

In the Soviet Union, as later on in China, agitation and propaganda have been utilized to a degree unparalleled in the non-totalitarian world. (The fascists, of course, did copy their Bolshevik mentors in this respect.) The Bolsheviks invented virtually every device that Mao has used, and intensified. The Soviets used wall newspapers, developed a wired radio system, made almost everyone attend agitation meetings at which, among other things, public newspaper reading took place. The Bolsheviks trained a large corps of oral agitators; they invented worker correspondents. They set up the apparatus of censorship, party fractions, central news agency, subscription promotion through post office, all of which the Chinese followed. However, orthodox mimicking of the Bolsheviks was represented by what the Chinese Communists did during their more bureaucratic periods of consolidation and internal construction. The crescendo of agitation that China has reached in the periods of mass campaigns was something that the Soviets never attained. It represents a step well beyond Lenin in belief in the power of mass persuasion to mold men.

Dr. Liu's book examines the organization and conduct of this agitation and propaganda, both in its normal bureaucratic manifestations and as it worked during the mass campaigns, at least up to the initiation of the Cultural Revolution.

Because in the West the mass media tend to be diverse and pluralistic, the literature on mass media growth in the non-communist world has tended to be rather non-political. The audience, its preferences and tastes, has been the favorite subject of research. The structure of media organizations and the content of media messages have been other subjects of research. Dr. Liu has done us a favor in looking at media growth in another perspective. In this book we are presented with a description of alternative patterns of media use and media organization as reflections of fundamental political strategy. By considering Mao's basic conception of human nature and his attempts at mass persuasion, Dr. Liu helps us to understand his extraordinary system of mass persuasion.

ITHIEL DE SOLA POOL

Massachusetts Institute of Technology
Cambridge, Massachusetts
November 1970

Preface

This is a study of the roles that the mass media in Communist China play in achieving national integration. Research for the study fell in two stages. Basic research on the structure and operation of the communications media in China was done at the Center for International Studies, Massachusetts Institute of Technology, from late 1963 to the beginning of 1967. It was part of a larger project on international communication sponsored by the Advanced Research Projects Agency of the Department of Defense (contract #920F–9717 and monitored by the Air Force Office of Scientific Research under contract AF 49 (638–1237). The whole project was carried out under the supervision of Professor Ithiel de Sola Pool.

The second stage of the research was carried out under the sponsorship of the Center for Chinese Studies, University of Michigan, when I joined its research staff in September 1967. In this stage of study, I concentrated on analyzing and interpreting the data already collected.

The main purpose of this book is to present the analytical and interpretive part of my research; reproduction of earlier reports is kept at minimum. I have, however, taken the opportunity to revise and update some of my original descriptions and data, particularly those dealing with the structure of the press. I have depended mainly on original Chinese Communist publications, particularly newspapers and journals. I believe that I have exhausted all sources that are publicly available in the United States and in major research institutes in Hong Kong and Taiwan. Insofar as data are available on every source and aspect of the communications media, I have traced their development from 1949 to the present.

I owe a very great debt to Professor Ithiel de Sola Pool of M.I.T., without whose patient reading and comments on my research throughout the years this book would never have been written, and to the Center for International Studies and the Department of Political Science at M.I.T. for their support of my research and study from 1963 to 1967. I am grateful also to the Center for Chinese Studies at the University of Michigan and to Dr. Alexander Eckstein, who directed the Center from 1967 to 1969, for their support of my research in its concluding stage. I would like to especially thank Professor Allen S. Whiting and Mrs. Janet Eckstein for their detailed comments on the first draft of the manuscript, and I am indebted to other teachers and colleagues for their critical comments and suggestions: Professors Lucian W. Pye, Rhoads Murphey, Richard H. Solomon, and Gayle D. Hollander. While at M.I.T. I greatly benefited from the wealth of knowledge about Communist China possessed by my friend Vincent S. King.

I am grateful to Professor Gordon Baker of the University of California, Santa Barbara, for extending to me some last-minute help to complete the book and to Martha Weir for her work in the final editing.

My research was made much easier by the help given me by these in charge of administration both in Ann Arbor and Cambridge: Jaqueline Evans, Maureen Shea, Alice Cashmen, and Karen Flitton.

Needless to say, the opinions contained in this book are mine; they do not necessarily represent the views of the two research sponsors.

Santa Barbara, California
September 1970

1

The Analytical Framework: Mass Communications and National Integration

The study of mass communications media in America has been directed mainly to statistical description and interpretations of audience behavior. This is largely because mass media in America are managed by private businesses and conducted for commercial purposes. But with the appearance of modern totalitarian states like the Soviet Union, Nazi Germany, and Communist China, where mass media have been used for overt political purposes, new research on mass media has explored interactions between the media and the total social system. A pioneering work using this new approach is Alex Inkeles' study of the media system in the Soviet Union.[1]

Since the end of the Second World War and with the proliferation of new nations in Asia and Africa, the approach which emphasizes interactions between mass media and social systems has been greatly enriched. While studies of mass media as a part of the propaganda apparatus of modern totalitarian states emphasize (perhaps excessively) the function of control, studies of the relationship between mass media and modernization or nation building in Afro-Asian nations go beyond that to deal with the role of media in various aspects of the nation-building process—such as, development of national identity, legitimization of a national government, and initiating and sustaining economic development.[2] Thus, if a totalitarian state happens also to be a developing nation, a scholar must focus on the broader political, social, and economic functions of the media in the nation-building process.

The present study is an attempt to continue exploring the complex relationship between mass media and social systems in the context of nation building. Communist China is both a totalitarian state and a developing nation. Therefore, a study of the media in China provides another opportunity to extend or consolidate our knowledge about this important relationship. Previous studies of the media system in Communist China have not adequately considered its political and social context, and thus have missed the most important part of the system: its function in the national integration of China. This aspect is the theme of the present study.[3]

The complex process of nation building has required scholars to focus on different aspects of it. Our focus will be on national integration, because it is the goal of all developing nations to achieve a new level of integration out of the dissolving old order. To begin with, the process of national integration needs to be discussed.

NATIONAL INTEGRATION: A GENERALIZATION

National integration can be conceived as occurring in two major phases—penetration and identification. In the penetration stage, the central government penetrates into regions that hitherto were autonomous politically and culturally. In this phase of integration, a central government usually employs coercive power more than any other kind of power.[4] Throughout this phase, the groundwork for various forms of cultural penetration is laid, such as the construction of modern transport to link up major regions, promotion of literacy and a common language, establishment of a system of mass communications, and a proliferation of new institutions to assimilate the young generation into the new national identity. The role of mass media in this phase of integration is to convey political authority to the people and to bring political consciousness or identity to the masses from without. The media then reflect not society but polity. In the meantime, the other integrative forces mentioned above will help the media gradually diffuse a set of common norms, values, and symbols among the population, especially the youth, so that identification, vertically between the ruler and the ruled and horizontally among citizens and groups, can be established. The predominance of coercive power will then be replaced by the power of common identification manifested in the development of a mass culture and a national language.[5] At this point, the media begin to mirror society rather than polity. With national identity sufficiently established, political leaders can enlarge feedback from society in order to gain more fundamental integration from below. This can take several forms. One of them is to loosen political control over the media completely. Another is to adjust the media, especially their content, to satisfy the growing cultural sophistication of the population.

These phases of penetration and identification in Communist China and the Soviet Union, however, also became problems of strategy to be decided by their political leaders. The problem of choosing one of the two arose in the Soviet Union in the early 1930s. Before that, the immediate need for control in an environment of social disintegration obviated any question of alternative strategies. The Communist Party in the Soviet Union (and in China, too) chose intensive political penetration as its strategy of integration in the initial years of the Soviet regime. But after a period of development, when political control over the country was no longer in danger, the leaders of the Soviet Union (and China) had to decide on a long-term integration strategy. This is the context of the changes in the Soviet policy on agitation and propaganda in the 1930s, such as the acceptance of intellectuals and managerial personnel as legitimate partners in the Soviet system and their recruitment to the propaganda apparatus, the emphasis on professionalism in journalistic work, an "educational-cultural" approach in mass indoctrination, and abandonment of the Proletcult policy in art and literature. As a result, the Soviets placed more emphasis on identification than on penetration.

Changes similar to those in the Soviet Union of the early

1930s occurred briefly in China after 1952. But debates soon developed on the top level of the Chinese Communist Party on the effectiveness and, perhaps more important, the legitimacy of this change in strategy. After a year of indecision during 1956 and 1957, the Chinese Communist Party abolished many of the changes instituted after 1952 and renewed its emphasis on political penetration, control, and regimentation.

It is one of the main theses of this book that the Cultural Revolution in Communist China represents, among other broad issues, a continuation of the debates over integration strategy among Communist leaders that first occurred in the late 1950s. The culmination of the debates in the political turmoil of the Cultural Revolution in China showed that the left-wing Chinese leaders, headed by Mao, rejected the path of identification as a basis of national integration. The destruction of the mass media in China during the Cultural Revolution represented the leftist leaders' attempt to prevent articulate social groups, especially intellectuals, from using the media to criticize the Party and to prevent non-leftist Party leaders from accommodating the wishes of these same social groups. Communist China has not yet attained the fundamental kind of national integration based on identification.

But whether a political regime chooses a strategy of penetration or identification as the basis of national integration, the role of mass media is essentially that of a facilitating agent. The effective functioning of the mass media as an integrative force depends on three interacting sets of factors: (1) the existence of a social infrastructure including a modern transport, a national language, and widespread literacy; (2) the type of political ideology; and (3) the administrative organization of the media themselves.

SOCIAL INFRASTRUCTURE

Modern transport, a national language, and widespread literacy are the grounding elements of national integration. They are also part and parcel of the all-inclusive process called modernization which is defined as "the totality of phenomena attending the transition of a society from a traditional (i.e., predominantly agrarian and rural) to a modern (i.e., industrial and urban) one." [6] But the important point is that these elements precede or accompany the development of mass media; the media cannot create national integration by themselves. The historical development of mass media in England and America shows that industrialization brought a revolution in transport, which in turn broke regional isolation. Subsequent urbanization greatly increased literacy and aided the growth of a national language. It was only after these elements had laid the foundation of social integration that mass media developed. The media reinforced the existing national unification and identity created originally by such a social infrastructure. Moreover, the media strengthened national integration in America and England by enlarging the feedback from society to the political system. Thus, the media in these two industrial nations did not really create national integration, but rather reinforced the existing integration and advanced it further.

As revolutionaries, the Communists claimed to have found a way to alter the historical process of the industrial West, a way which supposedly enables them to build society on a unique model. But with respect to the relationship between mass media and social infrastructure, the Soviet experience did not seem to break any new ground. As I shall elaborate later, the development of these social conditions in Russian society in 1917 was already quite advanced in comparison with China in 1949 and with most developing nations today. After the Bolshevik revolution, rapid industrialization in the Soviet Union strengthened and extended the existing social infrastructure much further, enabling the Soviet mass media to be institutionalized. The Soviet media, together with other modern institutions, were then able to reinforce and advance national integration by contributing to the consolidation of the Soviet political system and creating a greater degree of national identity among the Russian population, especially the young generation.[7]

In Communist China, the slow and uneven pace of industrialization after 1949 resulted in a correspondingly slow and uneven development of a social infrastructure. On the whole, the urban areas in China benefited most from the industrial programs of the Communist regime and the rural areas least. It is a main thesis of this book that, although the mass media in China helped the Communist regime extend its centralization over widespread regions and disseminate some basic facts about official ideology, the media did not succeed in creating fundamental national integration because of China's economic underdevelopment and political instability. In almost every aspect of its operation, the Chinese mass media reflected the fundamental divisions in the Chinese society, especially the urban-rural division. I will discuss this reflective aspect of the media in greater detail in later chapters.

The process of modernization in China has been going on slowly and tortuously for a long time; there is no sign that the process could be rolled back, though it could be prevented from having a smooth path forward. Politics is another matter. It is fluid and unfathomable. To examine how politics affected the media in China, we must discuss the core problem, the problem of ideology.

POLITICAL IDEOLOGY

The aspects of Chinese Communist ideology that concern us most are its conception of the functions of mass media and its general strategy of mass persuasion (or mass mobilization). We call this aspect of ideology the ideology of mass persuasion. Though formal Chinese Communist ideology includes other matters, mass persuasion is perhaps the most important idea in terms of national integration, for it determines the relationship between the leader and the led, and it determines how the Chinese people will participate in programs of national construction.

Communists in general, and Chinese Communists in particular, regard mass media as an important political instrument for national integration within the Communist ideological framework. According to the Leninist conception, the first and foremost function of mass media is to transmit the Party's or state's programs and instructions to the masses. The media, according to Lenin, are adjunct to the Party apparatus and must be controlled completely by it. Underlying this important function of mass media is the Communists' organizational approach to social mobilization. To make an organization effective, its members must be dedicated to the goals of the organization and competent in their professional skills. Similarly, the media in a Communist state must disseminate ideology and educational matter in order to transform its population into efficient and dedicated members of a Communist society.

But if unity of minds regarding the function of mass media existed among the leaders of Communist China or, for that matter, of the Soviet Union, the same cannot be said about the general strategy of mass persuasion. In the history of both regimes, there occurred debates among leaders on a proper strategy of mass persuasion in a certain period.

A fundamental issue of the debates concerned the nature of mass political consciousness. One view, held by the left-wing Party leaders, maintained that the political consciousness of the masses can be "precipitated." According to this view, firm political consciousness can be generated by intensive political indoctrination in concentrated campaigns. This group of leaders tended to rely on word-of-mouth propaganda because of its grassroots nature. The leftist leaders generally distrusted intellectuals and were contemptuous of formal cultural institutions, which they dismissed as useless at best and dangerous at worst. They were interested in mass media insofar as they could use the media to promote what they called "art and literature for workers and peasants." To the leftist leaders, any development of cultural sophistication and professionalism in the media system constituted a fundamental deviance from their goal of precipitating the political consciousness of the masses.

Yet there was another group of Party leaders who maintained that mass political consciousness could not be precipitated. These leaders believed that a long period of education was needed to cultivate a degree of intellectual sophistication in the people before they could be expected to have firm political consciousness. To the group of political leaders who held this non-leftist view on mass persuasion, political consciousness stemmed essentially from an identification from below, not intensive penetration and indoctrination from above. These leaders, however, recognized that oral agitation and campaigns were necessary during the initial years after the establishment of the revolutionary regime in order to familiarize the people with the new political order. But they emphasized that, in the long run, mass persuasion must be based on voluntary participation in mass media and that a degree of professionalism and cultural sophistication were necessary if the media were to function effectively in communicating between the leader and the led.*

The leftist ideology on mass persuasion was represented in the Soviet Union by the Proletcult school, which came into being immediately after the Bolshevik revolution and again during the early 1930s, when Stalin used mass mobilization to accelerate industrialization. But after that, Soviet policy gradually shifted from a leftist to a non-leftist view on mass persuasion. In China, Mao Tse-tung has consistently held the leftist view, and his ideology of mass persuasion is essentially a radicalized Proletcult.

Mao Tse-tung's leftist and anti-intellectual ideology had an empirical basis in the Chinese Communist revolutionary experiences. (Mao's ideology will be discussed further in Chapter 3.) Consequently, the Chinese Communist Party had developed a readymade code and system of mass persuasion to be applied to the whole Chinese mainland after 1949. This indigenous code conflicted with the intellectualism and professionalism brought forth later by the establishment of mass media. Mao's efforts to integrate the two systems or, rather, to permeate the media system with leftist ideology, ended in failure. The result was destruction of the mass media in the Cultural Revolution and revival of oral agitation and propaganda as developed in the Yenan period. In later chapters on the media in China, I will describe in some detail how the media bore the brunt of Mao's leftist ideology.

Social infrastructure and political ideology are two controlling factors in the effectiveness of mass media. But mass media are also distinctly modern institutions, and as such, they have their own institutional logic. The integrative effects of social

* For evidence of these differences in leadership thinking in Communist China, see the discussion of the propaganda apparatus in China in Chapter 4.

infrastructure and political ideology are, to a significant degree, influenced by the institutional characteristics of mass media. In the following section, I will discuss the specific institutional forms of the media in Communist China, and for that matter, in Communist nations in general.

ORGANIZATION OF MASS MEDIA

The specificity of the Communist media system can only be shown against the general characteristics of the media system in other non-Communist developing nations. The media system in developing nations has been well described elsewhere. Here, I will mention briefly some dominant characteristics.[8]

In reality, all the characteristics of mass media in non-Communist developing nations derive from one basic characteristic: their isolation in a few urban and relatively Westernized cities. This being so, the media in these nations also tend to be intellectually oriented. They appeal to a small group of people who have received some modern education. The media not only do not bridge but perpetuate existing social and cultural gaps. To the extent that the governments of these nations try to use mass media for national integration, they tend to use the negative forms of regulation and censorship rather than attempting positive integration of the media with political participation and economic development. This state of affairs is caused mainly by lack of social integration, unevenness of modernization, and absence of effective political leadership.

Against this background, the three characteristics of the Communist organization of mass media become meaningful. They are: structural integration, developmental integration, and linkage with face-to-face communication.

Structural integration refers to the integration between the territorial-administrative structure of the Communist Party, which in this case means the Chinese Communist Party, and that of the media.

Developmental integration refers to the close coordination between the stages of economic development that China went through from 1949 to 1966 and the changes of content in the mass media. This technique enabled the Communist regime to focus public opinion on the important tasks of national reconstruction in each period.

The linkage of mass media with face-to-face communication is a major innovation of the Communists. Such a linkage was made possible for China by the ability of the Communists to build a penetrative Party structure. With cadres to act as intermediaries between the media and oral communications among the masses, the Communist authority could overcome, to a certain degree, the lack of social integration—i.e., regionalism, lack of a common language, and a high illiteracy rate. The linkage between the media and word-of-mouth communication thus became a temporary substitute for social integration, which would have greatly facilitated communication through the media had it existed.

Yet, it should also be clear that this innovation of the Communists merely gave them a headstart in using the media for national integration, in contrast to other developing nations' inability to use the media effectively for the same purpose. The fundamental relationship between social integration and mass media in the process of national integration has not been changed by this organizational innovation. As will appear in later chapters, the Chinese Communists did their utmost to exploit this innovation in communication, but they were unable to create the kind of fundamental integration that has elsewhere been achieved only by a social infrastructure.

In addition to these organizational features of the mass media in China, I will also discuss the "medium characteristics" and their implications for national integration. Because radio and film are essentially oral media, they are better adapted to rural audiences than printed media. Rural residents are for the most part illiterate and lack intellectual sophistication. Thus, radio and film are media of agitation, in the Leninist sense of the word. They contribute to national integration by imparting vivid images of national symbols, disseminating basic facts about national government and politics, and focusing the attention of the masses on national reconstruction. Newspapers, journals, and books are more adapted to urban and educated residents. To use Lenin's definition again, the printed media are for propaganda. They contribute to national integration not only by complementing the work of audio-visual media, but also by providing seemingly unrelated events with an ideological (or cultural) context. In short, radio and film exhort, but press and books contextualize.

I have now described the components of the analytical framework of this book. The structure of this chapter reproduces briefly the rest of the book. Thus, I will begin the substance of the study—the actual communications process in Communist China—with discussion of social infrastructure and political ideology. Then, I will discuss the general headquarters of all the media of communication in China—the Propaganda Department of the Central Committee of the Communist Party— followed by chapters dealing with each medium: mass campaigns, radio, press, publishing, and films. The three essential parts of any mass medium—structure, content, and audience— are covered under the following five aspects: (1) integration between media organization and political structure; (2) the integration of media content with Communist ideology and integration strategy; (3) the linkage of each medium with face-to-face communication; (4) the impact of social infrastructure on each medium; and (5) the role that each medium plays in the national integration of China.

2

Social Infrastructure

Geographical unification, a national language, and literacy constitute the infrastructure for a national system of mass communication. In this chapter, I shall examine the efforts of the Chinese Communist regime to build up this infrastructure: the extension of modern transport to eradicate regionalism, the language reform program to establish a national language, and the anti-illiteracy campaigns in China after 1949.

REGIONALISM AND MODERN TRANSPORT

Historically, regionalism in China was always a haven for rebels and a nightmare for rulers. Favored by rugged terrain and primitive transport, regionalism took the form of a gross division between North and South, with further division into regional enclaves like Szechwan, Kwangtung, and Fukien in the South and Shansi and Shensi in the North. Almost every aspect of Chinese society bore the imprint of regionalism.

Perhaps in no other aspect was regionalism more conspicuous than in politics. It was manifested in the historical "regional kingdoms," which more often than not endured longer than the centralist dynasties. In the modern era, the most notorious manifestation of regionalism occurred during the warlord period (1916–1926). Regionalism probably contributed most to the survival of the Chinese Communist Party after the Nationalist-Communist split in 1927, when the Communists retreated to the interior and established "border areas" between provinces.

Regionalism was further reflected in cultural diversity. As recently as 1963, Radio Peking's schedule listed hours for "Hunan Folk Music," "Kwangtung Music," "Hanchow Music," "Shanghai Opera," and so forth. Another quite conspicuous aspect of regional diversity is the great number of dialects, which will be discussed in the next section.

These political and cultural divisions naturally gave rise to strong regional identities. Thus, after a visit in 1948 to one of the richest provinces in China, Szechwan, Barnett noted that the people there "have a regional consciousness, developed through centuries of relative isolation, which distinguishes them as Szechwanese. They think of themselves as being both Szechwanese and Chinese." [1]

The Chinese Communist leaders would not permit their ambitious program of nation-building to be thwarted by regionalism. To insure centralization, one requirement is modern roads and railways connecting the regions of China. Though modern transport will not bring cultural integration immediately, it certainly facilitates political integration. Railways and highways enable the national government to break autonomous regional political powers by sending soldiers, Party cadres, and propagandists into these regions. Through modern transport, institutions with a national orientation—such as mass media and schools which disseminate national symbols among the masses—can be set up in the hitherto isolated regions. This first step of physically linking the nation together by transport and organization is crucial.

From 1949 to 1958, the development of modern transport in China seemed to be aimed more at political integration than at economic development. Major railways and highways were designed for two purposes: to link the western and southwestern regions with central China and with the eastern and coastal areas; and to break up regional enclaves.

In 1950, three new railways were built—one linking the city of Tienshui with Lanchow in Kansu province in Northwest China; one from Chengtu to Chungking in the rugged terrain of Szechwan; and one from the border city of Laipin in Kwangsi province to Hanoi in North Vietnam (see map). As Alexander Eckstein has pointed out, the first railroad ran "through undeveloped dead space which can have only long-run economic significance." [2]

Almost all the major railroads built in the first eight years of the regime were in West China. In 1952, construction for the railroad running from Lanchow to Tihua in Sinkiang began. This line was significant politically. It extended the only east-west railway, the Lunghai railroad, all the way to the border area of Sinkiang. It thus facilitated Peking's effort to assimilate the minority race in Sinkiang into a Greater China. Eventually it was to be extended across the border to the Trans-Siberia line, linking China with the Soviet Union.

In 1955, a major railroad linking Inner Mongolia with the rest of China was begun, running from Lanchow to Paotou. The year 1957 saw three major landmarks in railway construction. One was the completion of a railroad of great significance to China's coastal defense, the line that runs from the city of Yingtan in Kiangsi province to the coastal city of Hsiamen in Fukien province. Through this railroad, Fukien province was linked with the main north-south railway and with other lines connecting major cities like Shanghai, Canton, and Nanking. The second important construction was the Yangtze River bridge in Wuhan. In the past, the main north-south railroad that links Inner Mongolia, Manchuria, Peking, and Canton had had to be interrupted in Wuhan for ferrying over the Yangtze River.[3] The third important event of 1957 was the completion of the railway that runs from Chengtu in Szechwan province to Paochi in Shensi province. The traditional geographical isolation of Szechwan was effectively broken. As a Communist report stated it, in the past the rich products of Szechwan were shipped to Northwest China in a roundabout way by the Wuhan-Peking railroad, but now a direct link between Szechwan and the Northwest had been made.[4] In 1959, another bridge over the Yangtze River at Chungking was completed that facilitated the link between Szechwan and the rest of Southwest China.

After 1958, the regime shifted its emphasis to East China. First, the entire north-south railway stretching from north of

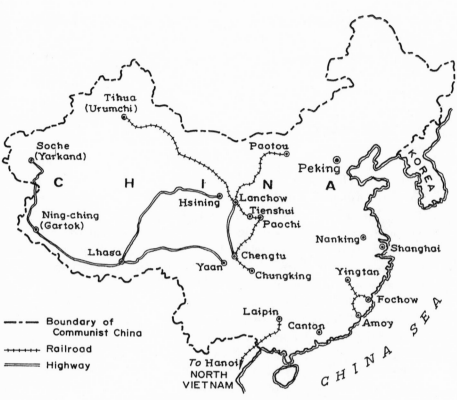

RAILROADS AND HIGHWAYS BUILT IN THE EARLY YEARS
OF THE CHINESE COMMUNIST REGIME

Harbin to Changsha, via Peking and Wuhan, is now double tracked, and so are the east-west Lunghai line from Chengchow to Paochi and the line from Peking to Paotou. At the same time, emphasis was shifted to building local transport to serve local needs.

The railway construction discussed above did not, however, cover the large area of Southwest China, including Chinghai, southern Sinkiang, Tibet, and western Yunnan, where the minority races reside. There the Communists built highways. The total mileage of highways in these areas increased from some 8,000 in 1950 to 20,000 in 1954. Over half of these new highways were built in areas where the minority races are concentrated. The main ones are the 2,255-mile highway from Yaen in Kweichou province, via Szechwan, to the capital city of Tibet, Lhasa; the 2,006-mile highway from Hsining in Chinghai province to Lhasa; and the road running from Chengtu to Lanchow, which further broke Szechwan's geographical isolation. In 1957, the 1,179-mile highway that runs from Soche in Sinkiang to Ningching in Tibet was completed.

In sum, the modern transportation system that the Chinese Communists built from 1950 to 1960 was extensive in type, linking regions and major cities. The system's major function was to extend central administration to those regions which had traditionally been isolated from the center. The coercive and persuasive powers of the national government were then brought to bear on the people of these regions.

The extensive highways and railways linking China proper with West and Southwest China undoubtedly also had economic and cultural impacts. They brought modern institutions like schools, hospitals, libraries, and mass media to the people of hitherto isolated regions. But immediate effects were limited to the few cities; the majority of the rural population there remained untouched. The addition of feeder lines to link villages with regional cities was a post-1960 phenomenon. This type of transport will deliver the *coup de grace* to regionalism in China, for economic transformation in the rural areas will ultimately orient people to a national identity and culture. However, this type of transportation still remains inadequate in China.

LANGUAGE REFORM

One of the clearest manifestations of regionalism is language diversity. The Chinese leaders are keenly aware of this serious obstruction to national integration. Chou En-lai said in 1958:

This diversity in dialects has an unfavorable effect on the political, economic, and cultural life of our people. From time to time, government workers are transferred from the north to the south, university students in the south are appointed to places in the north, and workers in the coastal cities go to the interior to reinforce their fellow-workers in industrial construction. Without a common speech, we shall, to greater or lesser extent, meet with difficulties in our national construction. It often happens that the listener fails to understand an important report or an important class lecture due to the dialectal barrier. Radio and the cinema are powerful publicity instruments. But as our common speech has not yet been made universal, their effectiveness in the districts where only local dialects are spoken is inevitably limited.[5]

By 1949, there was already an incipient national language in China. The spoken part of it was generally known as "common speech" (*pu-tong-hua*), which was a revised Mandarin. The written part was called *pai-hua*, which literally means "the vernacular language in its written form." [6] The problems of language reform consisted mainly of enlarging the use of the common speech among the Chinese people and simplifying the *pai-hua*, which is still based on difficult characters. The latter involved three things: first, limiting the number of characters in use by discarding the difficult and rarely used ones; second; simplifying the character structures; and, third, creating a Latinized alphabet.

In 1952, the government gathered scholars and language specialists and set up the Committee for the Reform of the Chinese Language to direct the overall efforts at language reform. This organization's first measure was to limit the number of characters used in publications. A list of the 1,500 most frequently used characters was published. The list was designed mainly for beginners in the Chinese language. Publications intended for popular reading were supposed to confine their usage of characters within this list as much as possible.[7]

In October 1956, the committee called a conference on the standardization of the Chinese language, which was attended by representatives of linguistic, literary, theatrical, broadcasting, and publishing professions. The conference resolved that the common speech would be actively promoted all over the nation from then on. A mass campaign to learn the common speech soon began. The Central Working Committee for Popularizing the Common Language was set up. Working branches of this central agency were established in twenty-two provinces and municipalities.[8] The first people to be trained in common speech were primary school teachers. In the same year, the committee on language reform published a list of 1,100 characters to be discarded from use.[9]

In 1956, two other major steps in language reform were taken. First, a scheme for simplifying Chinese characters was published. In all, 355 simplified characters were put to use in newspapers and journals.[10] Second, the draft scheme for a Chinese phonetic alphabet was also published. The Communists were particularly self-conscious about alphabetizing Chinese characters because this measure, more than any other, exposed the regime to the charge that they were destroying Chinese culture. To show that this scheme had popular support, the draft alphabet was given to the most authoritative mass organization in Communist China, the Chinese People's Political Consultative Council, for discussion. Through this mass organization and its regional branches, discussions of the draft scheme were carried on in twenty-two provinces, two autonomous regions, and some thirty cities. According to its own report, the committee on language reform received 4,300 letters containing suggestions, some from overseas Chinese, from February to September 1956.[11]

In his speech to the Chinese People's Political Consultative Council in January 1958, Chou En-lai emphasized that the alphabet was "not to replace the Chinese characters"; rather, its primary function was "to give the pronunciation of these characters."[12] Having made the point that the Communist government had no intention of destroying Chinese culture by doing away with characters, Chou went on to list other functions of the phonetic alphabet: to serve as a useful means of

teaching and learning the common speech; to serve as a common basis on which the minority races in China might create
or reform their written languages; and to help foreigners learn
Chinese and thus promote international cultural exchange.

By 1958, the language reform policy had been finally set. It
consisted of simplification of the Chinese characters, popularization of common speech, and use of the phonetic alphabet in publications. Progress in these three reform measures has been uneven. Popularization of the common speech has been most vig-
orously carried out. In 1956, the Central Broadcasting Station in
Peking and other provincial radio stations sponsored special
programs to teach the common speech, and more than two million people were reported to have listened to these programs.[13]
In Peking, Chekiang, Kiangsu, Hupei, Kwangsi, Szechwan, and
Yunnan, books on learning and teaching the common speech
were published; more than two million copies were sold in
1956. Based on statistical information from sixteen provinces
and municipalities in 1956, 27,493 primary school teachers all
over the nation had been sent to Peking for training in the
common language.[14] But even with these efforts, the result was
not satisfactory to the government. After the peak of the campaign in 1956, one source stated, the movement lost momentum
and in some areas the work stopped totally. Even in Peking,
half of the new high school teachers who came in 1957 from
other regions could not speak the common speech fluently.[15]

Undoubtedly, the group that adapted to language reform
most readily and effectively were primary school pupils. In an
inspection tour (possibly in 1956) in Sian, former Education
Minister Chang Hsi-jo found that many primary school pupils
there were speaking the common language very well.[16] Adults
resisted learning the new language rules for both physical and
psychological reasons. The most significant psychological obstacle was the ubiquitous regionalism. Wu Yu-chang, director
of the Committee for the Reform of the Chinese Language,
cited an interesting example of this:

At present, there still exists a tendency not conducive to the popularization of the common speech. For instance, some people sneer at, instead of encouraging, those who learn to speak the common speech.

When children speak it at home, some parents rebuke them for "showing off their Peking jargon," or "forgetting their native tongue." [17]

The simplification of characters met opposition from vested interests. Chou En-lai mentioned that after the publication of the scheme for simplification of characters,

some people had declared that "they would become illiterates." Such regrets or misgivings are unnecessary. Many of the simplified characters are familiar to us. How can we become "illiterate"? Of course, some characters may be unfamiliar. But if we use a little mental effort, the difficulties will be overcome. In the interest of the broad mass of the working people and the millions of children, the intellectuals should not begrudge the little extra thinking involved.[18]

The reform measure that has had the least success so far is alphabetization. Paul Serruys notes: "It is in the field of alphabetization that there have been the most signs of wavering and indecision" on the part of the Communist regime.[19] For a system of alphabetization to be effective, there must be a sufficient standardization of the common spoken language, which China has yet to accomplish. Thus, national leaders balked at the proposal to substitute an alphabetic orthographic script for the Chinese language. As things stand now, the government has merely ordered that all names on signs for institutes, schools, shops, meeting halls, streets, railroad stations, and government bureaus as well as all names of reviews and journals be written out alphabetically together with the Chinese characters.[20]

Though the results of language reforms fell far short of the Party's goals, a significant number of political and ideological terms have been widely diffused among the population. Western scholars who have interviewed refugees from China have been impressed by their respondents' assimilation of basic Marxist terms and jargon.[21] These commonly accepted terms not only enlarge the diffusion of a national language, not to mention the enrichment of the content, but also heighten a sense of national identity among the people, especially among the young. That is now corroborated by the Red Guard newspapers, which show that Chinese youth has indeed assimilated a great deal of the Communist political jargon, that a new political and national language has apparently been merged into the common speech.

THE ANTI-ILLITERACY CAMPAIGN

The main purpose of language reform in Communist China has been to increase literacy. Since 1952, the government has initiated numerous literacy campaigns for adults who cannot afford to return to the regular educational system. These campaigns took the form of "storming the fortress," and Party leaders hoped that such methods would yield quick results. In 1952, for example, a mass campaign of learning characters was initiated based on a simple scheme of phonetic transcript. The press began to report fantastic progress. In Peking, it was reported, workers in factories learned 1,800 characters within 38 hours, peasants learned 1,638 characters within 48 hours, and other residents learned 1,800 characters within 28 hours.[22] In Tientsin, a committee on character-learning was set up, and it planned to turn 320,000 illiterates in the city into literates within less than six months.[23]

The campaign for eradicating adult illiteracy continued in 1953, concentrated mainly in the cities. It was reported that 950,000 workers and other city residents participated in literacy classes all over the nation. Out of these, 200,000 were made literate, which means that they learned 1,200 to 2,000 characters, adequate for reading elementary books.[24]

In the countryside, adult peasants were organized into "winter schools" to learn characters, taking advantage of the fact that their work load was relatively light in winter. In 1953, some twenty million peasants were reported to be enrolled in these schools.[25] In 1955, another mass campaign was launched, but this time the emphasis was on the peasantry. This shift in policy seems to be correlated with the first wave of collectivization in agriculture, when the agricultural producers' cooperatives were organized. The provinces began to publish ambitious plans for turning masses of peasants into literates. Shangtung province pledged in November 1955 to turn 400,000 out of

4,000,000 peasants into literates by April 1956; Honan, 700,000 out of 4,000,000; and Liaoning, 220,000 out of 1,000,000 peasants.[26]

These plans exemplified the Chinese Communist conviction that political mobilization can transform Chinese society in fundamental ways within a fantastically short period. They were destined to fail. The authoritative *People's Daily (Jen-min Jih-pao)* reported in 1957 that in Liaoning, Shantung, Shansi, and Hupei, fifty percent of the original anti-illiteracy plans were accomplished by December 1956. In some areas, the paper reported, only ten percent of the planned number of peasants were enrolled in winter schools, and in other areas winter schools did not open at all.[27] The effectiveness of the winter schools was not mentioned.

Thus, the overall illiteracy rate in China remained high throughout the fifties and sixties. A report in 1955 stated that of 120,000,000 "youth" in China, only 4,000,000 were studying in regular schools. The remaining 116,000,000 worked in industry, agriculture, and administration. Among these, about seventy percent were illiterate or semi-literate. Half of the members of the Young Communist League were illiterate.[28] In an anonymous press report in 1957, it was said that in some areas the illiteracy rate was sixty to seventy percent among peasants in the age group from fourteen to forty. In other areas, the report said, the rate of illiteracy among peasants was even higher than that.[29] In this relatively sober report, it was projected that twelve years would be needed to eradicate illiteracy among the youth. A year later, in harmony with the spirit of the Great Leap Forward, the government claimed that, in fact, illiteracy in China could be eliminated within five to seven years.[30] Soon, the press was again filled with ambitious pledges from the provincial authorities to eliminate illiteracy in great strides. Yet by the end of 1958, when the Great Leap program was already experiencing drawbacks, a report stated that, based on an investigation of ten rural districts, the average rate of literate peasants lapsing back to illiteracy was thirty percent.[31]

Beginning in 1960, China again started campaigns of character learning based on phonetic alphabets. In 1964, Communist China's most prominent scholar-politician, Kuo Mo-jo,

Director of the Academy of Sciences, wrote a long article in the *People's Daily* summarizing the Japanese experience of language reform and urging the Chinese to learn from Japan. On illiteracy, Kuo said:

For more than ten years, we have been trying to eradicate illiteracy among the people. But our motherland is still a nation with masses of illiterates and semi-literates. Some counties once claimed that they had become literate counties. Yet soon they lapsed back to being illiterate counties. In order to improve the people's cultural standard and work efficiency, simplification and modernization of characters and language is a most important task.[32]

Today, we still have no exact information on the literacy rate in Communist China. Kuo's qualitative statement that "our motherland is still a nation with masses of illiterates and semi-literates" is the most recent and official statement on the subject.

The promotion of literacy, like language reform, is not solely a technical problem. Both measures are connected with the fundamental problems of industrialization and of changing people's attitudes. Whether one wants to be literate is a highly individual decision, one which is greatly affected by situational changes. When industrialization and urbanization advance steadily, many individuals are compelled to decide to be literate. Instead of perceiving this basic process of social change as mutual adjustment between individual decisions and situational changes, the Chinese Communists rely on political mobilization in the form of mass campaigns to promote universal literacy, when in fact the situation in rural areas rarely requires literacy. This blind application of the Soviet method of "storming the fortress" to a backward society such as rural China has limited effectiveness.

Of the three social conditions comprising the infrastructure of mass media that have been discussed here, certainly the Communist government has achieved its greatest success in the physical linkage of the whole nation. To be sure, regionalism in China has not yet been eliminated. But it is clear that the kind of regional autonomy that existed before 1949 has been weakened by the Communist regime. Success in political unification has enabled the Communist regime to establish a national network of mass communication controlled effectively by the Party.

The achievements in the creation of a national language and the eradication of illiteracy are less spectacular. The deficiency in these two social factors certainly has limited the integrative functions of the mass media; I will point out later, the media in China have fully reflected this deficiency.

3

Ideology of Mass Persuasion

The opinions of the Chinese leadership on the conception of the masses' political consciousness are divided. Over the years, the leftist view on mass persuasion has increasingly gained ascendance. Since this change of strategy greatly affected the operations of mass media, the leftist ideology of mass persuasion will be discussed in some detail in this chapter. This ideology has three components: Mao Tse-tung's conception of the uses of mass persuasion; the Chinese Communists' experiences during the guerrilla revolution in the interior; and Marxist-Leninist thought, which legitimized the first two components. Then, I will discuss the means of persuasion and the effects of the leftist ideology on the mass media.

MAO TSE-TUNG'S CONCEPTIONS AND IDIOSYNCRASIES

Mao Tse-tung's personality has had an extraordinary impact on the Chinese political system. The influence of Mao's personality is greatly strengthened by the convergence of two historical factors, the emphasis on the causal role of political leaders in Chinese political culture, and the fragmentation of Chinese society since the late nineteenth century. Four of Mao's personality traits have immediate bearing on mass persuasion: anti-intellectualism, emphasis on conflict, a penchant for social manipulation, and radicalism.

Several things in Mao's personal life contributed to his fundamental distrust—indeed, hatred—of Chinese intellectuals. One was his experience of being rejected by prominent intellectual leaders in the early Republican period, when he was a library assistant at Peking University. As Mao told Edgar Snow in 1936:

My office was so low that people avoided me. One of my tasks was to register the names of people who came to read newspapers, but to most of them I didn't exist as a human being. Among those who came to read I recognized the names of famous leaders of the renaissance movement, men like Fu Ssu-nien, Lo Chia-lung, and others, in whom I was intensely interested. I tried to begin conversations with them on political and cultural subjects, but they were very busy men. They had no time to listen to an assistant librarian speaking southern dialect.[1]

Later in his life, Mao's grievances against intellectuals were turned into contempt of them. The intellectuals who became political leaders, like Chen Tu-hsiu and the "returned students" from Moscow in the Communist Party, were ineffectual organizers and leaders.

Eventually, Mao found his strength and identity in the peasant movement. The spontaneous peasant rebellion in Hunan in 1927 impressed Mao with the power of simple political propaganda to fire the revolutionary enthusiasm of the masses. His attitude was characteristically anti-intellectual:

Even if ten thousand schools of law and political science had been opened, could they have brought as much political education to the people, men and women, young and old, all the way into the remotest corners of the country-side, as the peasant associations have done in so short a time? I don't think they could. "Down with imperialism!" "Down with the warlords!" "Down with the corrupt officials!" "Down with the local tyrants and evil gentry!"—these political slogans have grown wings, they have found their way to the young, the middle-aged and the old, to the women and children in countless villages, they have penetrated into their minds and are on their lips. . . .[2]

The guerrilla wars that Mao fought against the Nationalists, from 1927 to 1949, further required him to be near the peasant masses and to mobilize them for production and combat. In the meantime, the clumsiness and ambivalence of the Chinese intellectuals in organization and political leadership increased

Mao's contempt. It must have impressed Mao also that his chief opponent, then and now, Chiang Kai-shek, was much like himself—an action-oriented and anti-intellectual man who rose from the ranks and had very little formal education.

Mao does, however, believe in the power of ideas. Mingled with his contempt of intellectuals is his fear that, although the intellectuals are not capable of organizing the masses, they are capable of challenging political authority with their ideas. Contempt is thus mixed with distrust.

Mao Tse-tung also has what one scholar characterizes as the "combative spirit." [3] In contrast to the elite Confucian culture that emphasized harmony and compliance with authority, the "mass culture" of traditional China with which Mao, a more or less self-educated man, chose to identify, extolled conflicts, struggles, and rebellions. His passion for conflict was reinforced by the nationalistic spirit of the early Republican period. The ideal of reshaping Chinese culture and people according to a militaristic model has been shared by all revolutionary leaders in modern China.

Mao's experiences with the student movement, the revolutionary army, and then with peasant rebellions in the early part of his career taught him that emotional tension and ambivalence were common among a wide range of social groups, especially the intellectuals. In consonance with his emphasis on conflict, his revolutionary commitment to social change, and his knowledge of the intrigues and struggles in traditional Chinese bureaucratic politics, Mao refined the technique of manipulation.

Mao's manipulative tactics placed overwhelming importance on emotional tension. Later in his revolutionary career, he successfully exploited the class hatred between peasants and landlords and the ambivalent feelings of Chinese intellectuals toward the masses, i.e., their vacillation between elitism and romantic populism. These experiences gradually crystalized Mao's belief that given a proper technique of social manipulation, almost anything can be accomplished. Therein lies the cause of his unwavering insistence, after policy blunders such as the Great Leap Forward, that there was nothing wrong with his policy but rather that the cadres had not implemented it properly.

Mao's radicalism stemmed from his desperate desire to see institutionalized changes in government and society come out of the era of violent social change which had wrecked China since the late nineteenth century. He feared traditional Chinese inertia when confronted by social change.

Though Mao has a mystical belief in the revolutionary power of the masses, he is not without ambivalence toward the masses. He personally witnessed storm-like peasant revolts, but he is undoubtedly also aware of the mental narrowness and lethargy of the Chinese peasantry. These contradictions led Mao to the radical view that excess is not only inevitable in a revolution but also, in fact, desirable. For example, in 1945, when the Chinese Communists were implementing a radical form of land reform in their territory, Mao wrote:

Rent reduction must be the result of mass struggle, not a favor bestowed by the government. On this depends the success or failure of rent reduction. In the struggle for rent reduction, excesses can hardly be avoided; as long as it is really a conscious struggle of the broad masses, any excesses that have occurred can be corrected afterwards. . . .[4]

Mao's tactics of mass movement can be properly called successive waves of pushing. That is, the masses must be pushed all the way to the brink of their energy and willingness in order to accomplish anything. Any notion of adjustment to social equilibrium is, to Mao, reactionary.

Related to this idea is Mao's passion for total politicization of the individual's mind and action. This radical belief in the primacy, even monopoly, of politics in an individual's life seems to stem from Mao's projection of his personal life into the whole Chinese society. Mao is a totally politicized man, and his victory over the Chinese Nationalists tempted him to try to transform every Chinese after his own image so as to win an unprecedented victory—China's modernization.

THE PARTY'S EXPERIENCES IN GUERRILLA WAR

Leftist ideology also has a historical and empirical basis in the guerrilla experiences of the Chinese Communist Party. Four aspects of the guerrilla period seem to be relevant here: physical isolation, peasant mobilization, individual combat, and the united front.

Though physical isolation created hardships and deprivation for the Chinese Communists before 1945, it also enabled the leaders to insulate their people and their cadres from the inertia and demoralization of the wider society under the rule of the Nationalist government. Insulation made it possible for them to indoctrinate their people thoroughly and to instill in the minds of cadres and soldiers a firm Communist *weltanshauung*.

The need to mobilize the peasants in the guerrilla base areas compelled the Chinese Communists to shape their methods and doctrines of persuasion to the mentality of peasants. For example, Mao's anti-intellectualism became an asset here, for the Chinese peasantry's dislike of officialdom incorporated a strong sense of anti-intellectualism. Thus, this common element enabled the Party to appeal to the youthful peasants for cooperation.

The peasants' illiteracy and ignorance required an oral and emotional approach to mass persuasion. These factors were also the origin of one of the unique types of Chinese Communist political agitation—the use of slogans with numerical titles, such as Three-anti, Five-anti, Four-good Company, and Four-cleaning campaigns. This practice stemmed from the need to simplify in order to communicate with the peasants. Similarly, the kind of propaganda the Communists used was not subtle indirection but direct and one-sided argument.

The ignorance of the Chinese peasants seems to have strengthened Mao's radicalism. For example, in the Great Leap Forward, Mao advocated the theory that since China was a "poor" and "blank" country, she could be manipulated according to a master plan. As Stuart Schram explains:

In Mao's mind, the modernization of China and the transformation of the Chinese people are, of course, two sides of the same coin. Because the Chinese are poor, they are avid for change and are filled with revolutionary spirit; because they are "blank," that is to say, ignorant and innocent of the wiles of the modern world, they are also malleable. . . .[5]

During their guerrilla warfare against the Nationalist government, the Communist armed forces had to break up into small bands operating in isolated areas. The cadres needed a firm ideological outlook to be able to adjust to different situations. This required total politicization of the cadres' thought. Without a total transformation in his ideology, a cadre will not feel secure and free to make vital adjustments by himself. Thus Mao's image of himself as a totally politicized man, making adjustments of orthodox Marxism-Leninism to fit the Chinese situation, was now used to reshape his rank and file.

To survive and, moreover, to prepare for the final victory, the Communists needed allies in the Nationalist areas. The tactic of the united front was to ally itself with intellectuals, students, merchants, and other social groups in the Nationalist territories so as to isolate the government. To do so, the Communists had to manipulate the conflicts and tensions between and within groups. The success that they achieved in this effort greatly strengthened Mao's belief in manipulation and his interest in intellectuals as useful tools on certain occasions.

MARXISM-LENINISM

Mao's penchant for conflict, manipulation, and mass movement is in close harmony with Lenin's belief that individuals can and should intervene in the course of events. The ideological shift that occurred in the Soviet Union in the 1930s, with a heavy emphasis on men's "consciousness" in changing environment, also reinforces Mao's belief in radical social change.[6] The contradiction in Mao's belief in the power of ideas and his ingrained anti-intellectualism can be readily legitimized by Marx's emphasis on "practice" as a synthesis between spiritual and material matters.

IDEOLOGY OF MASS PERSUASION: A SYNTHESIS

The various parts of the Chinese Communist ideology of mass persuasion can be synthesized into four basic principles:

Insulation: Mass persuasion is most effective when people are insulated in an environment in which political propaganda and agitation penetrate every nook and corner.

Emotional arousal: The first objective of a persuasion campaign is the creation of emotional tension among the masses.

Simplification: Once the masses' emotions have been aroused, persuasion proceeds "in the manner of frontal assault by a mass of heavily weighted arguments rather than by subtle indirection." [7]

Politicization: Persuasion is not complete until a person has cultivated the habit of using some key ideological concepts to interpret his personal experiences.

Thus, when the Chinese Communists came to power over the mainland in 1949, they already possessed a well-tested ideology of mass persuasion. Furthermore, they had forged effective tools to implement that ideology.

INSTRUMENTS OF PERSUASION

The ideology of mass persuasion determined the means to carry it out, chiefly oral agitation. Two instruments for this were mass campaigns and small groups meetings, corresponding to Mao's two techniques of Party leadership: "general appeal" and "breakthroughs at particular points." [8]

The Chinese Communists used small groups extensively for cadre indoctrination. In small group discussions, both Party leaders and rank-and-file were participants. So far as political matters are concerned, the rank-and-file did not have any role in deciding policies. But the ranks were given decision-making power on relatively non-political matters such as food distribution and purchase. A false sense of democratic participation resulted, which was deliberately induced in order to elicit rank-and-file commitment to Party programs. The Chinese Communists, through their own trial-and-error, have discovered the same human reaction that American social scientists have found in group experiments: that mere participation in discussing the execution of a matter tends to influence participants to accept it. Furthermore, by requiring Party leaders to participate in group discussions, the general mood and reactions of the rank toward Party authority can be detected.

Mass campaigns were used to mobilize the population at large. The Chinese Communist idea of mass campaigns seems to be particularly inspired by guerrilla warfare, in which a few major targets are designated and then a superior force is organized to storm one target at a time. That is why, during the periods when the left-wing Party leaders controlled national development, some of the statements on mass persuasion were put in military terms. For example, in mid-1960, as part of the rearguard actions of the left-wing leaders in their retreat from the Great Leap, cadres were told to "occupy" the "thought positions," "empty points," or "empty areas" in society—meaning that the cadres must penetrate into the midst of the people to prevent any demoralization or loss of ideological militancy.[9]

Furthermore, in Communist China mass campaigns are also an expression of a basic attitude toward national development, an attitude which emphasizes mass and emotional participation regardless of the professional specialization of individuals or the different natures of various tasks. The power of ideology on human consciousness is exaggerated. Pushed to the extreme (and Mao has pushed it to the extreme), this conviction says that almost anything can be accomplished by "common men." Inherent in this attitude is an expectation of much good to come from single acts of innovation such as the Great Leap Forward. Those who hold this view, as Mao apparently does, are naturally attracted by oral, agitational, and campaign-like persuasion techniques.[10] But mass media as a modern institution cannot be totally adapted to this sort of mass persuasion. Let us look into this in some detail.

IDEOLOGY AND MASS MEDIA

First of all, oral agitation can meet the particular conditions of different social groups much more easily than mass media, which are essentially universalistic. The message of oral persuasion can be varied according to the kind of audience; the mass media must use a more generalized message. In addition, oral agitation and propaganda can be initiated and terminated at will, while mass media do not have this kind of flexibility.

Face-to-face persuasion is less restrained by the intellectual level of its audiences than are the media, especially the printed ones. A closely connected matter is professionalism. Oral agitation requires much less professionalism; in the revolutionary period, Party agitators and propagandists held a variety of concurrent jobs. Mass media, on the other hand, require a corps of full-time reporters, editors, and managers, all of whom have a professional identity.

Mao Tse-tung tried to permeate the media with leftist ideology and practice. He certainly did not want to see the development of a corps of professional journalists; in fact, editors and reporters were sent to the countryside to do manual labor while the newspapers were turned over to cadres and worker-peasant correspondents.

To realize his ideal of awakening the masses politically, Mao attempted to extend every mass medium, from radio to books, down to every village in China in the Great Leap, when the rural areas actually were not yet literate enough to use them. The failure of that effort was predetermined. Mao's frustration over the media's inability to storm the countryside eventually led him to destroy them, especially the printed media, during the Cultural Revolution and to revive the mobile oral agitation teams that had been used during the guerrilla period.

By contrast, the Soviets had long used the best of the two systems—oral persuasion and mass media—without favoring one at the expense of the other. The Soviets had used oral agitation to supplement the mass media. As Inkeles points out, although the Soviets did use the media for current political and economic propaganda, this was balanced by another type of content that had a long-term purpose, to promote mass culture. The Soviets also gradually abandoned the mobile oral agitation teams in favor of a more stable system of oral persuasion that was integrated into industrial, economic, and cultural institutions.[11]

The Chinese Communists, as we noted earlier, imitated the Soviet approach to mass persuasion from 1953 to 1957, but soon Mao and his left-wing followers asserted themselves and abandoned the Soviet methods. There is, perhaps, an element of irony in the Chinese development. Had the left-wing leaders in China not had a workable ideology and methods of mass persuasion that stemmed from their guerrilla experiences, they would perhaps have been more willing to recognize the special characteristics of mass media. Since they already had a doctrine which had worked quite well before 1949, they insisted in operating mass media in this anachronistic framework.

4

The Communication Process:
The Formal Organizations
of Propaganda

Although each individual medium of communication is technically an independent institution, it is also an integral part of a well-coordinated apparatus of propaganda. Until the system was disrupted by the Cultural Revolution, the policy-making and coordinating organization of this apparatus was the Propaganda Department of the Party Committee at each territorial level of administration. The general headquarters of this Party propaganda network was the Propaganda Department of the Central Committee. Under the guidance of this agency were four main branches: the Propaganda Departments of the regional Party Committees, the government Ministry of Culture, the mass organizations, and the mass media. Because the mass media will be discussed in some detail later, and the internal operation of the Ministry of Culture is not of immediate relevance, this chapter will deal only with the Propaganda Department and the mass organizations.

Although the Cultural Revolution has caused the suspension of the formal network of propaganda, there are still good reasons for wanting to study these organizations. First, it is unlikely that the Party will for long go without some organization of propaganda and agitation. Recently, the Maoists or ruling group of

the Party have been calling for rebuilding the Party structure.[1]
If this happens, then the propaganda apparatus is almost certain
to be rebuilt too. Given the emphasis on ideology in the Cultural Revolution, propaganda work in the future will be
strengthened and controlled from above even more than in the
past. It is therefore necessary to describe the past structure, so
that any new structure can be analyzed in comparative terms.

Second, the propaganda organizations, personnel, and mass
media bore the brunt of the attacks in the initial period of the
Cultural Revolution. An analysis of them will perhaps reveal
some underlying causes of the present turmoil in China.

THE STRUCTURE OF MASS PERSUASION

The structure of the Party Propaganda Departments was integrated with that of the Party and the state. In general, the educational system, run by the state, was in charge of "culture," which
meant the teaching of general subjects such as geography, language, science, and so forth. The Party was in charge of propaganda—political and ideological indoctrination—and policy-
making for education. Mass organizations stood nominally as an
independent system but, in fact, the Party exercised absolute
control over them.

The administration of the mass media was divided among the
three systems. The overall pattern of this elaborate structure is
presented in Chart 1. The chart reveals an interesting fact
unique to China among Communist governments: the state
itself had no press. In the Soviet Union, the state is represented
nationally by *Izvestia* and regionally by newspapers serving as
organs of Supreme Soviets of Workers' Deputies of union re-
publics and republic bodies.[2] There are two plausible reasons
for the Chinese Communist peculiarity in this. One is that the
Party wanted to secure complete control over the press, since
the Party had to rely on a substantial number of non-Communist journalists to operate the newspapers. The second is that
because of the low literacy rate among the Chinese people, the
Party press and the mass organization journals and newspapers
were able to meet the public demand fully.

CHART 1:

The Organizational Structure of Party Propaganda Network in Communist China

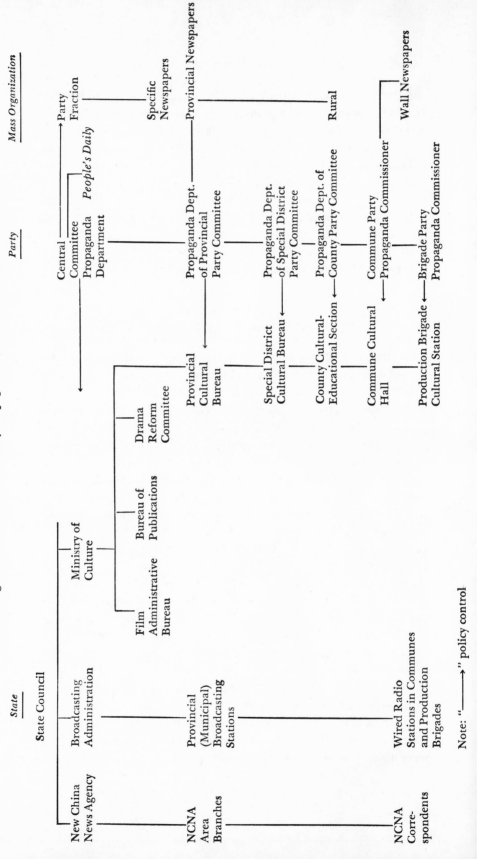

Note: "———→" policy control

1. Administration: general administration of the dep
2. Propaganda: propaganda policy-making in co the instructions and plans of the Central Party.
3. Science: supervision of scientific resear cluding such tasks as collection of int opments in other nations, productio suring instruments, and control dealing with scientific researc
4. Theoretical Education: ed cadres and publication of
5. Literature and Art: p ideological reform of All-China Litera schools and inst
6. Newspapers journals.
7. Press an press
8. Ed
9.

Cultu

ganda leadership. The purg
and at least five deputy directors, including Chou Yang
fields of work covered art and literature, press, education, broadcasting, and publishing. Except for Chen Po-ta, who has become an ardent supporter of Mao's Cultural Revolution, the fate of the remaining seven deputy directors who have not been publicly denounced is unknown.

As with all departments of the Central Committee, the work of the Propaganda Department was shrouded in secrecy. Only very sketchy information is available. According to one source, the department consisted of fifteen sections, displaying an extraordinarily wide scope of matters under its control and supervision. The duties of each of the sections are summarized as follows:

artment.

ordination with Committee of the

n and development, in-
lligence on scientific devel-
n of scientific tools and mea-
f Party cadres in organizations
and development.

cation and indoctrination of Party
documents for this purpose.

blication of classical and folk literature,
the traditional stage, and supervision of the
ure and Art Association and other related
tutes.

nd Journals: supervision of the Party press and

d Publication: general policy-making on publishing, the
nd publication censorship.

cation: educational policy, textbook publishing, and ideo-
gical reform of school teachers.

Public Health and Sports: policy making on public health, sports, and promotion of national sanitation and sports campaigns.

10. Cultural Education: supervision of special evening schools and short courses for cadres and promotion of literacy among cadres.

11. Marxism-Leninism Research: general Marxism-Leninism propaganda policy-making and coordination with the Publication and Translation Bureau of Works of Marx, Engels, Lenin, and Stalin of the Central Committee.

12. Editing and Translation: research on foreign works for internal propaganda.

13. Policy Research: implementation of Party policies and instructions for the benefit of the internal agencies of the Propaganda Department.

14. International Liaison: liaison with propaganda agencies of other Communist nations.

15. Political Department: supervision of political work within the Propaganda Department.[4]

This description of the inner structure of the Department reveals that the scope of its concern was extraordinarily broad—

even broader than that of its Soviet counterpart, Agit-Prop. Several sections in the Chinese Propaganda Department covered activities with which the Soviet Agit-Prop was not concerned. This perhaps shows some of the differences in the problems with which the two Communist Parties had to cope. The Chinese paid much more attention to the indoctrination of Party cadres than did the Soviets; two sections—Theoretical Education and Cultural Education—in the Chinese Department dealt with cadre indoctrination and education. That Marxism-Leninism was an alien doctrine that had to be assimilated by the Chinese was underscored by the two sections: Marxism-Leninism Research, and Editing and Translation.

Another interesting feature is the Public Health and Sports Section. Inkeles' description of the Soviet Agit-Prop mentions no similar sector, though it is plausible that the Sector for Cultural Enlightenment may cover sports and public health.[5] In any case, the Chinese concern with these subjects was substantially stronger than the Soviets. Modern Chinese political leaders, Communist and non-Communist, repeatedly professed their concern about the physical condition of the population. In fact, one of Mao's earliest writings was entitled *A Study of Physical Education*.[6] To every revolutionary-minded Chinese, one of the fundamental thought transformations necessary for the Chinese people was in their attitude toward physical exercise.

The Chinese Communists had to pay more attention than the Soviets did to problems like the low literacy rate among cadres and the population as a whole, "sinification" of the alien ideology of Marxism-Leninism, and instilling modern (industrial) attitudes in the people. This does not mean that the Soviets did not encounter such problems as illiteracy or cultivating modern attitudes among the Russian people. But the Soviet society in 1917, especially the urban sector, was much more modernized than was China in 1949. The wide scope of matters that the Propaganda Department was concerned with testifies to leadership thinking on these problems.

In adopting this Soviet type of propaganda organization, Mao and his veteran cadres stepped into a new field of work. Instead of the intensive type of communications work that they were familiar with, they now had to work through an extensive bureaucratic network. What is more, Mao had to use intellectuals or those cadres with intellectual backgrounds to manage such a complex organization. For example, in one way or another, the twelve deputy directors had been participants in either the "proletarian literature" movement of the early 1930s or Communist activities in universities during the pre-Communist period. Though Mao could and did retain the power to decide major policies in propaganda, he had to rely on these intellectual cadres and their subordinates to execute his policies. This inevitably caused Mao to fear the possibility of distortion and sabotage of his policies by intellectuals. The destruction of the Propaganda Department during the Cultural Revolution was explained on the grounds that the intellectuals and bureaucrats in the Party propaganda network had distorted and sabotaged many of Mao's decisions.

Information on the inner operation of the Propaganda Department is virtually non-existent. For an important Party organization, the Department was noted for receiving little or no publicity. Major decisions were always issued in the awesome name of The Central Committee of the Chinese Communist Party. The Propaganda Department itself was the subject of no propaganda. On the other hand, its power was regularly brought to public attention through the speeches and announcements of its director and deputy directors.

BUREAUCRATIC POLITICS AND DECISION-MAKING
IN THE PROPAGANDA APPARATUS

Publicly, all major propaganda policies were issued in the name of the Central Committee. However, over the years the size of the Central Committee had been progressively enlarged, diminishing its effective power. As Allen Whiting puts it: "the Central Committee is too large and meets too infrequently and too briefly to be the real decision-making center of the CCP."[7] The most plausible body for decision making in the Party was the Politburo, and sometimes not even all the members of the Politburo were consulted about major policies. In those cases, decisions were made by Mao and a few of his most trusted Party leaders. A decision with serious consequences for the Chinese people like the decision for people's communes in 1958 was made in this way.[8]

Because the propaganda program was an integral part of the Party's policy, a decision on policy in economics or other areas of development also prescribed a coordinated propaganda strategy. Given Mao's penchant for mass mobilization, it seems quite natural that Mao should have interfered more with the Party's propaganda work according to his personal preferences than he did with other types of work. In fact, it seems that Mao decided almost all major propaganda campaigns; sometimes he had to overrule others in order to have his way, as in the initiation of the campaign of free criticism in 1957.

Recent evidence reveals that Mao personally decided every major propaganda campaign that was closely related to the Cultural Revolution, starting from 1963. Mao usually made his decisions known to his colleagues and subordinates in the Party Central Committee in two ways. One was by formal speeches in either Politburo or Central Committee meetings. For example, the propaganda program of renewing the class struggle was decided by Mao and made known to other Party leaders in the Tenth Plenum of the Eighth Central Committee of the Party in 1962.[9] The decision on the "Socialist Education" campaign was announced by Mao to an enlarged meeting of the Politburo in May 1963. The Cultural Revolution is the most dramatic example of how Mao imposed his personal decision upon other leaders of the Party. The formal decision of the Cultural Revolution was announced in the Eleventh Plenum of the Eighth Central Committee in August 1966. Fearing possible opposition to his decision, Mao called in "revolutionary students and teachers" from colleges in Peking and members of the "Cultural Revolution Team of the Central Committee," headed by Mao's trusted Chen Po-ta, to participate in the meeting. According to an American analyst, Charles Neuhauser: "Several important provincial Party leaders evidently did not attend the plenum; the hall was packed with enthusiastic 'revolutionary' supporters of the Maoist position; voting may have been irregular."[10] Thus, decision-making at the top of the Chinese Communist power structure was highly personalized.

The second way that Mao made his decisions on propaganda known to his subordinates, especially to the Party leaders in the Propaganda Department, seems to have been through his "comments." Red Guard publications during the Cultural Revolution repeatedly accused the former Party leaders of that Department of ignoring Mao's "comments" on propaganda or preventing them from being implemented. The interesting question is how these "comments" were transmitted. A veteran political analyst in Hong Kong suggests that they were probably written on the work reports that the Propaganda Department submitted to Mao.[11] This seems to be a very plausible suggestion. According to Chinese Communist press reports, in 1963 and 1964 Mao made scathing attacks on the mass media and on Chinese journalists through these "comments," but top Party leaders in the Propaganda Department made only half-hearted responses to them.[12]

Although Mao's role in propaganda decisions was the dominant one, the bureaucracy of the Party Propaganda Department was still a large factor influencing decision making at the top level. This bureaucracy controlled communication between the lower and upper levels. Mao's decisions must have been at least partially based on the reports from the lower levels that went through the Propaganda Department. But perhaps more important than being the monitor of communication upward, the Department was an executive agency. It had the power to revise a communication transmitted from above, and it controlled access to mass organizations and the state bureaucracy on cultural affairs.

The deputy directors had the power to convene special conferences of writers, journalists, actors, educators, and so forth, to transmit important instructions from the Central Committee or any policy directives of their own. For example, Chou Yang was accused of convening a special conference in January 1964 which was ostensibly for the purpose of transmitting Mao's recent comments criticizing writers and journalists, but instead Chou, according to the accusation, covertly revised Mao's decision. One of the deputy directors on educational matters, Lin Mu-han, was said to have described Mao's criticism of the Ministry of Culture as a "joke" and to have said that there was "no need to transmit Mao's remarks downward." [13]

Chou Yang and other deputy directors of the Propaganda Department also had access to lower-level propaganda cadres. While Mao had the decision-making power, he still needed the deputy directors to activate the vast propaganda apparatus, whose arms extended throughout the whole nation.

Though the Propaganda Department as such received little publicity, its power was felt by the public through the appearances of its leading figures on many occasions. This was particularly true at the annual meetings of mass organizations, such as the All-China Playwrights' Association or the All-China Writers' Association. To these meetings, the Department always sent the deputy director who specialized in the work of the particular organization to deliver the major speech, which was essentially a policy directive to the organization. Such conferences were usually initiated by the Propaganda Department.

However, the propaganda apparatus' potential for decision making through bureaucratic execution should not be too exaggerated. At best, the Propaganda Department and its lower branches could revise some directives from Mao or the Politburo only marginally. The activities of the department until its collapse in 1966 revealed a strong tradition of compliance. Yet this compliance did not insure Mao's satisfaction with the performance of the department. There were substantial gaps between what Mao wanted Chinese propagandists to accomplish and what they had actually done. The gaps eventually led to the wholesale purge of propaganda personnel in 1966.

Furthermore, as a bureaucracy which executed policies decided at the top, the propaganda apparatus was, at times, handicapped by rival groups in the Central Committee or even in the Politburo. This seems to be a common problem for propagandists in totalitarian societies. As Friedrich and Brzezinski point out:

The final integration of totalitarian dictatorship does not preclude the occurrence of many intercine struggles; on the contrary, it lends to these struggles a fierceness and violence which is rarely seen in freer societies. This issue of the rival component elements in a particular totalitarian society poses very difficult problems for overall direction of propaganda. The chief propagandist often has to opt between such rival groups.[14]

The purge of the Propaganda Department of the Central Committee by Mao was due mainly to its compliance to a new set of policies by a different group of leaders, headed by Liu Shao-chi, between 1959 and 1965. According to Mao himself, the 1958 shuffle in leaders' roles in the Politburo was actually initiated by him.[15] Mao publicly stepped down from the chairmanship of the Chinese People's Republic while retaining the chairmanship of the Communist Party. Liu was made the chairman of the Republic. This change was necessary because Mao's Great Leap campaign had brought the nation's economy to the brink of total collapse. Now, with a different leader in charge after 1958, a new set of economic policies were implemented to tide the nation over the crisis. This is not the place to discuss the details of these new policies.[16] Suffice it to say that the new leadership and its policies were oriented toward reconciliation with the reality and desires of the population. The emphasis of national integration policy under Liu was more on identification than on penetration. Propaganda policy was naturally made to conform to this change in direction. Yet Mao soon became dissatisfied with the new policies, which, he felt, were leading China to the "restoration of capitalism." Because the propaganda apparatus of the Party complied with the new leadership, Mao deemed it disloyal to his own ideology and leadership. Thus, it is ironic that Mao purged the propaganda apparatus not because of its alleged opposition to the Party but because of its compliance to it when the Party was under the leadership of another faction.

As Alex Inkeles points out, the followers of a totalitarian dictator "are obliged themselves to have a substantial awareness of and commitment to the mystical commandments" of the dictator. The purges of the cadres of a totalitarian system are "not so much for what they have done as for what they have not done. . . . They are tried not so much for acting incorrectly, but for inaction, which is taken as a sign of waning devotion and doubt in the mystique." [17] Propagandists under the Propaganda Department of the Central Committee were cast out in 1966 by Mao and the left-wing faction because they did not defend Mao's mystique between 1959 and 1965, which would have required them to refuse to execute the current policies of the Party.

PROPAGANDA OPERATIONS AT LOWER LEVELS

Because of the Cultural Revolution, it has been necessary to devote much space to the problem of tensions and conflict among organizations at the national level. While the Party Propaganda Department itself has now been closed down, even today propaganda units in the important county Party Committees remain intact, though inactivated by the turmoils of the Cultural Revolution.[18] It is, therefore, important to describe the general functions of the provincial and lower-level propaganda departments in normal times.

A most important problem was coordination between the center and the regions. In the environment of diversity and geographical isolation previously described, regional adjustments of policies decided at the center were inevitable. The propaganda departments of the provincial Party Committees became the natural areas of decision, balanced between the center and the region.

The provincial propaganda department assumed the major responsibility for adapting a centrally decided propaganda policy to the regional situation. The communication between provincial and lower-level propaganda departments went through two types of channels, depending on the importance of the particular policy. Major policies were transmitted to lower levels in conferences of propaganda personnel from county and district Party Committees. Such a conference was usually chaired by the Secretary of the Provincial Party Committee, and his opening speech would announce and clarify the particular policy of the moment. The provincial propaganda department could also issue confidential instructions to lower levels, especially about any wrongdoing or deviations committed by base-level propaganda cadres.

Aside from these channels for communication of important and urgent matters, the provincial department maintained regular contacts with lower-level cadres by the periodic distribution of *Propaganda Handbooks* or *Handbooks of Information and Policy*. These were mostly confidential or semi-confidential publications, accessible only to propaganda cadres. The provincial propaganda department also maintained public communication by publishing instructions and materials for local cadres in the provincial newspaper.[19]

The meeting of open provincial or regional propaganda conferences and the use of press for transmitting propaganda instructions and materials apparently declined after 1953. In recent years, the Party seems to have convened conferences of propagandists secretly and relied mainly on confidential instructions for communication between the central, provincial, and lower-level propaganda units.

From the provincial headquarters on down, two local units became important centers of decision—the municipal and the county propaganda departments of the Party Committees. Although these two centers were at the receiving ends of covert instructions and regular propaganda pamphlets, they also relied on conferences for announcing and coordinating local propaganda activities. For example, according to a Shansi provincial broadcast in January 1965, the Lung County Party Committee called a propaganda conference that month and announced that in the New Year (February) period, the propaganda theme would be "Build the Proletariat, Eliminate Bourgeois Habits and Customs," which probably meant that the people in that county would be dissuaded from spending or celebrating extravagantly in the New Year season. It was also a coordinating action at the county level with a national mass campaign bearing the same name. Another report stated that in March 1965, the Peking Municipal Party Committee called a propaganda conference in which a drive to "Learn the Thought of Mao Tse-tung" was initiated. Thus, in normal times the Party propaganda apparatus succeeded in coordinating different units to carry out each mass campaign.

The structural and functional position of the provincial and municipal Party propaganda departments seems to fit Karl

Deutsch's category of "strategic middle-level communications and command," which he defined as follows:

It is that level of communication and command that is "vertically" close enough to the large mass of consumers, citizens, or common soldiers to forestall any continuing and effective direct communication between them and the "highest echelons"; and it must be far enough above the level of the large numbers of the rank and file to permit effective "horizontal" communication and organization among a sufficiently large portion of the men or units on its own level.[20]

The provincial and municipal propaganda apparatus had direct access to the regional units of mass organizations, local units of the Ministry of Culture, and the mass media. They were also in a good position to forestall or to facilitate communications between the masses and the central organization of the Communist Party in Peking. (At the risk of being called jargon-prone, language of cybernetics can be used to characterize the Propaganda Department of the Central Committee as a unit high in information but low in energy, and the provincial and municipal Party propaganda departments as high in energy but low in information.) The policies decided at the provincial and municipal levels had immediate action consequences, as the examples have shown. The provincial and municipal Party propaganda departments were "effectors" of propaganda at the mass level.

MASS ORGANIZATIONS

The mass organizations in Communist China were a counterpart of the Soviet public organizations. They were formal groups or associations nominally organized by people themselves on a functional or occupational basis. As such, they reflected the Soviet approach to social organization. Inkeles points out that this approach is similar to the views of the structural-functional school of modern sociology and anthropology in the West. The central assumption of this approach is that "the discrete institutions and institutional complexes in any society are intimately interrelated and interdependent so that the structure and operation of any given institutional pattern has important implications for other institutions and for the structure as a whole." [21] The Chinese mass organizations were created under the same assumption.

In 1964, there were 164 mass organizations in Communist China. They can be divided into five types:

The majority of mass organizations were created on occupational lines, such as the All-China Labor Union, All-China Journalists' Association, Union of Chinese Writers, and so forth.

The second type corresponded to specific interests, mainly sports societies and "friendship associations" with foreign nations. There were, for example, the All-China Athletic Federation, the Chinese People's Committee for World Peace, and the Friendship Association of China and Albania.

The third kind of mass organization was perhaps uniquely Chinese. These were nominally autonomous political parties and were supposedly cooperating voluntarily with the Chinese Communist Party in administering the nation. There were nine such parties in 1964. In the Soviet Union, we do not find any organizations corresponding to these non-communist political parties. The existence of such parties in Communist China seems to be a result of Peking's ideological pretense that the Chinese government was at that time an alliance of all major social classes; China had yet to achieve the integrated state in which the whole people would be of one proletarian class. The Soviet Union had long claimed that it had achieved such integration.[22]

The Young Communist League before 1966 stood as a category of its own because of its unique relationship with the Chinese Communist Party. The League was in essence the junior Communist Party. Its uniqueness can be seen in the fact that one chapter of the Chinese Communist Party Constitution was devoted to the organization of the League. The Young Communist League, according to the Party constitution, was to assist the Party and accepted the Party's leadership. A person usually became a League member before he was admitted to Party membership.

The fifth and last group of mass organizations were religious associations. In 1964, there were five of these.

The inner structure of the mass organizations was a copy of that of the Party. The purpose of this type of structure was to concentrate decision-making power step by step upward into a small group of leaders, who more often than not also held important Party or government positions. At the top of each organization, there was generally a National Congress, a Central Committee and its Standing Committee, and a Secretariat with various sub-committees. In theory, the decision-making power of each organization was vested in its National Congress. In reality, the Secretariat monopolized policy making and executed policies through the Central Committee.

All these mass organizations functioned primarily to mobilize different groups in society. Yet their importance to the Party varied. Their order of importance was shown in the extensiveness of their regional branches. By this measure, three mass organizations stood out as the Party's most important arms of mobilization: the All-China Labor Union Federation, the All-China Women's Association, and the Young Communist League. All three had branches down to the county commune and production brigade levels.[23]

The Propaganda Department of the Central Committee exercised day-to-day control over the mass organizations through the "Party Fraction" in these organizations. A Party Fraction was formed in any non-Party organization when there were more than three Party members occupying leadership positions in the group. The member with the highest position in a non-Party organization was the secretary of its Party Fraction. These secretaries were the main transmission belt between the Propaganda Department and the members of the mass organizations. For example in 1962, after the Central Committee decided to loosen political control over writers, it was Shao Chuan-lin, secretary of the Party Fraction in the Union of Chinese Writers, who passed on the new policy to the members of the union in a meeting. The specific instruction was that writers might now write about "middle-position characters," that is, characters other than Communist heroes, and "reactionary" villains.[24]

The mass organizations brought the largest number of people into direct organizational contact with the Communist regime. These organizations had both manifest and latent functions that were important in the integration of Chinese society. Manifestly, these organizations performed the functions of transmitting Party policies and organizing their members to carry out policies.

Whenever a Party policy was made, every major mass organization, particularly those directly affected by the policy, would call a national conference, to which the regional branches would send delegates. These delegates would be briefed on the content of Party policy, given relevant documents to read, and organized into discussion groups in which their questions and doubts were answered. The delegates would then return to their regional headquarters and, in turn, organize regional meetings. In this way, Party policies were transmitted directly to almost all the members of a mass organization.

The use of oral transmission probably helped the Party overcome the problem of language diversity and illiteracy. It also enabled it to control the diffusion of any particular message. In case of semi-confidential messages, the Party could close the transmission at any level in these organizations. For example, Mao's secret speech "On the Correct Handling of the Contradictions among the People" in 1957 was first made in a joint conference of government and Party officials and then was relayed orally to mass organizations.[25] The public learned it in published form much later than the members of mass organizations.

The Party also used the journals and newspapers of mass organizations for transmitting policies to the literate and elite group within the organizations. For example, the All-China Women's Association published the journal *Women in China;* the Young Communist League published the newspaper *China Youth Daily* and the journal *China Youth* (these three journals were suspended during the Cultural Revolution). Almost all professional organizations published their own journals, which dealt with politics and professional matters.

Another manifest function of the mass organizations was providing information on the attitudes of different social groups toward the Communist regime. The Party Fraction often called discussion meetings in which non-Party members of a mass organization would be invited to participate. These were relatively small discussion groups, and the secretary of the Party Fraction was able to detect the attitudes of non-Party members and their opinions about specific Party policies.

Aside from these manifest functions, a host of latent functions were also performed by mass organizations. They fundamentally altered the political and social life of the Chinese people. Almost every adult belonged to some mass organization; many belonged to more than one. The activities of these organizations reduced people's leisure time and made claims on their attention. Because these activities involved people in actions that called for new attitudes and values, they exposed people to "cross-pressure." They especially focused the conflict in people's minds between duties to the collectivity and duties to the family and other primary groups. By constantly reinforcing these conflicts, the mass organizations helped other persuasion media to change people's attitudes and opinions. In the meantime, the absorbing activities of the organizations dampened people's spontaneous social ties and so made them mobilizable, in the sense that they were loosened from their traditional socio-cultural grounding and were thus available for new patterns of socialization and behavior.[26]

To formerly unpolitical groups and persons, mass organizations offered an opportunity to gain knowledge about the Communist Party, its esoteric language, and the rules of the game. They were offered a chance to know the Party and to make themselves known to it also. Mass organizations were thus a channel for incorporating the aspiring elements of society into the Party.

The Cultural Revolution not only dealt a severe blow to the Propaganda Department of the Central Committee but also dissolved the major mass organizations, such as the All-China Labor Union Federation and the Young Communist League.* The fate of the All-China Women's Association is unknown.

---

* The Chinese Communist Party did not formally announce the "dissolution" of the Young Communist League, but in reality the organization no longer functions.

Most likely, it is not functioning. Numerous Red Guard organizations took the place of the previous organizations. Though students formed the core of the movement, workers and government employees also set up their own Red Guard organizations.

The dissolution of the Young Communist League and organizations on art and literature was a direct result of the purge of the Party propaganda apparatus. The dissolution of the All-China Labor Union Federation seems to be more a result of the downfall of Liu Shao-chi, who had been a leader in the labor movement in the early periods of the Chinese Communist Party and after 1949 became active in labor union reorganization. The labor unions were considered Liu's "sphere of influence."

THE GREAT PURGE IN THE CULTURAL REVOLUTION

The propaganda apparatus in Communist China bore the brunt of the Cultural Revolution, which formally got started in February 1966.[27] As we have noted, the immediate cause of the purge of propagandists seems to have been Mao's dissatisfaction with their compliance with Liu's policy of reconciliation. Yet to present a full picture of the Cultural Revolution and the propaganda apparatus in Communist China, we must search beyond the immediate cause. The following account is cast in both historical and analytical contexts.

Generally speaking, two types of factors can be used to analyze the purge of the propaganda apparatus during the Cultural Revolution. One type concerns mainly Mao's orientation toward propaganda work and Chinese intellectuals. The other concerns some circumstantial factors that existed within and without the propaganda apparatus from 1959 to 1965. The orientational factors provided the motive for Mao's purge, and the circumstantial factors, his strategy of purge. The major circumstantial factors are: first, the failure of Mao's Proletcult approach to propaganda in the Great Leap Forward Campaign of 1958; second, the new policy on art and literature under the leadership of Liu Shao-chi after 1959 that relegated Mao's policy of "art and literature for workers and peasants" to the background; third, appearance of disguised criticism of Mao's leadership in the press in 1961 and 1962; fourth, the appearance of factions within the decision-making level of the Propaganda Department and also at regional Party headquarters; and, fifth, the existence of a propaganda network in the army that served as an alternate channel for Mao to carry out his policy on art and literature. The last two circumstantial factors, factionalism and the autonomous army propaganda structure, crucially influenced Mao's strategy of purging the Party's propaganda apparatus. Yet, these factors by themselves could not have generated the violent purge of the Cultural Revolution. The violence and hysteria that marked the Cultural Revolution were generated by a fusion of these circumstantial factors with Mao's basic orientation toward intellectuals and propaganda work.

As I have said, Mao's attitude toward intellectuals is an ambivalent one. He has always shown his mistrust and contempt for Chinese intellectuals. Yet his own "revolutionary mystique" depends much on the power of ideas, which, in turn, means that Mao has to rely on a corps of intellectuals and propagandists to transform Chinese society. I have discussed Mao's approach to propaganda, which emphasized mass campaigns and intense oral agitation. To Mao, every Chinese intellectual in artistic and literary work and in Party propaganda must shed his penchant toward artistic sophistication. The intellectuals and propagandists of China, according to Mao, must popularize and simplify their work by adopting what he called the "language of the people." Furthermore, their work must concern contemporary political tasks. For the purpose of art and literature is political propaganda which can ignite what Mao sees as the latent "revolutionary spirit" in people and transform it into an earth-shaking material force. Thus, Mao's attitude toward propaganda consists of popularization, simplification, and intimate correlation with political tasks. His chief method of propaganda is the mass campaign, in which not only every intellectual must be present in every working site to conduct political agitation, but the greatest possible number of workers and peasants must also be brought to engage in propaganda work. In other words, popularization by professionals must be complemented by mass participation. Finally, Mao judges the devotion and loyalty of intellectuals and propagandists by the presence or absence of the "material force" that would carry Mao's program of economic and other types of development to success.

I. The Fiasco of the Great Leap Forward, 1958

The first crucial test of Mao's propaganda tactics was the Great Leap Forward campaign of 1958. It was designed by Mao to solve China's multiple social, economic, and political problems in a single mass campaign. Agricultural stagnancy was to be solved by mass labor mobilization and communization, which would then provide a base for accelerated industrial growth. To insure the success of this program, Mao mobilized the propaganda network to penetrate deeply into the population, especially the peasantry. As the then deputy director of the Propaganda Department of Party Central Committee explained it to a conference on broadcasting, there were two ways to conduct propaganda and cultural work. One was to rely on professionals and the process of building socialism by slow cultivation. The other way was to rely on "politics, the Party, and the masses." Mass participation could be used to accomplish "many things better, faster, and more economically." The Great Leap Forward was to take the latter path, the Maoist path of the mass campaign.[28]

To turn the latent revolutionary spirit of the peasantry into a powerful material force, the Communist Party in 1958 initiated an anti-intellectual "art and literature for workers and peasants" movement. The role of professionals in art, literature, and mass media was downgraded. Many professionals were sent down to the countryside to conduct person-to-person propaganda or to create instant works for on-the-spot agitation and propaganda. Mass media were arbitrarily extended to cover the rural area. In a few weeks "commune radio stations," "county newspapers," and "county theoretical journals" were created, symbolizing the spiritual transformation of the peasantry. To involve peasants and workers in propaganda, they were told that there was no mystery to artistic creativity. Thus, peasants were told to compose songs, write poems, and send stories to fill newspaper columns. For a few months in late 1958, the whole Chinese countryside was engaged in the romance of transforming revolutionary spirit into the great material force that, according to Mao, would bring the Communist millenium to China.

The Great Leap Forward turned out to be an impressive but futile exercise in political intervention. It failed disastrously because there was no social, economic, or political basis to sustain it. Though the failure of the Great Leap resulted in a severe economic crisis in China, its political consequences proved greater and less manageable than economic disaster. The prestige of Party leaders, especially that of Mao, suffered a drastic decline. The image of the Communist Party's invincibility was destroyed. The failure of the Great Leap also demoralized middle- and lower-echelon Party cadres, who received much of the blame for the disaster that followed. Last and not least, the failure of the Great Leap sowed the seed of dissension among leaders at the highest level of the Party; distrust now pervaded between Mao and his once close comrades-in-arms.

II. New Policy, 1959–1961

In November 1958, a change in the role and responsibility of Party leaders in the highest decision-making center—the Standing Committee of the Politburo—took place. The result was that Liu Shao-chi was given the power and responsibility to rescue the country from the disaster of the Great Leap. Mao resigned as chairman of the People's Republic and relinquished reluctantly his control of actual policy-making.[29] Under Liu, a policy of reconciliation was implemented.

So far as propaganda work is concerned, a general reduction of political penetration took place after 1959. In terms of Chou Yang's distinction between two ways of conducting propaganda, Liu's new policy emphasized reliance on professionals in art and literature instead of mass involvement. Instead of Mao's emphasis on quick transformation of the people's "revolutionary spirit," slow cultivation and education were preferred. Workers and peasants were no longer required to engage in instant artistic and literary creativity. Arbitrary extension of mass media to the countryside was halted and eventually abandoned. In short, Mao's Proletcult was discarded.

The Propaganda Department of the Central Committee issued a new directive in July 1961, titled "Ten Articles on Art and Literature." The articles reversed almost every aspect of Mao's approach to art and literature as implemented in the Great Leap. Mao's emphasis on the intimate correlation between art and literature and political tasks was denounced as one-sided and narrow-minded. To counter Mao's emphasis on politics, the new policy now stressed literary techniques and professionalism. Against the Maoist preference of contemporary (political) and Chinese works, the new policy of 1961 stressed the need to resurrect classical Chinese and fine foreign works, including those from capitalist nations. Mao's requirement of artists and writers to go down to the villages as laborers was severely curtailed, if not totally scrapped. The Party now "guaranteed" intellectuals and artists a degree of privacy and freedom in research and creation. In a statement that is directly opposed to Mao's orientation on propaganda, the "Ten Articles" stated: "To build the proletarian world outlook requires a long period of effort. It can not be done hastily. *In the meantime, those who do not have the correct world outlook are not necessarily anti-people and anti-socialism in politics.* Therefore, we can not always treat the problem of world outlook as a political matter." [30]

Under this new policy, the rallying slogan was changed from the Maoist "class struggle" to "whole people." In the dissemination of propaganda materials, those on "knowledge" matters outweighed those on "politics." In our analytical terms, the new policy on national integration under Liu was clearly based on identification rather than penetration.

The response to these new programs in propaganda, art, and literature can be seen in the growing number of "miscellaneous essays" in the press and journals, essays that had little relevance to current political tasks or Communist ideology; in the publication of classical plays and stories in the press and journals; in the production of several comedy movies that had mainly an entertainment function; and in the frequent performance of classical plays and operas that have always been popular among Chinese of all social classes.

As Mao later revealed, he was extremely dissatisfied with the policy under Liu and the response by intellectuals to it. What alarmed Mao most was that in essays and rewritten plays he saw thinly veiled attacks on his leadership. Mao's suspicion seems to have had some real basis. In the publications of 1961 and 1962, one can detect that Chinese writers had finally resorted to the time-honored device of making indirect political criticism by employing allegory. Chinese scholars now wrote about heroic officials of the past who had spoken out against despotic emperors on behalf of the oppressed peasants, despite their own personal risks. The most famous episode of this is the play written by Wu Han, then deputy mayor of Peking. Wu wrote about the Ming official Hai Jui, who lost his position because of his open criticism of the despotic emperor. To Mao, this was an implicit vindication of the former Defense Minister Marshall Peng Teh-hui, who criticized the Great Leap in a Central Committee meeting in 1959. Other essays and stories were more daring than the revised old plays. One branded Mao's talk about "East Wind now prevails over the West Wind" and other statements as "a great empty talk." [31]

Because these essays and plays were published in Party controlled newspapers, notably the *Peking Daily* and the journal, *Chien-hsien* (Front), of the Peking Municipal Party Committee, and, further, because their writers were high-ranking propaganda officials or renowned writers, Mao now suspected a plot among intellectuals within and without the Party to discredit him and his policies. To Mao, the proliferation of classical operas and the production of comedy movies that had no direct relation to politics were further proof that the party propaganda establishment was no longer loyal to his "revolutionary mystique." Herein lies Mao's motivation to purge the propaganda apparatus.

III. Propaganda in the Army, 1960–1961

The failure of the Great Leap and its consequent economic disaster affected the morale of the military as much as it did that of civilians. The army suffered particularly from low morale because most of the recruits came from the countryside. Mao's prestige and the credibility of the Communist Party were severely undermined even in the military.[32] As mentioned above, Marshal Peng Teh-hui openly challenged Mao's program in a Central Committee meeting in 1959. The subsequent purge of Marshal Peng and his associates brought Marshal Lin Piao to power. Lin quickly set about to rebuild morale in the army and restore Mao's prestige. Lin's present political eminence in China and Mao's use of the military in the Cultural Revolution both stemmed from Lin's success in rebuilding army morale and Mao's prestige in the military.

The main headquarters of propaganda work in the military was the General Political Department of the Ministry of Defense. This department was, in turn, controlled by the Military Affairs Committee of the Party Central Committee. The functions of the General Political Department were not confined only to political indoctrination of the troops. The department was in charge also of Party and Youth league organizations in the military and of the relationship between the military and the civilians. The General Political Department commanded a complex and penetrative propaganda apparatus in the military which was no less powerful than its civilian counterpart. The department operated a military press, the most authoritative publication being the national *Liberation Army Daily*. It also managed the military "August 1" Film Studio. The department maintained an independent policy on art and literature for the military, and the chief propaganda instrument of its policy was the system of Cultural Work Corps (*Wen-kun Tuan*).[33]

Under the General Political Department of the Ministry of Defense, there were Political Departments in various service headquarters. Between the service headquarters and the troop units was the military district system. China was divided into several First-level Military Districts, under which were Provincial Military Districts. The general headquarters of every military district commanded all military units within its territorial jurisdiction. In every district headquarters, there was a Political Department that, among other things, published a district military newspaper. From the General Political Department of the Defense Ministry to the Political Departments in service headquarters and military district headquarters a vertical chain of command was formed.[34] In troop units, from army corps to company, a system of political commissariat carried out propaganda work and other political activities as the arms of the General Political Department. In scope of function and depth of penetration, the political propaganda apparatus in the military paralleled the civilian propaganda organizations. Because of this parallel, the propaganda apparatus in the military was a ready-made alternate to the civilian one. To a manipulation-prone leader like Mao Tse-tung, the parallel apparatus served as an important instrument to purge the civilian propaganda apparatus.

Since Lin Piao was promoted by Mao to replace the purged Marshal Peng Teh-hui in 1959, Lin apparently considered it his first duty to restore Mao's prestige in the military. He lost little time in carrying out his obligation. At a Military Affairs Committee conference in late 1959, Lin attacked Peng's alleged emphasis on professionalism at the expense of political indoctrination. In the fall of 1960, Lin convened an enlarged meeting of the Military Affairs Committee to discuss political work in the army. A decision was made to intensify political indoctrination among troops. A mass indoctrination campaign was soon initiated in the military which consisted of three interrelated and essentially repetitious programs. One was the famous "four firsts" movement, which stressed the primacy of man over weapons and of political work over all other kinds. The second movement was the revival of the guerrilla tradition, emphasizing ideological firmness, frugality, and discipline. The third movement was learning the works of Mao. It is clear that all three movements were geared to bolster the prestige of Mao. As Philip Bridgham points out, the "four firsts" that put politics first over everything else, is merely a restatement of Mao's "mass line" approach to leadership.[35] The guerrilla tradition of the army involved mainly Mao's instructions to the Red Army during the Second World War. The indoctrination programs initiated by Lin were actually the forerunner of the Cultural Revolution.

To repair the damage that the Great Leap had done to

Mao's prestige in the army, Lin now blamed the disaster on middle- and lower-level cadres. These cadres, according to Lin's instructions to troops, had "created a communication block by failing to relay in time instructions of the Party and their superiors on the one hand and failing to submit reports to their superiors on the other." This tactic of blaming the middle-level cadres, according to Philip Bridgham, served to extricate Mao from the disaster of the Great Leap and, at the same time, provided legitimacy for the wholesale purge of the Party in the Cultural Revolution.[36] Lin then initiated a purge of the Party branches in the army in late 1960. According to a report, from July 1960 to February 1961, the Political Departments of the military had "cleaned and adjusted" about eighty-three percent of the Party branches in the armed forces. Over two thousand cadres in the military were either expelled from the Party or put on probation basis. New Party members were admitted, and over half of the squads now had Party members. Over eighty percent of the platoons were said to have Party teams, and all companies now had Party branches.[37] By this massive political penetration, Lin not only pleased Mao but also built up his own power base in the army.

In 1961, as China's countryside suffered severe food shortage and the troops' morale sank dangerously low, Lin Piao further intensified his political indoctrination program and the development of the cult of Mao. Lin initiated two mutually reinforcing movements in the army: the model "Four-good Company" and "Five-good Soldier." The emphasis of both was, again, "good in politics." To develop Mao's cult further, the general Political Department now published *Selected Readings of the Works of Mao Tse-tung* for use in the military. This was the first of the attempts to select parts of Mao's works for mass dissemination that finally resulted in the "little red books" of quotations from Mao which appeared in the Cultural Revolution. To counter the deteriorating troop morale, a mass campaign of oral agitation was staged among soldiers. The campaign consisted of mass participation in three types of activities: "recalling the past sufferings" before the Communists came to power, "speaking about the sweetness under the

Communist rule and thinking about its origin," and "discussing present politics and policies" about people's communes in order to see the merits of the communes.[38] Since most of the recruits were of poor peasant origin, this campaign, abbreviated as "recall and compare," was designed to arouse the class emotion of soldiers in order to achieve a catharsis. It was reported that when recalling their sufferings in the hands of landlords before the Communist rule, some soldiers were on the verge of tears. Like other campaigns initiated by Lin Piao this one also served to divert the soldiers' discontent from Mao and the Party Central Committee. Like other propaganda campaigns in the military from 1960 on, this one of "recall and compare" was later also applied to the civilian population.

Thus, glaring differences and contrasts existed between the propaganda, art, and literature sponsored by the Party Propaganda Department for the benefit of the civilian population and that sponsored by the General Political Department for the military. The two were almost antithetical to each other. While civilian propaganda stressed diversity, the military stressed the primacy of politics. While the civilian encouraged individual creativity and absorption of fine Western works, the military wanted the domination of the thought of Mao. Professionalism was preferred to mass participation in civilian propaganda, but in the military, the reverse was true. Civilian propaganda in 1960 and 1961 employed the unifying symbol of "whole people of China"; the military employed the revolutionary symbol of "class struggle."

Concerning these contrasts, it is important to know how they were interpreted by the Party leaders. In retrospect, we can see that Mao and Lin interpreted this as a struggle between "two lines," the socialist (or Maoist) and the capitalist (or revisionist) lines. The military approach to propaganda was naturally considered the socialist line. But civilian propagandists interpreted it otherwise. They perceived it as a natural difference between civilians and the military, a distinction that does not conform to Mao's desire to militarize the Chinese people.[39] Now, with the availability of the military propaganda apparatus, Mao could destroy the civilian apparatus in order to develop his own cult. This task was made easier by the appearance of the left-wing faction within the civilian propaganda apparatus.

IV. The Rise of the Left-wing Faction, 1962

The intellectuals and propagandists in Communist China were not a cohesive group. Divisions among them gave Mao an opportunity to exercise his talent of manipulation. Ever since 1957, the propaganda apparatus had been torn by a major dispute on strategy. It appeared openly for the first time in 1958, in the debate over the criterion of "Red" (ideological commitment) versus "expert" (professional competence) in cadre training, indoctrination, and education. Mao and other left-wing Party leaders overtly called for an integration between Red and expert, but there was no doubt in any cadre's mind that Mao wanted the primacy of Red over expert. The line of division among propagandists, then, was summarized by Chou Yang on "two ways of work" that we have already mentioned. The Great Leap Forward was a heyday for left-wing propagandists, who stressed massive political penetration in the form of mass campaigns.

As we know, the failure of the Great Leap discredited the leftist approach to propaganda and cultural work. And the new policy of reconciliation in propaganda and cultural work after 1959 thoroughly alarmed Mao. In the meantime, Lin Piao's approach to troop indoctrination was a genuine leftist one with its emphasis on politicization and mass campaigns. Mao's approval of Lin's program must have been noticed by leftists in the propaganda apparatus. By late 1962, a powerful figure had appeared in propaganda work who quickly bolstered the strength of the leftists. That was Chiang Ching, or Madame Mao.

That Chiang Ching assumed active political duty in 1962 is symptomatic of the anomaly of the Cultural Revolution. For until 1962, Chiang was an almost invisible figure who seldom appeared publicly with Mao, in contrast to the wives of other Chinese leaders like Liu Shao-chi and Chou En-lai. When in 1962 Chiang intervened in the propaganda apparatus' management of classical drama, she was without any formal official capacity. She acted purely as Mao's wife and his personal representative. In retrospect, both Mao's promotion of Lin and the use of Chiang Ching showed Mao's suspicion and distrust of the entire Party propaganda apparatus.

The appearance of Chiang Ching was a big morale booster for the leftists in the propaganda apparatus, for Chiang's conception of art and literary work was strictly leftist, or Maoist. Under her leadership, the leftists selected the proliferation of classical opera on China's stage as a pretext to launch a sustained attack on the professionals in the Party Propaganda Department. Chiang appeared to have gone to the midst of several drama troupes in Peking in 1962 and conducted a personal agitation campaign among the younger performers, urging them to criticize the established professionals for showing too many classical operas. She agitated for the showing of operas and plays that were intimately related to current political tasks. Instead of showing old emperors, queens, and generals, Chiang wanted the stage to show workers, peasants, and soldiers.[40] By eliminating classical operas, Chiang tried to accomplish two things. One was to eliminate the covert criticism against Mao, depriving the scholars of their allegorical devices. The other was to dispense with professionals on stage once and for all, as their skill was intimately related to the classical opera.

Then, in September 1962, Mao personally intervened to strengthen the leftists. In the Tenth Plenum of the Eighth Central Committee held in Peking, Mao made an important speech. He called on the Party to "never forget class struggle." As I have mentioned, "class struggle" was a rallying symbol for leftists in the Party. In statements resembling closely Stalin's justification for the great purge—claiming that the internal class struggle was becoming more and more acute as the nation moved toward socialism, Mao now said:

In the whole historical period of proletarian revolution and dictatorship, in the transition from capitalism to Communism (this may take some ten years, or more) there exists the class struggle between proletarians and the bourgeoisie, and between the two ways of socialism and capitalism. The overthrown reactionary ruling class will not be contented with being overthrown. They will try to restore their rule. Meanwhile, there exists in society influences of the bourgeoisie, the inertia of old society and some spontaneous capitalist tendencies among petit producers. Thus, there are some among the people who have not yet undergone socialist reform. Their number is small. But they grab at every opportunity to depart from socialism to take the capitalist road. Under these circumstances, class struggle is unavoidable.[41]

Having laid down a theoretical foundation for the leftists, Mao now turned on the current artistic and literary works, especially those suspected of containing covert political criticism. He regarded these works as necessary preparations in public opinion for the restoration of capitalism in China. This was a warning to scholars and intellectuals in the employ of the propaganda apparatus that they were engaging in counter-revolutionary conspiracy. Mao then made his wish known; he called for "reeducation of cadres" and initiation of a nation-wide campaign of socialist education.

V. The Intensification of Left-Wing Attack, 1963–1965

The Socialist Education campaign was a comprehensive one that included not only a sharp increase of political propaganda all over China, especially in rural areas, but also a Party "rectification" campaign. The latter dealt mainly with rural cadres. This discussion will focus on the propaganda aspect.

Because Mao had called for intensification of political propaganda in the nation, the Party propaganda apparatus had no alternative but to follow. But the officials in the Propaganda Department had no intention of repeating the radical political penetration of the Great Leap. Instead, they tried to toe a middle line between the policy of reconciliation, as expressed in the "Ten Articles on Art and Literature," and Mao's call for another wave of mass politicization. Their tactic was to start a campaign of "culture to villages" (*wen-hua hsia-hsiang*). In major cities of China, members of the professional drama, music, dance, art, literary, and science groups were organized into Rural Cultural Work Teams to go down to selected villages to entertain the peasants. In 1963, Peking led the way in this movement. The activities of these teams in villages were a combination of entertainment and general education. Political agitation, especially on "class struggle," was a minor part of their activity. In his speech to a Peking group, Chou Yang mentioned not "class struggle" but "labor struggle" in the countryside, i.e., facilitating production.[42] This was indeed an ingenious way of coping with Mao's demand. These Cultural Work Teams could partly satisfy Mao's penchant for enveloping the countryside with political propaganda. As they were mobile, they would not disturb the countryside for any prolonged period, thus maintaining the general direction of reducing political intervention in rural areas after 1959. Furthermore, members of these teams were professionals, whose performances could enliven rural life instead of creating tension and boredom by massive dosages of political propaganda.

By concentrating on the "culture to villages" movement, the Party Propaganda Department also sidetracked those major issues that Mao and the left-wing faction felt most objectionable. These were: criticism of Mao in the press, absence of modern plays with political themes, absence of adulation of Mao's thought, and lack of emphasis on "class struggle " in art and literature.

The left-wing faction gradually intensified its attack on the Party propaganda establishment in 1963. It appeared that a well-coordinated assault on professionals in the Party propaganda apparatus was worked out among Mao, Chiang Ching, and Lin Piao.

The military propaganda machinery openly encroached upon the civilian propaganda work first in 1963. In a comprehensive study on the development in Kwangtung province, Ezra Vogel reports that in January, 1963, at the Chinese New Year celebrations, "the army in Kwangtung went beyond its usual New Year's greeting to convey another specific message."

In the Swatow Special District, for example, army representatives addressed some 3,000-odd cadres and representatives of "the masses" to "propagandize the spirit of the Tenth Plenum of the Chinese Communist Party." The army's New Year's message was accompanied by the articles of the great success of socialist education in the army where campaigns for the "Four Good" teams (good in political thought, work style, military training, and management of living) and "Five Good Soldiers" (good in political thinking, military training, work style, accomplishing tasks, and physical training), based on the Thoughts of Mao Tse-tung, had been enormously successful.[43]

A more important development in the ascendency of the military propaganda machinery in 1963 was the Learn from Lei Feng, as published by the army, was filled with adulations of a soldier-martyr who died in a truck accident in 1962. He became a model for emulation because of his poor peasant background and his unswerving faith in Mao Tse-tung and the "proletarian stand of the socialist cause." The "diary" of Lei Feng, as published by the army, was filled with adulations of Mao's sayings. He was described as "one of Chairman Mao's good warriors." As Vogel points out, whether or not Lei Feng did really exist does not matter; he was "a symbol of all the virtues that the revolutionary Zealots wished to get across: absolute devotion to China, to socialism, to work, to children, to old ladies, and to Chairman Mao. The campaign was designed to restore faith in Mao and his correct policies." [44] Because Lei was supposed to have been a soldier and the emulation campaign was first started in the army, all propaganda materials about this campaign were issued by the army. In the civilian population, the campaign was most actively promoted in the Youth League. Later, the campaign was further extended to labor unions. This and other activities of the military propaganda machinery can be construed as implicit rebukes to the Party progaganda establishment for its failure to support Mao's leadership.

While Lin Piao's propaganda machinery was challenging the propaganda apparatus of the Party, Chiang Ching kept up her personal agitation among the opera groups in Peking and Shanghai. By the end of 1963, she was reported to have investigated about a thousand new and classical plays. All the while, she was backed by Mao's verbal rebukes to propaganda officials in charge of the stage. The propaganda apparatus could no longer ignore these pressures. In August 1963, the Ministry of Culture, which was controlled by the Propaganda Department of Party Central Committee, convened a conference on modern and classical plays. But the participants of the Conference, including Chou Yang, did not reach any conclusion on classical operas. Some were opposed to any tampering with the old plays, let alone banning them. Chiang's interferences in drama troupes in Peking were also resented by Party and state officials, especially those in the Peking municipal Party Committee and government.[45]

But in Shanghai, Chiang achieved a breakthrough. Shanghai was then the command center of the East China Bureau of the Party Politburo. In geopolitical terms, Shanghai is as strategic as Peking in the North and Canton in the South. These three represent the centers of three major geographical, cultural, and political regions in China. It was a major breakthrough for Chiang Ching and her leftist followers when the East China Bureau responded positively to her programs. The head of the East China Bureau then was Ko Ching-shih, who held the concurrent positions of member of the Politburo of Party Central Committee, Vice Premier of State Council, and First Secretary of the Shanghai Municipal Party Committee. In January 1963, Ko had spoken out against the policy of the "Ten Articles on Art and Literature." He called on intellectuals in East China to create works about the activities of workers, peasants, and soldiers since the establishment of the Communist rule. Whether Mao or Chiang had actively recruited Ko or Ko had decided to capitalize on the division between Mao and the propaganda apparatus to advance himself, does not matter. What matters is that now the left-wing faction had a regional base. In December 1963, Ko staged a grand and large-scale series of modern plays that lasted until the end of January 1964. It was called "A Review of the Modern Plays in the East China Region, 1963." Ko's opening speech echoed Mao's charge that the Chinese stage had been dominated by "dead men" and that the professionals in drama were "enthusiastic about bourgeois, feudalistic, foreign, and old matters" but "indifferent to socialist modern plays." [46] Ko's support for Chiang Ching's effort must have been crucial to Mao's decision in 1965 to go to Shanghai to launch his attack on the Peking Municipal Party Committee.

A further assault on the civilian propaganda apparatus was launched by the army in 1964. In February, a nationwide campaign of "Learn from the People's Liberation Army" was started. The methods that Lin Piao had used in rebuilding army morale and developing a cult for Mao in the military during 1960 and 1961 were now applied to the entire nation. Organizations in industry, agriculture, and commerce were told to compare their work with the army. Copying from the army, movements of "Five-good Employee," "Five-good Worker," or "Five-good Production Team" were staged in industry and agriculture. Meanwhile, the Party Central Committee and the Youth Publishing House published for mass distribution three versions of *Selected Readings of the Works of Mao Tse-tung*, which, as I mentioned, had been first used by Lin Piao in the army.

The army also moved to join forces with Chiang Ching in the field of modern plays. In Kwangtung, for example, the Army Political Department replaced Kwangtung's civilian troupes in presenting new plays to civilian audiences.[47] Under the joint pressure of the army and the left-wing faction, the Ministry of Culture now staged a national performance of modern Chinese opera in Peking from June to July. For the first time, Chiang Ching was publicly identified with the modern play movement, though she still bore no official title.[48] This national show in Peking marked Chiang Ching's victory in the drama field.

Mao Tse-tung now proceded to consolidate his initial gains, accomplished by Lin Piao and Chiang Ching, and to grapple with other problems of his concern. The most important problem, to Mao, was the veiled criticism of him by scholars and writers. Another concern was with artistic and literary works, especially films, that were produced after 1961 in response to the limited liberalization. Mao shrewdly did not call in the military to help him in this matter. He moved to split the ranks of the Party propaganda apparatus by establishing, sometime in mid-1964, an ad hoc group called the Cultural Revolution Section of the Central Committee, headed by then mayor of Peking, Peng Chen.[49] On the surface, this section did not encroach upon the functions of the Propaganda Department of Party Central Committee since the department's director, Lu Ting-i, was a member of the section. But in reality, the section was meant to supersede the Propaganda Department by virtue of its authority to review the entire field of art and literature. The specific tasks of this ad hoc section were clarified by Mao in June 1964 in a scathing attack on all the art and literary associations in China. Mao reportedly said:

The majority of the journals and publications (some were said to be all right) of these associations (not all of them) basically had not carried out the policy of the Party in the past fifteen years. They became officials and bureaucrats, unwilling to go near the workers and peasants or reflect socialist revolution and construction. In recent years they have gone near the edge of revisionism. If they do not seriously reform themselves, they will inevitably change into a group like the Petofi Club in Hungary.[50]

Thus, the job of Peng Chen was to start a "rectification" campaign among intellectuals and particularly to reverse the policy expressed in the "Ten Articles on Art and Literature."

Immediately after the creation of the Cultural Revolution Section in 1964, the Chinese press began to publish critiques of those who once had been spokesmen of the policy of reconciliation. The scope of the critique was extensive, ranging from subject matters in short stories to themes in historiography and the substance of ideological education of high-level cadres.[51] Yet all the criticisms had a common focus, the charge that those who were criticized either ignored or opposed the importance of sharp class distinctions, i.e., "class struggle." For example, the then secretary of the Party Fraction in the Writers' Association, Shao Chuan-lin, was criticized in the press for encouraging writers in 1962 to write about "middle characters," thus blurring the distinction between heroes, i.e., the proletariat, and "backward elements." Another significant aspect of this initial phase of rectification is that the majority of those who were attacked held high but mainly honorary positions in the Party and state. But they were professionals who had established their literary fame before the Communist rule. They were retained and given honorary positions after 1949, presumably as a showcase of united front tactics. The Cultural Revolution was eventually to wipe out this group of professionals.

Because most of these old professionals held positions in the cultural and educational organizations of the state apparatus, the Ministry of Culture was the first target of actual purge. In January 1965, the head of the Ministry, the famous novelist Sheng Yen-pin, and three well-known deputy ministers, Hsia Yen, Chi Yen-min, and Chen Huang-mei, were purged. Under Peng Chen's direction, four new deputy ministers were appointed. None of the four was of intellectual background, two being military officers and the other two, Party apparatchiki. The new minister, however, turned out to be the Director of the Party Propaganda Department, Lu Ting-i. It seems that Peng Chen was trying to maintain a balance between the left-wing faction and the established Party propaganda apparatus— at the expense of old intellectuals. The purge of these famous scholars and intellectuals from the ministry could not but please Mao. The selection of new deputy ministers from the military and other Party organizations was presumably intended to please the leftists, including Mao. To balance this new group, Lu Ting-i was then promoted to the position of cultural minister. It could be that Peng, as a veteran organization specialist, tried to protect the established Party apparatus. Suggestive evidence of Peng's effort to blunt Mao's attack on intellectuals and propagandists is the way this first move of rectification was conducted. The campaign was carried out in an academic fashion. The purged officials were criticized by their younger colleagues in the press, more like a debate in Communist scholasticism than like the populist campaigns of anti-intellectualism that the left-wing faction favored. Mao Tse-tung complained in 1966 that this rectification under Peng Chen did not arouse much attention.[52] It is highly plausible that this was a deliberate attempt by Peng to limit the extent of disruption.

But in the eyes of Mao and his left-wing followers, the greatest sin that Peng Chen had committed in this rectification campaign was one of omission rather than commission. Peng had sidetracked the burning issue of covert criticism of Mao by several high-ranking Party officials in the propaganda organization of Peking Municipal Party Committee and government— the most conspicuous culprit being the deputy mayor, Wu Han. Finally in September 1965, Mao was reported to have confronted Peng personally about the issue of covert attacks, particularly Wu Han's play *Hai Jui*. The occasion of that confrontation was a conference of the Politburo. The conference lasted for two months, which suggests not only that a large number of matters were brought up in the conference, but also that consensus was difficult to reach among members of the Politburo. Peng was said to have replied to Mao that only "some aspects" of Wu Han's works could be criticized.[53] Whether this is indeed true is hard to determine. But one thing is certain. Mao felt that he had met active opposition from Peng and other members of the Politburo and that, short of a total attack on the Party structure in Peking, Mao could not force his will on Peng and his association. Immediately after the conference, Mao left Peking for Shanghai. He was to stay there until the total destruction of the Peking Party apparatus in mid-1966. Mao's departure from Peking marked a major escalation of the leftist attack on the entire propaganda apparatus. The Cultural Revolution now quickly moved toward its "mass" phase, when the Party as a whole was subject to mass attack.

VI. The Destruction of the Party Propaganda Apparatus, 1966

As described above, the leadership of the Shanghai Party apparatus had aligned itself with the left-wing faction as early as 1963. It was logical, then, for Mao to go to Shanghai to mobilize the leftists for an attack on his real or imaginary opponents in Peking. The Party chief who brought Shanghai to the leftist faction, Ko Ching-shih, however, died in April 1965. But he had staffed the Party apparatus with supporters of the left-wing faction before his death. Thus, Mao's work in Shanghai was not hampered by Ko's death.

On November 10, 1965, the Shanghai newspaper *Wen-hui Daily* initiated the first attack on the previously mentioned play by the deputy mayor of Peking, Wu Han. The newspaper carried an article by Yao Wen-yuan, who was then the chief editor of the *Liberation Daily,* the organ of the Shanghai Municipal Party Committee. According to a later and official account, Yao's attack on Wu Han was actually initiated by Mao. The attack, as this account goes, lifted "the curtain of the Great Cultural Revolution." [54] There are two revealing aspects to Yao's attack. First, the attack on a major political personality was initiated by a local newspaper, not by the Party Central Committee; and, second, the attack was printed in a non-Party newspaper. Yao could have published his attack in his own paper, the *Liberation Daily,* which, as the organ of Shanghai Party Committee, would have imparted more authority to his essay. It is very plausible that Mao intended this to be a test to see how the other Party leaders at the national and regional levels reacted to it. Their reaction, one might infer, would determine for Mao who could be recruited to the leftist faction. Mao, through his wife, had used the issue of modern plays to test the reaction of Party officials and had thus recruited the late Ko Ching-shih and his East China Bureau. Now, Mao used Yao's article once more to test Party officials. That is why he deliberately used an obscure Party-line intellectual like Yao to attack the renowned Wu Han in a non-Party newspaper.

Reactions to Yao's article must have been disappointing to Mao. For, of all the major national and regional newspapers including the most authoritative *People's Daily*—organ of the Central Committee—only the military organ, the *Liberation Army Daily* "responded" to Yao's attack by denouncing Wu Han's work as "poisonous weed." The term "poisonous weed" had been hitherto used to denounce "rightists" in the Hundred Flowers campaign of 1957, i.e., those who criticized the Party during the campaign. It was equivalent to charging a person with "anti-Party" activities, a serious charge indeed. All the other newspapers, organs of mass organizations or regional Party headquarters, had called for discussions and debates instead of denunciation. [55]

But Peng Chen could hardly ignore this matter, especially when the military had openly challenged the Propaganda Department by differing with the *People's Daily*. Peng reportedly had another personal encounter with Mao in December over Wu Han. Peng was later accused by Red Guard newspapers of fabricating an agreement between him and Mao on the "non-political nature" of Wu's work. Under pressure from the left, however, Peng did order Wu to conduct a self-criticism in the press. Peng seems to have tried to sidetrack this matter by using his old method of making the issue a sort of intellectual debate.[56] Peng was, in fact, struggling for personal survival. For he knew well that only a topmost leader like Mao could be free of "collective responsibility." Mao would be adulated even while his one-time heir, Liu, was denounced as an "internal traitor," "thief," and "revisionist." But a mayor must be held responsible for the actions of the deputy mayor. Peng was reported to have said, "Before truth, everyone is equal," but he must have known that in Communist Party politics, some are more equal than others.

By now, Mao must have concluded either that Peng had failed the test of personal loyalty to Mao, or that Peng had exhausted his usefulness. The leftists then moved quickly to close their ranks. In other words, the downfall of Peng and the entire Party propaganda apparatus were imminent at the beginning of 1966.

In February 1966, Marshal Lin Piao moved to consolidate the power of the leftists, a move presumably either initiated or at least approved by Mao. Lin invited Chiang Ching to convene a Conference on Art and Literary Work in the Armed Forces. The conference was held in Shanghai without publicity. The attendants were mostly high-ranking officers in the apparatus of the General Political Department. Though Chiang Ching was formally invited merely to lecture on art and literature in the military, she was actually made the director of all artistic and literary work in the military. Lin Piao reportedly instructed the officers at the conference to "submit to her all documents on the art and literary work in the armed forces from there on." [57] Thus, an alliance was formally created between the military propaganda apparatus and the leftists under Chiang Ching.

The content of Chiang's lecture to the conference on art and literary work in the armed forces made it clear that it was intended for the use of the entire nation, not just the military. Chiang denounced the entire policy of reconciliation that was implemented after the failure of the Great Leap. She accused the intellectuals and professionals in art and literature of anti-Mao and anti-socialist activities. She called on the military to "assume an important role" in the "Great Socialist Cultural

Revolution." The future artistic and literary work, according to Chiang, must be based on "mass line." She declared her determination to reeducate and reorganize the ranks of workers in these fields. Chiang's lecture was later read and revised by Mao three times before it was dispatched to be circulated in the military.[58]

Lin's legitimization of Chiang's position in the military in February 1966 seems to have been in anticipation of the activities of Peng Chen. As we know, Peng was appointed by Mao in 1964 to head the Cultural Revolution Section under the Central Committee. He was to deal with the many objectionable aspects of artistic and literary production, particularly covert criticism of Mao. I have described how Peng carried out his work. Now, in February 1966, Peng was also preparing a document to serve as a guide in the Cultural Revolution. Meanwhile, Mao and the leftists under his wife had already lost their trust in Peng. There was thus a need to counter Peng's forthcoming policy statement. Chiang's lecture to the military served this function. Peng's statement on policy in artistic and literary work was a mere confirmation of what he had already done. He had diverted the attack on intellectuals and writers out of political and into academic channels.

We can see that Peng was in a particularly trying position because the most daring criticisms of Mao had come from three high-ranking officials of the Peking Party and state apparatus. They were Teng To, one-time editor-in-chief of the authoritative *People's Daily*, who held the positions of secretary of Peking Municipal Party Committee and editor-in-chief of the organ journal *Chien-hsien* (Front) in 1966; Liao Mu-sai, a veteran journalist who was the director of the United Front Division of Peking Municipal Party Committee; and Wu Han, renowned scholar and historian, who was Peking's deputy mayor in 1966. This group of important Peking intellectuals had published their works in the organs of the Peking Municipal Party Committee, the journal *Chien-hsien* and the *Peking Daily*. That Peng could not treat these intellectual dissidents as political opponents of Mao is understandable, for Peng himself was the mayor of Peking and the first secretary of the Peking Party structure. Furthermore, once Mao had expressed his dissatisfaction with these officials, their works were no longer published. The essays by Teng, for example, disappeared immediately after Mao's speech in the Central Committee in September 1962. By the end of 1964, these dissidents' works had completely disappeared. Peng must have assumed that the suspension of these works had mollified Mao's dissatisfaction. Like others, Peng seems to have underestimated Mao's determination to eliminate the influence of the established intellectuals once and for all.

Since Mao had already lost trust in Peng over the Wu Han affair, Peng's proposal in February 1966 had the negative effect of provoking Mao. Reportedly, Mao warned Peng in March that if he continued to protect the intellectuals under him, then the Peking Party Committee "must be dissolved." [59] Under this pressure, the *Peking Daily* began to publish criticisms of the three officials in April. Meanwhile, the military propaganda machinery, under the direction of Chiang Ching, formally announced the start of Cultural Revolution in the *Liberation Army Daily* in an editorial on April 18. As one analyst points out, a major mass campaign like this had always been announced by the most authoritative Party organ, the *People's Daily*.[60] But in this instance, the military newspaper had got the lead and the Party organ followed it. That Mao's wife, Chiang, was the leader behind the scene in this episode is borne out by the content of the *Liberation Army Daily* editorial of April 18, which contains excerpts from Chiang's speech to the military political workers in February. The fall of the *People's Daily* from its position of authority signified the imminent purge of the Propaganda Department of Party Central Committee.

In May, Mao Tse-tung, now residing in the scenic city Hangchow, ordered the dissolution of the Cultural Revolution Section headed by Peng Chen and invalidation of Peng's policy submitted in February. Mao further stated openly his real purpose in the Cultural Revolution. In his words: "The goal of this great struggle was to criticize Wu Han and a large group of anti-Party and anti-socialism bourgeois representatives. (There are such people in the Central Committee and its agencies and at provincial, municipal, and autonomous region levels.).''[61] Mao's intention of a wholesale purge is made clear in this statement. To put the purge under the direct control of the leftists, Mao reorganized the Cultural Revolution Section. This group was now put under the Standing Committee of the Politburo and headed by Mao's faithful personal secretary Chen Po-ta; Chiang Ching was the deputy chief of the group.[62]

The die was cast. Like a series of dominoes, Peng Chen, Peking Municipal Party Committee, Lu Ting-i, Chou Yang, and the Propaganda Department of Party Central Committee fell one after another between May and the end of June 1966. Lu Ting-i, the former director of Propaganda Department, was accused of neglecting "appropriate measures against the anti-party, anti-socialist tendencies in the propaganda, educational, and cultural fields" and helping "the off-stage activity of the anti-party group."[63] On July 30, a rally was called in the former Propaganda Department to denounce Chou Yang. The rally was presided over by a new deputy director of the department who was formerly the head of the Political Department of Hunan Military District. Chou Yang was accused of committing the multiple sins of refusing to advocate "art and literature for workers and peasants," calling for "literature and art for the whole people," affirming "the theory of human nature" and repudiating "class struggle," and "worshipping of foreign works." Chou was also accused, like Lu, of failing to take measures to stop the anti-party tendencies in art and literature and ignoring Mao's repeated criticisms of art and literature.[64] Though the charges against Chou Yang were more specific than those against Lu Ting-i, they were largely spurious. As Merle Goldman observes, in reality, "Chou Yang had been the most ardent advocate of Mao's cultural line since the Yenan days. . . ." And "the frenzied, highly emotional charges hurled against Chou Yang revealed Mao's utter frustration with the intellectuals, particularly the literary intellectuals, who had been responsible for shaping the mind of China. Chou Yang was blamed for the fact that after almost twenty-five years of unceasing indoctrination and thought reform, the intellectuals still resisted Mao's direction."[65] As we observed earlier, Inkeles' comment on the totalitarian mystique, which, in this case, means Mao's thought, is quite applicable to the purge of the propaganda specialists in China. Lu Ting-i and Chou Yang were purged "not so much for what they have done as for what they have not done. They are cast out not for bashing in the wrong heads, but for not bashing in enough heads." [66]

Though Lu Ting-i and Chou Yang were cast out by June 1966, the skeleton of the Propaganda Department remained. A new director was appointed. He was Tao Chu, first secretary and director of the Propaganda Department of the Central-South China Bureau of the Party Politburo. Yet within six months, in December, Tao was cast out too. As to the causes of the quick rise and fall of Tao, Mao himself offered an explanation. In a talk to the Cultural Revolution Section of the Politburo Standing Committee, Mao was reported to have said that the former secretary-general of the Chinese Communist Party, Teng Hsiao-ping, recommended Tao to the post of propaganda director. Since Mao's antagonism toward Teng was even more intense than that toward Liu Shao-chi, and since both were cast out eventually, Tao's fall was natural.[67] But a more substantial reason for Tao's quick descent was that he had never been accepted by the left-wing faction dominated by Chiang Ching and Chen Po-ta. Tao had not responded positively to Chiang's modern plays movement in 1963, as the late Ko Ching-shih did. Both, however, held the strategic position of first secretary of a regional bureau of the Politburo. Tao had implemented the policy of reconciliation in art and literature without reservation. After Mao had gradually enlarged his attack on the propaganda apparatus and relied on the military from 1962 on, Tao tried to balance the two sides in his Central-South Region.[68] Because of this reluctance to throw in his lot early with Chiang Ching, as the late Ko Ching-shih did in East China, Tao earned the hatred of Chiang. In a talk with Red Guards, Chiang accused Tao of trying to restrain her Cultural Revolution Section. He was accused of allowing a picture of Teng Hsiao-ping to appear in the press. Chen Po-ta charged Tao with ignoring the Cultural Revolution Section and complying with Liu Shao-chi and Teng Hsiao-ping.[69] Be that as it may, Tao was cast out primarily because of the left-wing faction's unwillingness to share its

power with an outsider. The episode of Tao Chu is symptomatic of the factional conflicts that were to follow as the Cultural Revolution progressed.

With the downfall of the Peking Party structure and the
Propaganda Department in June 1966, Mao then concluded
his sojourn in Shanghai and proceeded leisurely back to Peking
whence he had departed in disgust in November 1965.* Once
Mao was back in Peking, on July 18, 1966, he started the Red
Guard movement and the purge of the topmost leaders like
Liu and Teng. This phase of the Cultural Revolution is not
within the scope of this discussion, and an authoritative study
is available, so I will not dwell upon it here.[70]

Once Mao was back in Peking and the old propaganda apparatus ruined, the prestige of Chiang Ching quickly reached
a new height. On November 28, a rally was called by the Cultural Revolution Section to further the alliance of the military
and the leftists, particularly to exalt the position of Chiang
Ching. At the rally, an army representative from the General
Political Department announced the appointment of Chiang
Ching as the advisor on cultural work in the army and the
incorporation of the four most prestigious musical and dramatic groups into the military. These were: First Peking Opera
Company of Peking City, National Peking Opera Theatre,
Central Philharmonic Society, and the ballet troupes and or-
chestra of the Central Song and Dance Ensemble. Chiang then
made her first formal speech in front of a mass audience in the
Cultural Revolution. She called for a further struggle and
criticism campaign against the already paralyzed Propaganda
Department and the Ministry of Culture. She warned the
Peking opera group that had just been put under military
control to "break clear" of the old Peking Municipal Party
Committee for, in her words, "there is only one way out for
you." [71]

VII. The Politics of New Factions, 1967–1970

Responding to Chiang Ching's call for furthering the attacks
on the propaganda apparatus, a wave of purges took place in

---

* He stopped by in Wuhan in July and took a dip in the Yangtze River. This
event was highly publicized in the world press. Its symbolic meaning will be discussed in Chapter 5, "Mass Campaigns."

provinces and cities. The directors of the Propaganda Departments in provincial and municipal Party structures were toppled one after another. Starting from January, the purge had been transformed into a "power seizure" from below, i.e., in the form of Red Guards, or "revolutionary rebels" (cadres, workers, bureaucrats). Young staff members of major newspapers and radio stations formed revolutionary groups and announced their take-over of the newspaper or the radio station. For example, on January 12, the former organ of the Central-South Bureau of the Central Committee Politburo, *Southern Daily,* was taken over by two groups, called "Mao Tse-tung Thought *Southern Daily* Workers Rebellion Headquarters" and "*Southern Daily* Mao Tse-tung's Thought Revolutionary Rebellion Unified Command." On January 17, Radio Peking was seized by Red Guards. On the same day, the Provincial Shensi People's Broadcasting Station was taken over by a revolutionary group. Before the end of January, five more radio stations were taken over by rebel groups. Yet, surprisingly, the disruption of normal broadcasting was not extensive. As one report stated, Mao had ordered the army to take active control of all radio stations in January. Broadcasting programs were supplied by the army.[72] This wave of power seizure in the media system is part of the Red Guard movement that the leftists engineered in August 1966. The leftists were soon to lose control of the movement, which developed its own factional politics. Meanwhile, the Cultural Revolution Section under the command of Chen Po-ta and Chiang Ching had virtually taken over the former Propaganda Department of Party Central Committee, the Ministry of Culture, the Ministry of Education, and the New China News Agency. The Cultural Revolution Section was reported to have three subsections, one each on propaganda and publishing, art and film, and education. On the whole, the main division of labor was between Chen, who controlled propaganda, and Chiang, who controlled art and literature.[73] They had destroyed the entire Party propaganda apparatus that many had labored for two decades to build. Now, they faced the formidable task of building up their own following and, more important, the task of controlling it.

We have noted that in 1962, as Chiang Ching began to intervene in the propaganda field, she had conducted a personal
agitation campaign among the younger members of the dramatic groups in Peking. In her talk to the military propagandists in February 1966, Chiang had declared her determination
to reeducate cadres and train new ones. The new cadres logi-
cally stemmed from the younger members in the former propaganda apparatus whose grievances against the established
professionals Chiang had exploited to the full. Chiang soon
found that the attack on the Party had opened a Pandora's box.
Factional conflicts among the young rebels were rampant. To
call a halt to factionalism and to present a semblance of unity,
a rally was called in June 1967 for the followers of the leftists.
It was attended by 14,000 "fighters in literature and art," representing artistic and literary groups, academics in art and
literature, the film industry, libraries, and museums. This was
supposed to be the Cultural Revolution Section's "first militant
massive review of the ranks" of the left. But the rally was called
for defensive reasons. As the report on this rally stated, "considerable contradictions and dissensions exist among them due
to differences in viewpoint and the influence of anarchism,
sectarianism, small-group mentality, and selfish thinking. . . ." [74]

Furthermore, the values of professionalism to which Mao
and the leftists so strongly objected were by no means weakened by the attacks on old professionals. On July 4, 1967,
Wen-hui Daily, the paper that fired the first salvo of the Cultural Revolution, published an editorial appealing for a
"great alliance" among drama groups. The editorial not only
expressed concern over factionalism but also revealed that
"large number of youth and other people" were corroded by
the "three famous" and "three highs" principles. Both were
the sins of professionals. "Three famous" meant that literary
and art workers strived only to be famous writers, directors,
and actors. "Three highs" meant high salaries, royalties, and
awards. The editorial concluded on an almost despairing note:
"Some units in literature and art have not yet effectively
brought about a revolutionary great alliance. Some engage in
endless 'civil wars.' "

Factionalism and "civil wars," however, were originated

from above, from Mao. It is not surprising, then, that in late 1967, the Cultural Revolution Section itself was rocked by a major factional struggle. The full picture of this struggle has not yet been made clear. But by December 1967, three important and once active members of Chiang Ching's entourage in the Cultural Revolution suddenly disappeared from the public. Among them were Wang Li, who briefly took over the post of director of the Propaganda Department of Party Central Committee after Tao Chu was cast out, and Chi Pen-yu, who had been the chief writer in the attacks on the Peking Municipal Party Committee and later was the author of the attack on Liu Shao-chi. All three were deputy editors of the chief ideological journal *Hung Chi* (Red Flag). Because of their expulsion in late 1967, the journal ceased publications for several issues. It was only in April 1968 that Red Guard newspapers published charges against the three. They were accused of encouraging mobs to disrupt the Chinese foreign office and attack British diplomats. Chi was accused of attempting to disrupt the State Council and spy on Chou En-lai. The three were further charged with collecting information about their boss, Chiang Ching, and attacking the military.[75] It seems that by the end of 1967, the leftists had overplayed their hand. Nationwide disruptions and faction struggles had brought disrepute to Chiang and other leftwing leaders. Meanwhile, once in power, Chiang Ching and her military ally Lin Piao were now also interested in conserving, especially in striking an alliance with such a powerful central figure as Chou En-lai, who controlled the vital state apparatus. It is also quite plausible that since both had accomplished their purpose of gaining national eminence, Chiang Ching and Lin Piao may now have had conflicts of interest.[76] The three leftists who were purged in late 1967 were probably sacrificed for the sake of "power politics" at the top.

From 1967 to 1969, no institutionalization took place in propaganda work. The Cultural Revolution Section had the main preoccupation of combating factions among their "followers." Yet, the leftists could devise no innovative method to deal with factions. In 1967, they had tried to resort to the old method of sending rebels in artistic and literary work to the countryside in order to divert them from cities and fragment their ranks so they could be controlled by the Party and military in the countryside. When this did not work, the leftist leaders tried to use faction to fight faction. In 1968, in addition to the use of military to counter factionalism all over China, a new type of group was formed. These were the "workers propaganda teams," whose ostensible function was to reeducate intellectuals and students in schools and cultural institutes. In actuality, the real function of these workers propaganda teams was to act as intermediaries between the military and civilians, to blunt the antagonism especially existing between students and the military.[77] But instead of performing such a moderating function, antagonism arose between workers and students. The cure seems to have been worse than the disease.[78] I shall have more to say about these propaganda teams in later chapters.

Meanwhile, policy on propaganda and cultural work was dominated by Chiang Ching and two of her trusted lieutenants, both recruited from the former Shanghai Party structure. They were Yao Wen-yuan and Chang Chun-chiao. Although both were lower rank Party officials before Chiang brought them to national prominence, they were also professionals in literary and journalistic work. Yao was the youngest of the three-member group. Information about his early background is not yet available. Until Yao became the editor-in-chief of the *Liberation Daily,* organ of Shanghai Municipal Party Committee, sometime in the mid-1960s, his work was in youth leagues and mass organizations in art and literary fields. He was known as an activist who frequently contributed literary criticisms to journals espousing his Proletcult views. Yao probably had caught the eyes of Mao and his wife in the Hundred Flowers Campaign of 1957, when Chinese intellectuals, especially those in journalistic work, attacked the Communist Party for its control of the press. In that campaign Yao had stood out to defend the Party-line approach to newspaper work and had attempted on his own to expose the "bourgeois tendency" of the Shanghai paper *Wen-hui Daily.*[79]

In comparison with Yao, Chang Chun-chiao had extensive experience in the Communist Party's propaganda work. During the war, he had done artistic and literary work in the Communist base areas in the Northwest. He was the Communist representative who took over the Nationalist government's news agency, the Central News Agency, in 1949. He was the editor-in-chief of the *Liberation Daily* in Shanghai in 1954. Afterwards, he assumed various administrative jobs in the field of culture. Chang was probably recruited by Chiang Ching in 1964 when she was conducting her personal campaign for modern plays.[80] Thus, both Yao and Chang were professionals in propaganda work. Yao, however, seems to be more an ideologue than Chang, who had more experience in administrative work on propaganda. Seen from the background of these two and from Chiang Ching's own background as an obscure actress in stage and films in the 1930s, the Cultural Revolution can also be portrayed as the "outs" attacking the "ins."[81] Certainly in terms of professional careers, none of the three-member group had attained the literary fame of those who had been cast out. But the "outs" had grasped the reality in China, the reality of "politics takes command," and "political power grows out of the barrel of a gun."

The leftists had got power with guns. But they now found it difficult to realize the next step in Mao's principle: "the Party commands the gun; the gun shall never be allowed to command the Party." From 1969 onward, signs of conflict between the three-member clique headed by Chiang Ching and the military became more visible. On the eve of China's Army Day of August 1, 1970, broadcasts in Shanghai, which were controlled by Yao and Chang, contained challenges to the role of the military in politics. According to one newspaper account:

The Shanghai broadcast carried a series of quotations on the role of the army taken from the works of Chairman Mao. One quotation was viewed here [Hong Kong] as especially significant in the light of Shanghai's leftist orientation.

It stated, "The people's armed forces of a socialist country must always be placed under the leadership of the political party of the proletariat and the supervision of the masses of the people."

Political analysts here said that, by focusing attention on this quotation, the broadcast called into question the present situation in which the army exerted considerable political influence and blocked the mass organizations from gaining power.[82]

In September, a new director of the General Political Department of the military was appointed. An obscure former army corps commander, Li Teh-sheng, assumed this important post that commands the entire propaganda apparatus in the military. A professional soldier, Li had no experience in political indoctrination. His appointment was interpreted by some as "a tactical gain for the leftist forces in China and their mentor, Chiang Ching," for Li had no known historical affiliation with the man who commands the gun, Lin Piao.[83]

CONCLUSION

The Cultural Revolution has been a wrecking operation. The old leadership of the Party propaganda apparatus was wiped out and its organization wrecked because its members failed to realize Mao's revolutionary mystique of transforming mass "revolutionary latency" into the great material force that he envisioned. Now, a new corps of leaders has taken over headed by Mao's wife. In the process of wrecking the old, Mao and his wife freed the disintegrative forces that they and the old propaganda apparatus had labored to suppress in the past. Factionalism is now rampant and regionalism has again become an important facet of Chinese politics. Thus, when the Shanghai broadcasts of August 1970 challenged the dominant role of the army in current Chinese politics, it is reported that "vigorous defense of the army's role came from Hupeh and Honan."[84] The military again became the most important integrative force in China. In the meantime, a massive politicization campaign has been underway to rebuild the prestige and legitimacy of Mao and the Communist Party. In other words, the course of China's political development from 1949 to 1970 has gone a full circle.

In 1949, the Communist Party relied mainly on the military to achieve a degree of integration in the nation. At the same time, the Party staged a massive propaganda campaign to build up the authority of the new regime over the land. As institutionalization proceeded forward, the Party was able to relegate the military to the background and put the base of integration more on identification between the population and the new political authority. In 1970, the Cultural Revolution has returned the military to the forefront of China's integration, and the Communist Party has to be rebuilt. But in 1949, Party construction and national integration were facilitated by a spirit of optimism, revolutionary elan, and dynamism among the cadres, soldiers, and politically active groups in society, mainly students and intellectuals. By 1970, much of that spirit was gone. Mao's tactics of setting one group off against another and his purge of topmost Party leaders have resulted in widespread cynicism, albeit hidden behind the facade of revolutionary fervor. The rebuilding process from 1970 on is certain to be long and hard. The presence of the military and other coercive powers will not be reduced for a long time to come.

This description, however, is not intended to imply that what the old propaganda apparatus had accomplished has been totally undone. At the time of its paralysis in 1966, the Propaganda Department had existed for seventeen years. In this time, it had built the mass media on a national basis, organized professional writers and journalists, and launched a series of mass campaigns involving almost all adult members of the population. These activities must have left an imprint upon the Chinese people. Undoubtedly symbols of national identity and facts about Communist ideology had been widely diffused among the public. As a result, national consciousness was heightened. It is plausible that Mao recognized these accomplishments of the old propaganda apparatus and that he purged it precisely because he knew that with the heightened sense of national identity among the people, especially the younger generation, total disintegration of Chinese society would not occur even when the propaganda apparatus was not functioning. Furthermore, the unifying symbol among the "rebels" of the Cultural Revolution was the personality of Mao, which the propaganda apparatus itself had helped to build up.

Though the purge in the Cultural Revolution has wiped out the leadership corps of the old propaganda apparatus, the vast number of middle- and lower-rank cadres remains in the structure. These base-level cadres are certain to be recalled to duty, as they are the only group of trained personnel in propaganda work. Their training was conducted by the old propaganda establishment. The Propaganda Department also played a crucial role in the building up of the middle and lower cadres of the entire Party in the transition period from 1949 to the early 1950s. Through the work of the Department, training manuals and study guides were centrally distributed. The Department ran a system of formal and informal Party schools to train old and new cadres. All these efforts had created a large degree of organizational integration. A common Marxist-Leninist language was disseminated. A centripetal orientation was instilled in the cadres. Indeed, the overall centripetal orientation in and out of the Party created by the hard work of the old propaganda apparatus had made its own demise possible in the Cultural Revolution.

It was the propaganda apparatus before the Cultural Revolution that had achieved a breakthrough in the pattern of political life in China. Throughout the years, Party propagandists altered the thinking of ordinary Chinese about politics. A vast number of people, formerly non-participants in politics, were mobilized by means of mass campaigns. Mass mobilization overthrew the traditional pattern in which the state relied heavily on spontaneous social control by the family and the communal authority. The Communist propagandists reoriented the Chinese people toward a new form of control in which national identity, political ideology, and organization were more important than parochialism, the family, and regional loyalty. The new form of control may be more tyrannical than the old, but it is more in conformity with modernization.

Thus, the purge of the propaganda apparatus was not without elements of irony. Although the propaganda apparatus failed to satisfy Mao, it nevertheless had succeeded in increasing the national integration of China. In Communist jargon, the Party propaganda establishment of pre-1966 had fulfilled its "historical mission."

5

Mass Campaigns

Of all the means of communication between the leaders and the led in Communist China, mass campaigns were perhaps the most reflective of the Communist Party's strategy of national development. The shifts and turns of the Party's political and economic policies after 1949 were all expressed in changes in the nature of mass campaigns. The Party used the campaigns to mobilize the Chinese people to participate in its political and economic programs.

A mass campaign consisted of a series of organized, planned actions for a particular purpose. An ad hoc command organization was created for each campaign, and a large number of people were mobilized to engage in highly visible, intensive, and concentrated activities. Each campaign had a life cycle with a number of different stages. When a campaign ended, the ad hoc organization was dissolved and its participants returned to their routine work.

The past campaigns can be categorized by cross-tabulating them on two dimensions. One of these is whether or not a campaign included a specific target group designated as an "enemy." For example, the Suppression of Counterrevolutionaries campaign has a target group; the Hundred Flowers movement did not. The second is whether a campaign performed specific or diffuse functions. The functionally specific campaigns such as the Three-anti movement, were designed mainly to enlist people in a Party action. The functionally diffuse campaigns, such as Learn from Lei Feng, were designed mainly to create a new value system among the people. These aimed at reforming the "thought" of the people. These categories are somewhat arbitrary because to some degree all campaigns had the function of creating a new value system. A list of mass campaigns grouped according to these dimensions is given in the Appendix.

ORGANIZATION OF MASS CAMPAIGNS

To describe the organization of mass campaigns, let us first examine a typical campaign and then observe how different kinds of campaigns deviated from it. To begin with, all campaigns were decided by the top Party leadership in Peking. Apparently, the provincial Party leaders either were participants in the meetings with top-level Party leaders that decided on any particular campaign or were informed immediately after the decision had been made at the top level. During the first stage of internal decision-making and preparation, main operational features such as the organization of ad hoc command groups, training of special cadres, and designation of target groups must have been worked out between national and provincial Party leaders.

The second stage of a typical campaign began with a public announcement in the mass media. The announcement was usually vague and formalistic. At the same time, much unpublicized activity went forward within the regional apparatus. Special cadres were trained at the provincial level to be dispatched to cities and counties to direct local campaign operations. Peripheral activities prepared the public psychologically and aroused their attention—and, perhaps, even their anxiety and tension.

The third stage marked a transition from activities at the national and provincial levels to the municipal and lower-level Party headquarters. The transmission belt was provided by specially trained cadres, who now arrived to direct campaign operations in cities and rural towns. These cadres performed three important functions. First, they briefed local Party cadres with detailed instructions for the campaign. With these authoritative instructions, the whole municipal or county Party machinery began to work at a quick tempo. One meeting followed another. Second, they served as supervisors and judges of regional cadres, representing the national Party authority. Their function was to see if any centrifugal force had developed. Third, they organized local activists to assist local Party cadres in operating the campaign. The function of activists was to establish some informal contacts between the national Party authority and the society. The use of activists not only served to tap the force of the revolutionary elements in society but also to prevent the campaign from being revised by the possible inertia of the bureaucratic Party apparatus.

When this third stage was completed, the Party had an organized force of propagandists (activists) as storm troops and an ad hoc organization composed of three groups: the special cadres representing the central Party authority, local Party cadres, and activists representing the masses. This ad hoc organization was not merely local; some campaigns, like the Three-anti and Five-anti, had their own national command structure. For example, the national organization for the Three-anti campaign was the Central Government Economy Inspection Committee headed by Po Yi-po, then vice chairman of the Finance Committee of the Administrative Council and head of the North China Bureau of the Party Central Committee. At provincial and municipal levels, branch committees were set up. In some campaigns, ad hoc local organizations were set up, such as the Suppression of Counterrevolutionaries Committees in major cities, which consisted of representatives from municipal People's Congress, government, Public Security Bureau, People's Court and Procurator, Party Committee, militia, peasant associations, city Residents' Committee, and housewives.[1]

The ad hoc organizations insured that a campaign was effective down to the very bottom of the normal Party apparatus. We have already noted that by using specially trained cadres, the national Party leaders by-passed the middle-level Party apparatus. They insured that a campaign would not be carried out perfunctorily by the bureaucratized cadres. The other function of these organizations was to forge a direct link between the Party headquarters and the people. The results were not only to incorporate some dynamic elements of society into the Party power structure and exploit group tensions but also to make local Party cadres feel insecure. Hence, these organizations tended to increase local cadres' awareness of the power of the Party center.

Once the ad hoc organizations had been formed and a force of activists organized, a mass campaign went into its fourth and climatic stage. All mass media focused their coverage on the campaign, and the masses were organized into meetings and discussion groups. This was the stage of "fermentation." For example, in the Three-anti campaign in 1952, the ad hoc organization in Peking formed another group called the Work Team of the Mayor, which consisted of 923 members, of whom 500 were cadres of the Public Security Bureau, 93 were college professors, and 330 were college students. The team was divided into 253 small groups. Each of the groups was assigned an area, roughly identical with a police administrative division. Upon entering its area, a group would first consult the police to identify the local activists. The group would then talk with the activists; after that, the activists would transmit news of the arrival of the work team to the residents in the area. A mass meeting was called, at which members of the work team explained the Party's policies and delivered propaganda speeches. In this particular campaign (Three-anti), the target group was corrupt Party cadres and bureaucrats. Thus, cadres and state officials were forbidden to attend these mass meetings because the masses were supposed to express their criticism of cadres and officials in these meetings. If necessary, individual interviews were conducted by the members of the work team in order to gain genuine information on cadre corruption.[2]

In this stage of fermentation, the Party provided an overall guideline for cadres and activists. This was the principle of *fan-sou fa-tung chuan-chung*, which literally means "release your hands (control) on the masses and ignite them." In other words, cadres were to excite the masses into an emotional frenzy so as to create an upsurge of emotional responses.

Sometimes, the fermentation stage of a campaign was divided into substages. For example, in Shanghai, where the Five-anti campaign was particularly intensive, this stage was divided into three "phases of battle." News media employed military language to report the progress of the campaign. Headlines would proclaim "The First Phase of the Five-anti Battle Has Been Opened," or report that "the great troops of Five-anti campaign workers staged a battle rally and were soon to take their battle positions." [3] This military language may have been designed to create terror among the general population, particularly among the target group. It perhaps also enhanced the morale of the campaign workers. During the Five-anti campaign, employees and clerks had to be persuaded to accuse their employers of wrongdoing; the atmosphere of tension and fear created by military language may have helped campaign workers to intimidate them into making the accusations.

After the fermentation stage, the campaign went into the fifth or legitimation stage. By this time, the target groups were already harassed into submission, and the attacking groups were either mobilized to a fever pitch or intimidated into accepting the Party's instructions. Then, a mass meeting would be called in which the target group would be publicly abused by the attacking group. Finally, punishments would be meted out to the target groups, and the legitimation stage was complete.

The final stage of a campaign was the usual review meeting in which the special cadres sent from above would review the performances of local Party cadres and activists. Those activists who had performed well would be rewarded, the highest reward being admission to the Party. As a former school teacher stated: "After each campaign the Party was always able to absorb a group of new people, and the Party and the [Youth] League grew just that much bigger. The Communists have a well-known saying for this: 'You grow in mass movements.' " [4] With the completion of a campaign, the ad hoc organizations were dissolved.

The campaigns before 1953, especially those involving target groups, conformed most closely to the typical campaign we have described. But the majority of campaigns after 1953, especially those without target groups, deviated significantly from it. For example, in the campaign of Study the General Line of Socialist Transition in 1953, there was no ad hoc command structure, and hence no specially trained cadres dispatched from the center to regions. In this campaign, regional Party headquarters organized special propagandists to explain the Party's policy on industrialization to various groups and to hold discussion meetings. Because there was no target group, there was no fermentation and arousal of emotional tension. Mass organizations played an important role in these campaigns without target groups. They organized members to listen to reports by special propagandists and helped organize discussion meetings.

CHANGES IN STRATEGY, 1949–1966

On the whole, changes in campaign styles were an indication of shifts in the Party's strategy. We can analyze the changing goals and functions of the major campaigns over six periods of time and show their relationship to the Party's integration strategy in each period.

I. 1949–1952

In the first three years of the Chinese Communist regime, the Party, following a strategy of penetration, subjected the population to a series of radical mass campaigns that were designed primarily to instill in the minds of the people a respect for the new political authority.

Every one of the major campaigns launched between 1950 and 1952, such as the Land Reform, New Marriage Law, Suppression of Counterrevolutionaries, Three-anti and Five-anti campaigns, emphasized the theme of "class struggle." * It was the element of "struggle" in these campaigns that created a reign of terror on the mainland at that time. Yet, terror was tempered by the element of progress in these campaigns, for each of them carried out major social reforms, such as equaliza-

---

* The Three-anti campaign was initiated in August 1951 to cope with corruption among cadres. The three specific "antis" were: anti-corruption, anti-waste and anti-bureaucratism. The Five-anti campaign was initiated in December 1951 and carried through 1952 to strike at the urban bourgeoisie in China. The five sins that the Chinese bourgeoisie were accused of by the Party were: bribery, tax evasion, stealing of state property, cheating on government contracts, and stealing of "state economic intelligence."

tion of land ownership, equality for women, and purging corruption in the bureaucracy. The campaigns embodied the new regime's plan to build its authority by demonstrating simultaneously its power of coercion and its ideology of social progress. However, not every campaign in this period balanced terror with reform. The Suppression of Counterrevolutionaries campaign seemed to be aimed solely at instilling terror among the people.

The combined use of terror and reform conceivably performed the mobilizational function of loosening people from their parochial roots and integrating them into the new political and social system.[5] Though in most cases, people were compelled to participate in these campaigns, they could not but acquire some new knowledge and expectations about the Communist regime.

One campaign in this period, Anti-America Aid-Korea, did not adhere to the patterns described above. It concerned neither the class struggle nor social reform. Most probably this was due to the fact that Communist China did not originally expect to participate in the Korean War; it was not part of Peking's master plan in 1950.[6] However, the campaign still served important integrative functions by transforming the class struggle into a national struggle against a foreign enemy. The Korean War supplied the new regime with the convenient integrative symbol of "foreign enemy," which has been exploited by leaders of other developing nations.

II. 1953–1957

The year 1953 marked a major shift in Communist China's integration strategy, from one of political penetration to identification. Apparently the regime felt confident that the campaigns of 1949–1952 had effectively established the Party's authority over the country. In the meantime, the economy had recovered from the destruction of the civil war. The first Five-Year Plan was started formally in 1953. In consonance with the goal of industrialization, the regime shifted its appeal from the class struggle to patriotism or nationalism. The leaders' attention turned to creating political legitimacy by institutionalizing a formal government system of "socialist democracy," based on nationwide and regional elections of delegates to a People's Congress.[7]

The strategic shift in 1953 resulted in a marked decline in the number of mass campaigns. The major campaigns in this period were all connected with establishing political legitimacy: Study of Election Law (1953), Study of General Line of Socialist Transition (1953), Discussion of the Draft of the National Constitution (1954), and so forth.

That the Communists consciously used different campaigns at different stages of development is shown by the following editorial in the *People's Daily* on the national election of 1953:

In the initial period of the People's Republic of China, the liberation of the whole mainland was yet incomplete. In most areas, Land Reform had yet to be carried out thoroughly. The Supression of Counterrevolutionaries and other democratic reform campaigns had not been carried out in full scale. The masses of people had not been thoroughly organized. Under that circumstance, it was impossible for us to have national elections. . . .

Now, our country has accomplished an unprecedented degree of unification. We have realized a series of democratic reforms and victoriously carried out the Suppression of Counterrevolutionaries and the great Anti-America Aid-Korea campaigns. We are now in transition from the rehabilitation of the national economy to a period of large-scale economic construction. The present situation is thus drastically different from the past. In order to carry out the great historical mission, we must enable the state to link with the masses more directly and closely. The transient organizations of the past that were used as substitutes for people's congresses are no longer adequate. It is necessary for us to have national elections to replace the transient measures so as to enhance the masses' revolutionary positivism and creativity. . . .[8]

In other words, the Party was ready to shift its integration strategy from penetration to identification.

However, in the last two years of this period there were debates among Party officials and propagandists over further integration strategy. In addition to the widening gap in productivity between the stagnant agriculture and the burgeoning industry, the Communist government faced other domestic problems that had accumulated over the years. In 1956, amidst unrest in East European nations and a tense situation in rural China, where a radical collectivization campaign had just concluded, the Chinese Communist Party had to find a formula that would allow sufficient dissent by the Chinese people to release their pent-up resentment toward the Communist authority without endangering the Party's overall control over society. In terms of integration strategy, the Party had to decide which measure would increase national unity and motivate the population to work harder—liberty or discipline.[9] This political problem was closely tied to the economic necessity of increasing agricultural productivity. The question here concerned the degree of material incentives and individual efforts that the Party should allow the peasants. The choice was political control versus spontaneous social action.

Against this background, the inconsistencies of the campaigns of 1956 can be explained. In early 1956, the second wave of the Suppression of Counterrevolutionaries campaign was organized. It began in reaction to literary dissent by a prominent Party intellectual named Hu Feng. The campaign seemed to express the Party's decision to clamp down on further loosening of political control. Yet after a few months, the Party organized the Hundred Flowers campaign, which briefly allowed a wide range of political dissent—in violent contradiction to the campaign of suppressing the counterrevolutionaries. Then, after the Hundred Flowers campaign got out of the Party's control, the Party again went to the other extreme of suppression, in the Anti-rightists campaign.

In sum, before 1956 the Party seemed to have a coherent strategy of integration and was confident of its ability to direct society to the desired course of development. But this sense of confidence was lost in 1956, and integration strategy wavered. The vacillations and uncertain actions shown in the campaigns in 1956 seem to bear this out. It is also interesting to note that many accusations made against former propaganda officials during the Cultural Revolution traced these officials' "anti-Chairman Mao" actions to 1956–1957.

III. *1958–1959*

Having decided to loosen political control in 1953 and then having experienced the uncertainties of 1956 regarding further liberalization, the Chinese Communist Party was no longer a cohesive organization by 1958. The decision for the Great Leap Forward marked the rise of Mao and his left-wing followers in the Party. They immediately redirected the integration strategy toward further political penetration. Mao's romantic conception of the political consciousness of the masses became the rationalization for a series of radical mass campaigns. The All People Participate in Industrialization and All People Participate in Scientific and Technological Innovation campaigns were aimed at mobilizing the peasantry to increase agricultural production.

Though the left-wing leadership did not revive the call for "class struggle," they disguised it in the appeal for collectivism and populism. Chinese peasants were exhorted to "storm the intellectual fortress" and to despise experts and professionals. Meanwhile students, intellectuals, and professionals were sent to villages to do manual labor. As the Party propaganda stated it, the goal of this combination of mental and manual labor was to create a new Communist man and society.

IV. 1960–1962

The economic crisis that followed the Great Leap Forward compelled the Communist regime to reduce drastically all types of political regimentation in order to keep the public quiescent. Three major campaigns were launched in 1960: Army Love the People, Police Love the People, and Cadres and the People Get Together. All these were localized campaigns, and they did not require the people to take any specific action. But they required soldiers, police, and cadres to be near the masses—perhaps to maintain surveillance.

To preserve stability in the crisis, the Chinese regime acted as the Soviets did in World War II: they appealed to people's patriotic sentiments toward their nation and culture. They even rehabilitated Confucius and his teachings in the mass media in order to keep the nation together.

On the whole, then, there was no militant, penetrative, and nationwide mass campaign in this period. Whatever local campaigns were undertaken in this period were for the immediate purpose of maintaining stability in crisis.

V. 1963–1965

It has been noted that the failure of the Great Leap had resulted in a shuffle in leadership in the central committee. Mao became the leader, in his own words, in the "rear line" while Liu Shao-chi was the leader in the "front line." The general reduction of political penetration between 1960 and 1962 was a major tactical adjustment of Liu's policy of reconciliation. Yet, as described in Chapter 4, Mao became increasingly dissatisfied with the new direction set by Liu. Hence, in late 1962, Mao intervened and at the Tenth Plenum of the Eighth Central Committee called on the Party rank and file to "never forget class struggle." As a result, political penetration by the Party into society was sharply intensified. The number of mass campaigns was greatly increased. The unique feature of the campaigns in this period, as analyzed in Chapter 4, was the division between those sponsored by the Party propaganda apparatus and those by the military propaganda apparatus. It is not necessary to dwell on these campaigns in this section.

What is interesting about the campaigns in this period, including those directed by the army, is that the atmosphere and spirit of "fortress storming" which had so characterized the pre-1953 campaigns under the call for class struggle was slow to emerge in 1963. In fact, the campaigns after 1963 were all carried out very gradually and moderately. The Socialist Education campaign, which was designed to mobilize the militancy of poor peasants to carry out the planned new Great Leap, was, as Charles Neuhauser notes, an extremely leisurely affair.[10] The same can be said about the series of emulation campaigns, in which people were exhorted to learn from various army heroes. Though these campaigns emphasized class hatred and love of Communist collectivism, no real target group was designated to be struggled against. Instead, the people's voluntary emulation was emphasized.

The most plausible reason for this moderate style of political penetration was the growing ineffectuality of the militant type of mass campaigns that had dominated the pre-1953 period. This loss of effectiveness came not suddenly but gradually, over the years. It is an ironic development that, as the Chinese people's national identity was heightened by Communist propaganda, disillusionment with the Communist regime and political apathy also grew steadily among the people, also as a result of the regime's propaganda. The disillusionment was mainly due to excessive political regimentation and the gap between people's economic expectations and the regime's ability or willingness to meet their economic needs. A young former official of the Foreign Ministry commented on the best known campaign of emulation in this period, Learn from Lei Feng:

The "spirit of Lei Feng" was more than another political campaign; it was a revolutionary change in the propaganda line. For the first decade and more of the Communist regime in China, we were exhorted to work hard, make sacrifices, and obey the leaders on the constantly repeated promises of fantastic prosperity. We were told over and over again that materialism—the goods and services with which the degree of living standard could be marked—was the basis of all social progress and that socialism under Communist Party leadership was best because with it this progress was made faster. After the failure of the Leap, however, the fall in food production because of the commune system, the promises of great prosperity just around the corner aroused only bitterness and resentment. Even the slowest wit in the country knew now that long years of drudgery were ahead before we could have once again even the inadequate living standard of 1958. Thus the only possible approach in propaganda was to attempt to make us accept our suffering cheerfully. And no one ever suffered more—or enjoyed it more—than that fictionalized character named Lei Feng.[11]

The Learn from Lei Feng campaign is representative of all the campaigns for emulating army heroes in this period. They had a highly moralistic tone. They emphasized "self-cultivation" in the face of suffering and hardship. One can almost say that these campaigns sponsored by the army implicitly employed the Confucian mode of persuasion, which emphasized self-cultivation and the emulation of moral personalities. The difference between Confucian persuasion and the mass campaigns of 1963–1965 lies in the substance of persuasion and object of emulation. Army models like Lei Feng were a medium through which the Chinese people were supposed to identify themselves with Mao. Lei Feng was emulated because he was "one of Chairman Mao's good warriors" and had made Mao's thought his own.

We know that the army had assumed the responsibility of building up Mao's prestige after 1963. By emphasizing the spirit of self-cultivation, Confucian moral uprightness, and Maoist ideological purity in the face of material deprivation, the army propagandists tried to build up Mao's prestige, disassociate Mao from the economic setbacks, and prepare people psychologically for a long period of deprivation that lay ahead.

VI. Cultural Revolution, 1966–1968

Because the causes and major events of the Cultural Revolution have already been described, our focus in this section is on the tactics of mass mobilization. On the whole, the leftist faction employed the same technique of mass mobilization in this period that the Communist Party had used frequently in past campaigns. Specifically, it included the following three features: the designation of specific target groups for the public to struggle against, the dispatch of special cadres from the center to the regions to conduct the struggle, and an ad hoc command structure. The attack on literary intellectuals and leadership in propaganda apparatus provides the outstanding example of the first feature; the dispatch of army officers to various localities to conduct propaganda of learning Mao's works and the use of liaison men by the Cultural Revolution Section are illustrations of the second; and the Cultural Revolution Section headed by Chen Po-ta and Chiang Ching is an example of the third.

The Cultural Revolution as a mass campaign also has unique features. The major ones are: the extraordinary efforts by the leftists and military propagandists to popularize Mao as a genuine populist leader; the pervasive role of the army; the organization of youth into Red Guards; and the use of Red Guards to attack Party leaders. Although this discussion will cover all four, its focus will be on the popularization of Mao and functions of Red Guards. These two constitute the major dynamic forces in the mass phase of the Cultural Revolution.

Popularization of Mao Tse-tung. Marshal Lin Piao began the effort to restore Mao's prestige in the army in 1960. In the civilian population, the emulation campaigns of 1963–1965 were designed to accomplish the same purpose. However, a more specific goal of the leftists was to link Mao with students, for the latter had been designated to mount the assault on the Party. The symbol of Mao could provide legitimation and inspiration to the students.

But this is not an easy task—to popularize Mao. To most Chinese on the mainland, Mao must have been an aloof and rarely visible leader. He has no talent of public speech and his written words are laden with esoteric classical allusions that "proletarians" may not comprehend.[12] In the Hundred Flowers campaign in 1957 and in the crisis of 1959–1961, Mao's aloofness had been criticized by students and soldiers.[13] The leftists and their military allies must have noted this in their attempt to link Mao with youth in the Cultural Revolution. They made a concerted effort to increase direct contacts between Mao and the students.

The series of events that were designed to link Mao with Chinese youth began with Mao's famous dip in the Yangtze River on July 16, 1966, in Wuhan City. It turned out to be a carefully prepared event. News about Mao's intention to swim on that day, which was the occasion of a swimming contest, was circulated widely the day before. Thus, when Mao arrived, he was greeted with a mass ovation. He was seen mingling with youthful swimmers.[14] As mentioned earlier, by July 1966 the Cultural Revolution was well underway and its first victim was the Peking Party structure. Mao was proceeding back to Peking to initiate the mass phase of the movement. The swimming episode was designed to popularize Mao's image among the youth, laying the foundation of the mass phase of the Cultural Revolution.

Meanwhile, the leftists under Chiang Ching's direction had already set the stage for Mao to initiate the Red Guard movement in Peking. For, by July 1966, the students in Peking University were already mobilized to attack their president. Mao had earlier urged Party leaders, including leaders like Liu Shao-chi, to send special "work teams" to the colleges in Peking to observe the Cultural Revolution on campus. Unaware of Mao's real motivation or his wife's, these leaders in Peking assigned the "work teams" their conventional function as special cadres dispatched from the center to direct a mass campaign. The teams had then imposed discipline and restraint on student rebels. By doing so, these Party leaders fell into a trap set by the leftists. After Mao's return to Peking, he accused these leaders of suppressing student revolutionaries, and he ordered all "work teams" withdrawn from schools.[15] Thus, Mao was portrayed as the liberator and Liu Shao-chi the oppressor of students.

To link Mao further with students, a selected group of students were admitted to the meeting of the Central Committee that Mao called for August 1 to August 12, 1966. The functions of these students in the Central Committee meeting were mainly two. First, the students' presence served to build Mao up as the true populist leader among the youth. Second, it intimidated Mao's potential opponents. The meeting resulted in elevating Lin Piao to a position as the heir apparent of Mao.[16] Mao then went a step further to identify himself with the student revolutionaries. Knowing that the students in Peking had put up big-character-posters to attack the president and faculty of their school, Mao now wrote a big-character-poster himself on August 5 entitled "Bombard the Headquarters." By "headquarters" he meant Liu Shao-chi, Teng Hsiao-ping, and other leaders in Central Committee that Mao suspected to be his opponents. Mao's poster charged Liu and his associates with "standing facts on their heads and juggling black and white, encircling and suppressing revolutionaries, stifling opinions differing from their own, imposing a White Terror. . . ." [17] Mao now literally joined the student rebels in attacking the Party leadership.

After publication of Mao's poster and the conclusion of the Central Committee meeting on August 12, the Red Guards that had hitherto been confined to schools were turned loose. There is no question that the first batches of Red Guards were not spontaneously formed by students. They must have been created by members of the leftist faction. The declarations of the first group of Red Guards, those from the Middle School of National Tsinghua University, were identical in content to the speech delivered by Lin Piao at the first mass rally of the Red Guards on August 18.[18] To link Mao with the Red Guards, mass rallies were staged. From August to November 1966, Mao personally reviewed Red Guards eleven times during these mass rallies. In the first rally on August 18, Mao had appeared, for the first time, in the olive-color uniform of the army. He allowed a young girl to put the Red Guard arm band on him. The significance of Mao's wearing the army uniform was pointed out explicitly by the *Liberation Army Daily* the next day. An editorial stated: "Chairman Mao's wearing of his military uniform is the greatest honor for our army, and indicates his greatest confidence and inspiration in us, and his greatest expectation from us. We feel boundlessly happy and boundlessly proud." Mao now became the symbol of the alliance between the Maoist revolutionaries (youth) and the military.

Red Guards and Wall Posters. In regard to the functions of the Red Guards, Mao's own remarks in several occasions are highly revealing. One of these remarks seems to suggest that Mao intended the Red Guards to arouse the attention of the people to the Cultural Revolution. In a meeting on October 25, 1966, Mao stated that the activities of the Cultural Revolution in the first half of that year did not arouse people's attention. "But once the big-character-posters and Red Guards began to charge forward, public attention was immediately aroused." [19] We can recall Mao's early writings on thought reform in which he suggests that in order to reform a man, he must be shocked first, as one might shock a patient by shouting, "You are sick!" The Red Guards, then, were intended to produce a shocking effect on Chinese society. Another remark of Mao's suggests that Red Guards were used to attack prominent scholars and intellectuals because, being young and ignorant, they were not intimidated by the prestige of scholarship. Commenting on the prominent historian Chien Po-chan in a meeting, Mao said, "Chien Po-chan has written so many books. You think you can struggle against him? But the masses dared to attack him. They said, a small temple usually has strong ghostly wind and a shallow pond is infested with turtles." [20] Mao meant that a man with half-knowledge (like Chien, in Mao's opinion) is particularly prone to have wrong (or, dangerous) ideas. The Red Guards could see through this, but Party cadres tended to be awed by the prestige of scholars. Thirdly, the Red Guards' attacks on officials enabled Mao and others in the left-wing faction to legitimize the numerous purges on populist grounds. Thus, commenting on the purge of Tao Chu, Mao said in a meeting of the Cultural Revolution Section, "As to the problem of Tao Chu, I could not solve it. You could not either. But with the arousal of Red Guards, the problem was solved instantly." [21] Tao was attacked first in a Red Guard wall paper in November 1966 before he was formally cast out.[22] Although not every official attacked by Red Guard papers was purged, wall newspapers enabled the leftists to be highly flexible in their power maneuver.

The main instrument that the Red Guards used to attack intellectuals and the Party as directed by the leftists were the "big-character-posters" and small tabloids. The proliferation of these papers created an impression of spontaneity. One western reporter described the great number of tabloids in China as "the nearest thing to a free press that the mainland has ever had under Communist rule." [23] The leftists in the Party justified the use of these media in the same terms. After being transformed into a paper of the left-wing group in June 1966, the *People's Daily* stated:

The great proletarian cultural revolution is now in full spate. We must stand at the forefront of this movement and actively guide it. It is necessary to arouse the masses without reservation and adopt the method of full or frank expression of views and opinions, of putting up posters written in big characters, and of carrying out great debates. It is necessary to let the masses speak out fully, expose all the representatives of the bourgeoisie who oppose the Communist Party, socialism, and Mao Tse-tung's thought, expose all the monsters and demons, and, one by one, smash to pieces the reactionary bastions of the bourgeoisie.

Chairman Mao Tse-tung says: "Posters written in big characters are an extremely useful new type of weapon." The revolutionary big-character posters are very good! They are a "monster-detector" to unmask the monsters and demons of all kinds. With everybody putting up such posters, it is possible, quickly and from all sides, to reveal the true fact of the sinister antiparty and antisocialist gangs.[24]

In actuality, the degree of spontaneity in the publication of these papers and posters was limited. As the above report stated, the posters were a weapon to unmask "the monsters and demons of all kinds." In other words, these seemingly spontaneous media were actually a tool of the left-wing faction. The Cultural Revolution Section controlled by Mao's wife seemed to have significant control over the posters in Peking. One account told how Chiang Ching ordered the deputy editor-in-chief of the journal *Red Flag* to publish Mao's criticism of Liu Shao-chi in wall newspapers in January 1967.[25] Another report stated that an explicit order was issued by the "Capital City University and College Red Guard Representatives" to all its affiliated organizations to stop all attacks on Chou En-lai in wall newspapers.[26] The organization that issued the order seems to have been one of those control and coordinating units set up by the leftists from September to October 1966 to restrain excesses of the Red Guards.[27] There is little doubt that the order to stop attacks on Chou came from the top. Another indication of the controlled nature of these newspapers and posters was their sudden disappearance in Peking in September 1967. This moved a Japanese correspondent in Peking to remark: "Such a sudden change in the situation makes one feel that he is almost living in another world, poles apart from the Peking where wall newspaper reports on rivalries and confrontations between revolutionary organizations in almost every region and every work site prevailed only a short while ago. . . ." [28] As the same reporter concluded, the disappearance of the wall newspapers must have been associated with the emphasis on the "great alliance" among revolutionaries in September 1967; hence, no more reporting of factional conflicts was permitted.

The chief function of the wall posters and tabloids was to discredit and humiliate Mao's real or imaginary opponents, for these media contained little of what is generally regarded as "news." They were almost exclusively devoted to sensational exposés of those who were cast out. The language of the posters was even more bombastic and hysterical than the later tabloids, whose "reportorial style is long on mood, atmosphere, and political diatribe and short of facts." [29] According to the *People's Daily*:

By presenting the cardinal issues of right and wrong and getting everybody to discuss, examine, and critically appraise them, the revolutionary big-character posters concentrate twenty years' education of the masses in a day, particularly in raising the proletarian consciousness of the younger generation. In a big way, the revolutionary posters fortify the high resolve of the proletariat of the masses of the workers, peasants, and soldiers, and in a big way deflate the arrogance of all the antiparty and antisocialist reactionaries and the high and mighty bourgeois "authorities." [30]

This is only repeating what Mao had said in 1927 about his impressions of the peasant revolt in Hunan. Mao wrote then that "ten thousand schools of law and political science" could not have accomplished what a few simple political slogans like "Down with imperialism!" "Down with the warlords!" and "Down with the corrupt officials!" had done in few months in provoking peasants to strike down traditional authority. Mao had learned then that illiterate peasants could use slogans to destroy the prestige and the respectful aura of all kinds of authority. In the Cultural Revolution, Mao enriched this tool to pursue his old tactics. Slogans aside, the little red books of Mao's quotations were used to intimidate anyone suspected of anti-Party actions. Wall posters and tabloids were used for the same purpose. In 1927, simple slogans and mob violence had struck at the prestige and power of gentry and landlords. In 1966, quotations from Mao, wall posters, tabloids, and Red Guard violence struck at the prestige and power of intellectuals, scholars, and Party officials suspected of engaging in anti-Maoist activities.

VII. 1969–1970

The Ninth Party Congress of April 1969 symbolically marked the beginning of the reconstruction of the Party after the destruction of the Cultural Revolution. Leftists who now dominated the policy-making machine at the top, in an uneasy alliance with the military, found their task of reintegration staggering.[31] During the Cultural Revolution, the deposed leadership of the propaganda apparatus was invariably accused of thwarting the dissemination of Mao's works to the masses. Now, after the purge is largely over, the new leftist-military leadership has initiated an unprecedented campaign of learning Mao's works. From 1966 to 1968, close to three billion copies of Mao's works, in various forms, were published and circulated over China.[32] Political penetration has indeed reached a peak in China today.

This massive campaign of disseminating Mao's works has been gathering momentum since the beginning of the Cultural Revolution in 1966. The movement was spearheaded by the army, as I have described already. From 1966 to 1968, the army sent out mobile propaganda teams to civilian organizations and communities to conduct mass reading of Mao's works. The army had also established "study classes" of Mao's works in civilian institutions. In 1968, the army further organized the "worker Mao Tse-tung thought propaganda teams" to reinforce the ranks of army propagandists in schools and cultural institutions.

In 1969, the worker propaganda teams had already been stationed in cultural organizations like the Chinese Academy of Sciences and Ministry of Culture. There, they organized staff members of these formerly prestigious institutions to study repeatedly Mao's works. Because the intellectual gap between the workers and the members of these institutions is so great, one cannot take seriously the official contention that the workers have changed the mental outlook of the intellectuals in these institutions. The most plausible function of these worker propaganda teams was to reduce somewhat the omnipresence of the army and, at the same time, keep the intellectuals under continuous surveillance. There are signs that these teams may have already been gradually phased out as the Maoists tried to return China to normalcy. On July 6, 1969, the Shanghai newspaper *Wen-hui Pao* entitled its whole front page with the oblique headline: "What should worker propaganda teams do in the new situation?" The newspaper editor acknowledged that the worker teams had "met with some new problems in carrying through to the end the great proletarian cultural revolution." Although the editor ritualistically called for a strengthening of the reeducation of intellectuals, he concluded by stating the need to "step up the ideological and organizational building of the worker propaganda teams." In other words, the mission of these teams was formerly to educate others; now, the teams were told to educate themselves. The leftists may thus be dispensing with the workers, as they have already dispensed with the Red Guards.

Another major indication of the gradual reduction of the worker propaganda teams is that an apparent change in propaganda technique took place in 1970. Instead of relying on mobile propaganda teams, the emphasis now is on studying Mao's works within every institution. The main form of such propaganda is the "Mao Tse-tung thought study class." As one report stated it: "A new situation has emerged, with the leading cadres taking the initiative in studying and applying and the masses actively participating." [33] This downplay of mobile propaganda teams and the corresponding emphasis on on-the-job propaganda are in conformity with the Party leadership's policy of reconstruction after the Ninth Party Congress in April 1969. The hope of the leftist leadership was to institutionalize mass learning of Mao's works. In border areas and other interior provinces where the excesses of the Cultural Revolution have not yet been brought under control, the army propaganda teams are still active, one such province being Kweichow.[34]

The study classes are now widespread in China. As one report described it: "Mao Tse-tung study classes are organized in factories, at railway stations, on the docks, and in dormitories. Meetings to exchange experience in study and application are held at all levels in a variety of ways. 'Study everyday' has become a habit." [35] As in the penetration campaign during the Great Leap, individual privacy has been reduced and leisure time is regimented. In one residential area in Shanghai, whose occupants were mostly workers, the residents were organized into propaganda teams to disseminate Mao's thought in the neighborhood. A report in the *Wen-hui Pao* stated: "The neighborhood is an extremely important position from which to consolidate the dictatorship of the proletariat. It is both a rear area in which to build socialism and an outpost of the struggle between the proletariat and the bourgeoisie." [36]

In rural areas too, a repetition of the mass politicization of the Great Leap has occurred. Following the lead of the army and worker propaganda teams, "poor and lower-middle peasant propaganda teams" were organized in many provinces in 1969. The organizing force behind these teams was the ubiquitous army. For a while, these teams roamed in their community from one production team to another to conduct propaganda for

Mao's works.[37] By 1970, a pervasive network of "political evening schools" and "Mao Tse-tung's thought study classes" had been set up in the countryside. A report on several model evening schools in Chekiang province said: "These political evening schools have been run continuously throughout the year, regardless of busy or slack farm work. . . . Despite their fatigue after a day's work and no matter what the weather, they [the peasants] attend the political evening school after supper every day." [38] These schools were said to have been organized on the basis of production teams, or the smallest aggregate within natural villages. The schools, however, do not replace the "Mao Tse-tung thought study classes," which are held in the field, at work sites, or in gatherings of several households. Penetration has reportedly been extended even to the families of peasants. One report on northern Kiangsi said, "the homes of ordinary commune members have become classrooms for the living study and living application of Mao Tse-tung's thought. Everywhere one can see fathers and sons, husbands and wives, mother-in-law and daughters-in-law and sisters-in-law study Chairman Mao's works together . . . and discuss national affairs together." [39] Accompanying all these propaganda activities was continuous emotional agitation—the method of "recall past bitterness and compare it with the present happiness."

This massive political penetration seems to have three intended functions.

The first is a further communalization of communication in Chinese society.[40] The leftists who now control the Party see the dangers of bourgeois contamination and corruption everywhere in society. Hence, it has become necessary to communalize every type of spontaneously developed social relations or communications. The report quoted above on the need to politicize city neighborhoods is an example of the leftist attitude. In the countryside, this effort to penetrate informal communication is made even clearer:

Because of the establishment of political evening schools in various production teams, the spare time of the commune members is filled with politics. . . . in many villages in South China, the peasants spent their spare time in tea houses, cooling themselves in summer and sitting around a furnace for warmth in winter and chatting freely.

The handful of class enemies often took this chance to spread the poison of feudalism, capitalism, and revisionism. After the political evening schools were set up, the commune members went to take part in political study during their spare time. They talked about the revolution, discussed the affairs of the state [sic] and told stories about the heroes [sic]. They spent their spare time in a way completely different from that of the past.[41]

One aim of this massive politicization is, then, to insulate the Chinese people totally from undesirable (from the leadership's standpoint) ideas and influences. With monopoly of information and collectivization of almost every facet of human life, the leftist leaders hope to realize their dream of spiritual transformation of the Chinese population.

The second function of such a campaign is to prepare the public for a possible revival of the Great Leap Forward. In factories, the campaign to study Mao's works was accompanied by repudiation of "the counterrevolutionary revisionist fallacies spread by Liu Shao-chi on putting production, profits, and technology in command and 'placing bonuses in command.' "[42] In the countryside, peasants were similarly urged to attack Liu Shao-chi as the representative of anti-collectivist economy.

The third and most ambitious function that this massive campaign of studying Mao's works is designed to serve is to institutionalize Mao's works as a kind of Chinese Communist "protestant ethic." This effort appears most explicitly in certain moralistic works of Mao, called "three old pieces" (*lao-san-pien*), that everyone on mainland China is required to learn by rote. It also appears in the emphasis on the "living study" of Mao's works, i.e., using Mao's thoughts in practical action. The "three old pieces" were *In Memory of Norman Bethune,* which told of a Canadian doctor who died serving the Red Army in 1939; *Serve the People,* which is also a memorial to a soldier killed in action; and, *The Foolish Old Man Who Removed the Mountains,* in which Mao used allegory to encourage the ranks of the Party in 1945 to brace themselves for the long fight with the Nationalists.[43] Each work focuses on the same moral lesson: devotion to a transcendental cause. Yet, this cause is also understood to be bound up with the practical actions of the people. Thus, the Chinese people are told not only to internalize Mao's thoughts, but also to use them as guide in all kinds of action. As one article says about the drive to study Mao's works among factory workers: "People go to Chairman Mao's works when they are seeking answers to specific questions. They use the basic theories they learn from these writings to analyze and solve their problems." [44] The study drive is also said to aim at "organizing and bringing into play the inexhaustible enthusiasm for socialism latent in the masses in the high tide of the socialist revolution and socialist construction." [45] In other words, Mao's words are to be the tonic that will brace the Chinese people for the revolutionary struggle ahead (to be defined by Mao from time to time), as the "protestant ethic" was the tonic that braced the European bourgeoisie for their conflict with the aristocracy.[46]

But it is in the countryside, in communes, production brigades, and teams, that the substitution of Mao's works for the old religion is most actively pursued. Take, for example, the following report on a certain Tunt'ou production brigade in Chekiang province:

The setting up of the political evening schools and the wide popularization of Mao Tse-tung's thought brings about a great change in social practice. Now in Tunt'ou, all commune members, father and son, husband and wife, brothers and sisters, take Mao Tse-tung's thought as the criterion for their words and deeds, whether in the collective or at home. . . .when a wedding or a funeral is held, they do not give feasts or presents. On festivals, they neither worship gods nor offer sacrifices to their dead ancestors. On the eve of the Spring Festival in 1969, the commune members of various production teams broke with their old habit. They did not take the traditional New Year's Eve meal and did not offer sacrifices to the gods. Instead, they set up battlefields in various political evening schools to criticize feudalism, capitalism, and revisionism and to recall past bitterness and think about the present happiness. On the Spring Festival Day, more than 150 people in the whole brigade were organized to go to the hill to reclaim wasteland.[47]

Judging from the lessons of the Great Leap, the prospect of this massive campaign of politicization is not good. But the campaign and its wider base, the Cultural Revolution, serve to illustrate the conceptualization and the techniques of mass persuasion and political mobilization used by the left-wing faction. These have been discussed in detail in the chapter on the ideology of mass persuasion in China.*

INTEGRATIVE EFFECTS OF MASS CAMPAIGNS

Because they rely chiefly on oral communication, mass campaigns were particularly effective in the first few years of the Communist state. First, they counteracted the inadequacy of the mass media in China at that time and enabled the government to communicate with more people than it would otherwise have been able to. Second, the campaigns made it possible for a wide range of social groups, especially youth and women, to participate in the Communist political system, thus facilitating their identification with the new Communist authority.

The initial effectiveness of the mass campaigns, however, was dependent upon three factors. First was the inadequacy of mass media, which made the campaigns the only extensive propaganda effort. As a result, though the campaigns intruded into people's privacy, the intrusion was not regarded as excessive. The second factor was the popular enthusiasm for the new regime. Mass campaigns then were an important means by which people could transform their enthusiasm into meaningful political action. The third factor was the absence of other political, economic, and cultural institutions that would enable the people to participate in the new system.

Over the years, however, mass media and other political, economic, and cultural institutions were developed, and the people's participation in the overall Communist system was enlarged. Propaganda to the people by means other than the campaigns became quite extensive. Popular enthusiasm for the Communist regime, meanwhile, inevitably waned. Consequently, the mass campaigns gradually lost their effectiveness. Though the campaigns still were useful for linking the media with face-to-face communication, they became too intrusive to

* Compare the technique of the study of Mao's works campaign with the discussion of the ideology of mass persuasion in Chapter 3 of this book, especially the section "A Synthesis."

CHART 2:

Campaign Styles and Integration Strategy: A Summary

Year	Strategy	Symbol of Appeal	Goal
1949–52	Penetration	Class Struggle	1. Building political authority 2. Creation of new mass political attitudes
1953–57	Identification	Patriotism (or, nationalism)	1. Creation of political legitimacy 2. Industrialization
1958–59	Penetration	Collectivism	Creation of Communist man and society
1960–62	Identification	Patriotism (or, nationalism)	Stability in crisis (or, public quiescence)
1963–65	Penetration	Class Struggle	Creation of Communist man and society
1966–68	Penetration	The Great Proletarian Cultural Revolution	Purge of "Party Opponents"
1969–70	Penetration	Building a New Party	Institutionalization of the Thought of Mao Tse-tung

be received by the people favorably. They had created a constant sense of anxiety among cadres [48] and general resentment among the public. The Party had overplayed the campaigns, and that reduced their effectiveness.

Not surprisingly, there were high-ranking Party officials who realized these problems and called for changes. But their criticisms went beyond the campaigns' role as a means of mass persuasion. They said that mass campaigns were an anachronistic carry over of the combat experience of the Party and attacked their use as a general strategy of action. For example, in an article commemorating the tenth anniversary of the formal establishment of the Chinese Communist state, Chou En-lai mentioned that there were critics who attributed the penchant for mass campaigns to "petty-bourgeois fanaticism." [49] Another official, writing on the same occasion, was more specific:

There has been quite a bit of argument within our Party over the question of launching large-scale mass movements in socialist construction and, above all, on the industrial front. Some say that "mass movements are all right for revolutionary struggles but not for construction." Others say that it is a rather complex thing to run modern industry and in this respect, instead of organizing mass movements, we should establish a "regular regime." Still others say that mass movements may be all very well in carrying out political reforms in factories and businesses, but that in carrying out technical reforms we should rely on systematic "scientific methods" instead of mass movements, and so on and so forth. The basic standpoint is that the Party's mass line in socialist construction should be replaced by a set of "regular" methods, and lively and vigorous movements by bare administrative orders. They even call their methods "normal," "scientific," truly Marxist-Leninist methods and call mass movements "abnormal," "unscientific" methods which, according to them, run counter to Marxism-Leninism.[50]

As it turned out, this dispute on mass campaign was also part of the divisions within the propaganda apparatus that were analyzed earlier. Those who favored the mass campaigns were the leftists. The passage quoted above was written by the late Ko Ching-shih, former First Secretary of East China Bureau of Party Politburo, the man who joined Mao's wife at the beginning of the modern play movement in 1963. But aside from the initial impact of mass campaigns and the dispute over their continuous usefulness, mass campaigns in Communist China have performed some long-term integrative effects.

The first and perhaps the most important integrative effect of the campaigns in China has been the dissemination of a mass political language. As the late T. A. Hsia, an authority on Communist manipulation of language, noted: "The invasion of the people's vocabulary by a large number of terms and expressions, imported, invented, or resuscitated by the Communists, and, in many instances, by Mao himself, is one of the most significant linguistic phenomena in Communist China." [51] The mass campaigns have been the chief instrument used to invade and enlarge the Chinese people's vocabulary. According to Hsia,

> Anyone who has not lived through a mass movement in Communist China can hardly feel the power of words when backed up by the power of the party-state. For it is words that incite the people to action; it is slogans uttered by the men on top and echoed by the propaganda machine that start what is often described in the Communist press as the "tidal waves" or the "conflagration that reaches the sky." [52]

Relying on a pervasive propaganda apparatus and motivated by a Promethean sense of changing man and society, the Chinese Communist Party has mobilized a very large percentage of the national population through wave upon wave of mass campaigns. Each of these campaigns nationalized people's attention with a uniformity of language. In the long run, the integrative effect of this uniform political language is indisputable.

Another long-run integrative effect of the mass campaign is mass experience of organization and coordinated action. So far I have mainly discussed those campaigns that were clearly directed toward political purposes. Yet, as mentioned above, mass campaign has become the general strategy of action of the Communist Party, especially the left-wing faction. Aside from the campaigns discussed, there were numerous others, and some of them bordered on ludicrousness, as, for example, the mass extermination of sparrows in 1958. Yet, as T. A. Hsia noted, the important thing is the psychological impact of these seemingly ludicrous campaigns: "the people learned therefrom a useful lesson in military organization and coordinated action. And the lesson was put across through military language." [53] Mass experience in nationwide coordinated action is a major breakaway from traditional family and clan centered group actions.

In the language of social sciences, the effect of all these campaigns in Communist China is "social mobilization"—"the process in which major clusters of old social, economic and psychological commitments are eroded or broken and people become available for new patterns of socialization and behavior." [54] The mass campaigns in China have not yet integrated

the Chinese people into "new patterns of socialization and behavior," as evidenced in the Cultural Revolution. But the campaigns have laid the necessary psychological and physical
foundations for new patterns of national integration.

Aside from the impact on national integration, the mass campaigns have had one major institutional impact on the overall
propaganda enterprise. They had made it possible to dispense
with a separate system of oral agitation. In the Soviet Union,
the reverse is true. A well-established system of oral agitation
has obviated the use of nationwide mass campaigns, such as
those we see in China.[55]

However, in 1951, the Chinese Communist Party did establish a Soviet type of oral agitation network, called "propagandists and reporters." The former actually performed what Lenin
called agitation, i.e., political propaganda toward a mass audience, and the latter, propaganda, i.e., sophisticated political
indoctrination to the literate class in society.[56] Employing a
large number of enthusiastic youths, this system performed its
designated function of familiarizing the Chinese population
with the policies and nature of the new Communist government. In that period of transition, this system of propagandists
and reporters contributed greatly to the stabilization of the
Communist power. By using various means on the basis of
person-to-person communication, such as loudspeakers and wall
news bulletins, the instructions of the Communist Party were
transmitted throughout the land. This was no mean task, given
China's high rate of illiteracy and diversity in dialects.

Yet, the system of propagandists and reporters quickly
atrophied after 1953. That was when the Communist Party
shifted its integration strategy from penetration to participation
and identification. As later reports revealed, the system of oral
agitation was cast away by many regional Party officials because
of its superfluity and its interference with production.[57] The
Party, however, never seriously made an attempt to revive this
system. A major reason is that in each mass campaign, the Party
mobilized ad hoc groups for mass oral agitation. Thus, in 1953,

after the Party proclaimed the policy of "transition to socialism," thousands of workers, students, and cadres were organized in various parts of China to conduct oral agitation on
Party policy.[58] Each wave of the collectivization campaign in
the countryside since the mid-1950s was accompanied by suc-
ceeding corps of agitators and propagandists, instead of a separate and stable corps of professional agitators. In the post-Great
Leap period, prime examples of this situation were the many
"cultural work teams" in the drive of "culture to villages" in
1963. In the two years of 1963 and 1964, the Party propaganda
apparatus mobilized students and people of all walks of life to
engage in the "story-telling" movement, i.e., stories about "past
bitterness and present happiness." [59] The preference for using
ad hoc and temporary oral agitation teams is well illustrated in
the proliferation of all types of propaganda teams during the
Cultural Revolution, such as the army propaganda teams, Red
Guard teams, workers' propaganda teams, lower and middle
peasant propaganda teams, and propaganda teams of regional
Revolutionary Committees.

Suspending the separate system of oral agitation in favor of
mass campaigns is another testimony to the Chinese Communist
Party's emphasis on mass involvement in politics. The continuous change in the ranks of oral agitation as one campaign suc-
ceeds another has the advantage of involving more people in
propaganda work than does a separate system of professional
agitators. Another intended advantage of such a campaign approach to oral agitation is, perhaps, to avoid the growth of
"formalism" in agitation work, which beset the Soviet system
of oral agitation by professionals.[60] With a continuous flow of
new faces into the ranks of oral agitation, the system can thus
be invigorated rather than routinized. Meanwhile, new members will keep up a high morale. New members in agitation
work may also escape somewhat the dilemma faced by a stabilized group of professional agitators, the dilemma of an agitator's commitment to his work group versus that to the Party.[61]

But the mobile system of oral agitation used in Communist
China also has major disadvantages, corresponding to its advantages. First, mass involvement was achieved at the expense
of quality of work. The ad hoc and temporary columns of agi-

tators trained for each mass campaign in China cannot possibly develop their skills to the degree of veteran and professional agitators. Second, formalism in work is by no means eliminated. Short-term and intense propaganda may encourage zealots as well as opportunists. Third, new members in agitation work, especially when "new" also means "outsiders," may escape the dilemma of the in-versus-out group commitment somewhat. But lack of any social or emotional ties with the recipients of propaganda does not work to the advantage of the persuader. In short, group members cannot "identify" with a new agitator sent from outside and his persuasiveness is bound to be reduced.

Political agitation in totalitarian nations like Communist China and the Soviet Union is not an enviable profession. Communist agitators are sandwiched between the Party and the masses. They bear the brunt of the masses' hostility toward the Party and of the Party's stringent requirements which are, more often than not, unrealistic. Inkeles has noted the extremely high turnover in the ranks of Soviet agitators.[62] By using the campaign approach to oral agitation, the Chinese Communists virtually legislated high turnover in order to turn it to Party's advantage. But the results are not clear-cut. The advantages and disadvantages in both the Chinese type of mass involvement and the Soviet type of agitation by professionals tend to balance out. The Chinese Communist campaign-centered oral agitation, however, does have the image and reality of a more passionate desire to politicize the *weltanschauung* of every man and woman, while the Soviet system of professional oral agitation has been largely oriented toward production promotion.

6

Radio Broadcasting

Radio is an invaluable tool for national integration. It possesses the flexibility of oral communication, and yet it can be controlled and manipulated easily. As an oral medium, radio is highly adaptive to the cultural diversity and particularism of a developing nation. It is an important transmission belt between political authority and the masses.

INTEGRATION BETWEEN RADIO STRUCTURE AND POLITICS

Like the Soviets, the Chinese Communists organized their radio broadcasting network on three operational levels—central, regional, and local—which corresponded to the three major geographic divisions of administration. Each level of broadcasting represents its respective political authority.

The central level is operated by the Central People's Broadcasting Station (Radio Peking), representing the voice of the Central Committee of the Communist Party. Regional broadcasting consists of two levels, the networks of provincial and municipal People's Broadcasting Stations. Many stations presumably handle both types of regional broadcasting, as provincial capitals have their own municipal stations which also serve as the center of provincial broadcasting.*

Local broadcasting consists of wired radio stations in communes, factories, schools, and mining areas. This network is

* For a statistical portrayal of the development of these stations and their regional distribution, see Appendix 2.

118

like the Soviet system of radio diffusion exchanges. In every county seat, an ordinary radio station was built; it monitors programs from central, provincial, and municipal stations, and it initiates its own county programs. From the county radio station, wires were extended to all the villages within its jurisdiction and connected to loudspeakers mounted on poles in marketplaces, on the roofs of government buildings, and sometimes even on the walls of individual peasants' homes. By 1964, there were six million such loudspeakers in China. It was then reported that ninety-five percent of the counties and towns in rural China had been connected by this wired radio network.[1] The Cultural Revolution does not seem to have damaged the wired radio network seriously. Since 1968, the Communist Party has initiated a campaign to extend the wired network from county towns to communes and production brigades, which are subdivisions of the county in China.[2] In any case, the link-up of ninety-five percent of counties and towns in the countryside is already a major achievement for the Communists, enabling them to penetrate deeply into the hitherto isolated and politically apathetic rural society.

The main impetus to the growth of wired broadcasting came from above, not below. As Table 1 shows, there was a sudden increase in wired stations and loudspeakers during the two radical agricultural collectivization campaigns in 1956 and 1958. The sudden extension of wired radio stations to rural areas was a part of the leftward turn in political and economic development in these years. As we have noted, the leftists believed in precipitating the political consciousness of the masses. Wired broadcasting was designed to agitate the peasants to accomplish the collectivization campaigns. But the 1958 campaign failed, and as we can see from Table 1, the number of county radio stations "declined" from 11,124 in 1959 to 1,975 in 1964. It is also very plausible that there was no decline because the "growth" of 1958 might well be due to false reporting by cadres, which was quite common then.

Little is known about the Party's control over radio broadcasting. Technically, broadcasting is a government enterprise. But there is no doubt that the propaganda department of the Party Committee at every territorial level controlled the con-

TABLE 1

Number of Rural Wired Broadcasting Stations
and Loudspeakers in China, 1949–1964

Year	Stations	Loudspeakers	Number of Loudspeakers Per Station
1949	8	500	62.5
1950	51	2,200	43.1
1951	183	6,100	33.4
1952	327	16,200	49.5
1953	541	31,800	58.7
1954	577	47,500	82.3
1955	835	90,500	108.3
1956	1,490	515,700	346.1
1957	1,700	993,200	584.2
1958	6,772	2,987,500	441.1
1959	11,124	4,570,000	411.7
1960	—	—	—
1961	—	—	—
1962	—	—	—
1963	—	4,500,000	—
1964	1,975	6,000,000	3,037.9

SOURCES: Figures from 1949 to 1958 are from *Ten Great Years* (Peking, 1960), p. 208; figures for 1959 are from *Communist China Digest*, no. 20 (July 26, 1960), p. 56. Of the 11,124 stations, 1,689 were county stations. The figure for 1963 is based on a New China News Agency release of August 7, 1963, which reported that the number of loudspeakers was "more than 4.5 million" in 1963. The 1964 data are from *Jen-min Jih-pao*, November 21, 1964.

tent and operation of the broadcasting stations within its jurisdiction. An indication of this is that during the Cultural Revolution, whenever a purge within a given regional Party Committee occurred, the radio stations in that region stopped broadcasting local and regional news completely and instead only rebroadcast news from Radio Peking.[3]

The Cultural Revolution did not alter the pattern of control of radio broadcasting. The content of broadcasting was most affected, and this will be discussed later. On the whole, the centralized system of broadcasting served the Communist regime well. It greatly redressed the geographical unevenness in radio broadcasting that had existed in the pre-Communist era. It broke the urban concentration by installing wired broadcasting in rural areas. The linking of political organization with broadcasting enabled the Party to communicate with the masses regularly in every part of the country.[4]

INTEGRATION BETWEEN CONTENT AND POLITICS

The purpose of integrating the structure of broadcasting with that of political organization was of course to control programing. The criterion for controlling and planning radio programs is ideology. Chou Yang, former deputy director of the Propaganda Department of the Party Central Committee, stated in 1958: "All propaganda media must submit themselves to situational needs, because they are an instrument of class struggle and they have to serve politics at all times. . . . Broadcasting cannot have any mission independent of that demanded by the current situation. . . . We decide political missions according to the situation, and we decide propaganda missions according to political missions."[5] Consequently, as the regime changed its policies from time to time, the radio programs changed accordingly. In this section, I shall trace the changes in radio programing since 1949 to see the relationship between broadcasting and the regime's strategy.*

During the years from 1949 to 1952, when the Communists were preoccupied with building their authority, mass campaigns were used to create new political attitudes among the Chinese people. Radio broadcasting in this period performed the same functions. The most prominent programs then were live broadcasts of mass rallies and trials during each mass campaign. There was also extensive use of collective listening in "broadcasting assemblies." The emphasis on live broadcasting of mass campaigns can be seen in this report in 1951:

The broadcasting stations all over the nation performed great propaganda and education functions in diffusing and deepening the Anti-America Aid-Korea Campaign. There were about two million (excluding audiences in the armed forces) who listened to the reports

* For a quantitative analysis of the content of radio programs, see Appendix 3.

by the representatives of Chinese Volunteers [in Korea]. In Shanghai alone, 500,000 listened to the program. . . . In the live broadcasting of the mass accusation meeting in the Anti-America Aid-Korea Campaign on March 7, the Honan People's Broadcasting Station mobilized 30,599 people out of its audiences of 60,000 to sign the petition for a peace treaty. . . .

A majority of People's Broadcasting Stations organized the broad urban population to listen to the discussion on Suppression of Counterrevolutionaries by the local People's Representative Council. The people thus received a great political education. According to an incomplete survey, the numbers of people organized to listen to the campaign in major cities were as follows: 300,000 in Peking, 430,000 in Nanking, 300,000 in Chunking, and 150,000 in Chinan.[6]

Radio broadcasting in this period was used as an adjunct to mass campaigns. The dominant style of broadcasting was mass agitation rather than propaganda. The differences in functions were a matter of emphasis. Radio programs naturally included music, news, and literary works, though they were overshadowed by the live broadcasts of mass campaigns.

As the government shifted its goals in 1953 from building authority to creating legitimacy and increasing industrialization, the emphasis in radio broadcasting also changed. In terms of style, broadcasting from 1953 to 1957 was for mass propaganda or, more specifically, mass education. Similarly, the form of listening also changed, from collective to individual reception. A major policy statement on radio broadcasting that appeared in the authoritative *People's Daily* on February 6, 1954, clarified the new mission of radio:

Collective listening, or forcefully feeding people long and dull materials, obviously does not suit the characteristics of broadcasting. Therefore, these are not the future directions of our broadcasting. (Broadcasting assembly is just a propaganda form that, under specific conditions, is suitable for large-scale campaigns.) The direction of our broadcasting should be to make it the most ideal propaganda medium for every family and individual. If after a day's tension and labor, the masses can turn on their radios and enjoy light and pleasant music, brief news and lectures, and easily comprehensible study lessons, then the masses will be greatly interested in sitting around their radios.[7]

The new policy called for a balanced and sophisticated presentation of literary, educational, and political programs. National, provincial, and municipal radio stations were told to mobilize musicians, playwrights, writers, and folk singers to strengthen cultural broadcasting. Western classical music (including Russian) was to be systematically introduced to Chinese audiences. In the meantime, important literary and ideological works were to be popularized, especially for the benefit of urban workers. Thus, in this period, the dominant function of broadcasting coincided with that of the Soviet radio, the transformation of the nation into "a country of complete literacy and high culture." [8]

During the Great Leap Forward, radio broadcasting returned to mass agitation rather than propaganda. Instead of promoting literacy and high culture, radio stations were now required to propagandize "literature of workers and peasants" for increasing agricultural and industrial production. In line with the anti-intellectualism of the leftist ideology, the Party demanded that the literary and musical programs be "nationalistic and populistic," not "intellectual and foreign." [9] The policy of the preceding period was totally repudiated.

The most important development in propaganda themes at this time was the emphasis on the role of soldiers in national construction. According to Chou Yang: "the defense of the motherland is not our soldiers' only duty. They now must also participate in socialist construction." [10] This new emphasis was obviously a result of a long debate within the military on its role in China's modernization, which ended in the victory of the anti-professional and militia-oriented group of China's military leadership. [11]

The failure of the Great Leap temporarily discredited Mao's leftist policy. Though detailed information is lacking, radio programing from 1961 to the breakout of the Cultural Revolution in 1966 seems to have resembled closely that of 1953 to 1957; that is, programs were oriented more to popular tastes than they had been during the period of the Great Leap. Although political propaganda was by no means dropped, it was subtly packaged in entertainment programs. According to an analysis made of the scheduled and actual broadcasts of Radio

Peking on February 23, 1964: "'Propaganda through entertainment' seems to be Radio Peking's motto. Entertainment is a vital element in overall programming."[12] This type of broadcasting was certainly in harmony with the regime's integration policy at this period: to reduce political penetration and to keep the population quiescent.

The Cultural Revolution repudiated this policy. Under the populist slogans of "Down with the Bourgeois Monopoly of Art and Literature" and "Let Workers, Peasants, and Soldiers Grasp Theory and Ideology Directly," political propaganda permeated radio broadcasting to an unprecedented degree.* Programs such as "Quotations from Chairman Mao," "Selective Reading of Chairman Mao's Works," and "Workers, Peasants, and Soldiers Learn Chairman Mao's Works" replaced the literary and musical programs of the past. The new literary and musical programs were "revolutionary songs and dances." The radical politicization of all media content in this period was designed to create a favorable climate of opinion for the Cultural Revolution, to heighten the morale of Mao's followers, and to intimidate and isolate Mao's real or imagined opponents.

There are advantages and disadvantages to the close integration of radio programs with the overall national policy. The most important advantage is, as I have mentioned, the nationalization of public attention. Radio broadcasting helped the Party to focus people's attention on the immediate and dominant task of the nation in each period.

But extreme pragmatism in radio programing had one major disadvantage. It sacrificed those musical and literary programs that were not immediately related to the current political and economic tasks, such as Western classical music and Chinese works of art and literature. The elimination of this type of program occurred always during the periods when the leftists in the Party dominated policy-making. Had this kind of program been permitted, it would have made broadcasting more diversified and more attractive to a wider audience. These programs could have balanced the crudeness of purely political programs and made them more acceptable to sophisticated audiences. But Mao's anti-intellectualism and his radical ideas

* See the quantitative analysis in Appendix 3.

about mass persuasion based on peasant mobilization prevented him from using literary and musical programs for the long-range benefits of national integration.

RADIO AND FACE-TO-FACE COMMUNICATION

The Communists' success in integrating broadcasting with political organization enabled them to link radio with face-to-face communication through collective listening. At first, collective listening was both a necessity, because of the limited number of radio sets, and a device for intensive political penetration. The use of collective listening thus was affected by both economic and political factors.

The period of 1950 to 1952 was marked by one mass campaign after another, and hence also by collective listening. Collective listening not only maximized the usefulness of the limited number of radio sets then at the regime's disposal but also increased the "impression of universality" that is one of the characteristics of radio communication.[13] Collective listening in this period occurred primarily in two ways, broadcasting assemblies and institutional listening.

In a broadcasting assembly, a heterogeneous audience, presided over by Party cadres, was gathered around a radio set or loudspeaker to listen to some designated programs. Between 1950 and 1952, this form of collective listening was used extensively in three mass campaigns: Anti-America Aid-Korea, Suppression of Counterrevolutionaries, and Destruction of Reactionary Secret Societies. One purpose of these mass campaigns was to create a centripetal orientation among the people. Collective listening facilitated this objective, for in a group setting the pressure to conform to collective standards was high, and individuality was submerged. As a result, the collective symbol, the Party, was strengthened.

Institutional listening took place in factories, schools, and governmental offices, where wired loudspeakers were installed and where the employees, students, or workers were a captive audience. During 1951 and 1952, factory broadcasting was particularly active because of the "democratic reform" programs to reorganize labor unions and factory management.

As the period of building authority was succeeded by that of creating political legitimacy in 1953, the assembly type of collective listening was drastically reduced in urban areas. Individual listening was encouraged instead. However, the institutional type of collective listening became part of the daily routine for urban employees.

In rural areas, because of the low literacy, shortage of radio sets, and language diversity, broadcasting assemblies still predominated after 1953. Indeed, they increased from 1955 to 1959 with the collectivization campaigns. It was reported, for example, that in 1958 the Party Committees in thirteen provinces organized 303 broadcasting assemblies and the audiences totaled several millions.[14]

After the failure of the Great Leap, however, collective listening was reduced even in rural areas. For example, in describing a certain county in South China, Barnett states: "When the Party wished to ensure that certain instructions or information would effectively reach everyone in the county, local Party propaganda personnel were directed to organize radio listening groups . . . at the brigade and team levels. Otherwise, listening was not normally compulsory." [15]

The Cultural Revolution once more increased collective listening all over China. Take, for example, the report from Shanghai on August 9, 1966, the day after Radio Peking had broadcast the Central Committee's decision on the Cultural Revolution:

The broad revolutionary people enthusiastically listened to the broadcast of the Central Committee's decision last night. Early this morning, parade columns appeared in major streets of Shanghai. . . . The commune members in the suburbs, who were kept busy in reaping and planting, listened to the broadcast and were greatly excited.[16]

Similar reports were published about other major cities in China whenever an important decision was broadcast over the nationwide radio network.

The combination of broadcasting and face-to-face communication had advantages for the Party. Collective listening enabled the Party to insure that the people received what was intended for them. It enlarged the utility of a limited number of radio sets and overcame, to a certain degree, language diversity. However, it also tended to provide resentment because of the coercive nature of collective listening. That the Chinese Communists recognized this defect can be seen in the change to individual listening in urban areas after 1953. But the left-wing Party leaders, true to their ideology, invariably criticized such a compromise with popular reaction. To them, collective listening was the only way to envelop the population with political indoctrination and assure mass political awakening. But their efforts often boomeranged because of the people's resistance to excessive political regimentation.

LIMITATIONS ON THE EFFECTIVENESS OF RADIO

Communist ideology transformed Chinese broadcasting into a centralized system of public communication and made it a vital part of the state's integration strategy. Yet, the new system had to cope with some of the basic facts of China's underdevelopment which restrained the effectiveness of ideology and organization. Language diversity and the absence of a common culture in China hindered radio broadcasting from exerting its full potentiality for integration.

Though radio can bypass the barrier of illiteracy in communication, it cannot bypass the absence of a standard language in China. In a little-publicized speech to the conference on the standardization of the Chinese language in 1955, a representative of the broadcasting industry revealed that of the existing fifty-five stations (wireless), provincial and municipal, fifteen had to use both Mandarin and dialects in their programs. Altogether eighteen dialects were used. According to the Wenchou Municipal People's Broadcasting Station of Chekiang province, only five percent of its audiences were able to understand Mandarin. And even the Wenchou dialect could be understood only by those residents within a radius of thirty-four miles of the station. The Kwangsi provincial station had to use three languages alternately to broadcast a single program: Mandarin, Cantonese, and a local dialect. In major industrial towns where workers from all parts of the country gathered, local radio stations often found it extremely difficult to select a language that could be understood by the majority of their audiences.[17]

The specific radio stations mentioned in the above report were all in South China; there the diversity of dialects is most serious. Language diversity plagued provincial and municipal stations particularly, because they had a more heterogeneous audience than rural wired radio stations. But in the latter, the Party escaped the problem of language only to be confronted by ideology. For, since the wired stations were permitted to broadcast part of their programs in the local dialect, localism might just be strengthened. The wired stations were therefore required to relay the Mandarin news programs from the Central People's Broadcasting Station and their provincial and municipal stations.

Cultural diversity also affected Chinese radio broadcasting. There were gaps between literates and illiterates and between modernists and traditionalists. The mass media in general were controlled by the literate and modernists. The media content naturally reflected their cosmopolitan values. In 1954, for example, the *People's Daily* criticized radio for its lack of programs suitable to the taste of workers and peasants.[18] In 1958, Mei Yi, director of the Broadcasting Bureau, stated that "there is no common language between our laboring people and some of our editing cadres." [19] There is perhaps a grain of truth in Mao's bitter charge, during the Cultural Revolution, that the media specialists in China were not willing "to go near the worker and peasant masses." But such cultural diversity is caused by the gross unevenness, among regions, in China's modernization. The aloofness of the media specialists is a result rather than the cause of such cultural gaps.

RADIO BROADCASTING AND NATIONAL INTEGRATION

In the end, what can we say about the overall integrative effects of radio broadcasting in Communist China?

First, because of its physical extension and uniformity of content, radio broadcasting must have heightened the people's national identity. It is likely that this effect was most pronounced in rural areas and among the young. As one report described it: "Every evening at 8:30 [in a village in Shantung], when the National Anthem inaugurates the half-hour relay of the Central People's Broadcasting Station's daily report of national and international events, even small children clap their hands and proclaim, 'Peking speaking!' " [20] The vague image of national authority that Chinese peasants had in the past must have been sharpened by now.[21]

A heightened sense of nationhood must have been furthered also by radio's dissemination of some key political terms all over China. Terms like "imperialism," "colonialism," "exploitation," "struggle," "class," and other more positive terms concerning the Communist system enlarged the political vocabulary of the common people, particularly the previously inarticulate peasants.[22] In the long run, this new political language will not only contribute to the growth of a national language but also inculcate in the people some basic concepts about society and politics which broadly conform to Communist ideology.

To the extent that rural broadcasting disseminated simple facts about sanitation and agricultural production, then perhaps it could have some effects, albeit minor, on economic development in rural China. But the official Chinese claims about rural broadcasting's motivating the people to change in a "modern" or "collectivist" way must be treated with caution. Mass media alone have not been found to be capable of changing people's deep-rooted attitudes. The most intensive uses of rural wired radios and the most fantastic claims for their effectiveness in motivating peasants were made during the Great Leap Forward period, in 1958 and 1959. Since then, the "commune radio stations," which were supposed to have numbered around 9,435 in 1959 (Table 1) have disappeared, and the government has granted peasants a degree of autonomy and has conceded to traditional marketing activities. These policy changes are a strong testimony to the limitations of rural broadcasting or, for that matter, the use of other media as well, as instruments of rural modernization.

7

The Press

Technologically, the press is a much less complicated medium of communication than radio. But in terms of social and cultural factors, the press as a mass medium is far more complex. A press based on mass circulation needs a high rate of literacy in society, and literacy, in turn, is a result of modernization.[1] The impact of social conditions on the press is much greater than it is on radio.

On the other hand, the press has some advantages over radio. For example, a newspaper is better able to communicate complex ideas in a sophisticated manner than is a radio program. Moreover, written communication is much more durable and controllable than the spoken message. For a regime that is dedicated to transforming a nation's ideology, the press is indispensable, for it can put the varied actions of the regime into a coherent ideological context, and it is suitable for repeated "study" in indoctrination sessions.

INTEGRATION BETWEEN PRESS STRUCTURE AND POLITICS

The structure of the press in Communist China was more complicated than that of radio broadcasting. In terms of ownership, there were five types of newspapers. The most important was the Party press, organized in national, regional, and local levels, corresponding to the organizational structure of the Party. At the national level, there was the *People's Daily*, the organ of the Central Committee. At the regional level, every provincial and municipal Party Committee published a newspaper as the organ of its Central Committee. The county Party Committees did not publish papers of their own. (A number of attempts to do so were made, but they failed.) Instead, the provincial newspapers published "rural editions" to serve the counties and communes within every province.

The second type were newspapers owned by mass organizations, such as the former *China Youth Daily* of the Young Communist League and the present *Kuang-ming Daily* of the Democratic Alliance. These mass "front" organizations were designed to mobilize and control different social groups.

Third, there was the institutional press, published by public institutions such as schools, colleges, factories, and other public agencies. These papers were mainly for internal circulation and were used as a complement to the public press.

The fourth type of papers had no organizational base. They were papers that had existed before 1949 and had been retained by the Communist regime because of their previous pro-Communist views. They were used to give some substance to the united front policy, in which the state is proclaimed to be an alliance of proletariat, peasantry, national bourgeoisie, and petit bourgeoisie. These papers were designated to represent the latter two groups. So far as I can determine, there were only three such papers, *Ta-kung Pao* (Impartial Daily), *Wen-hui Pao* (Wen-Hui Daily), and *Shanghai Wan-pao* (Shanghai Evening News). *Ta-kung Pao* seems to have circulated in several major cities, mostly in the eastern part of the country. The other two seem to have circulated only in Shanghai, where they had been published before 1949. The social groups that they served are similarly concentrated in the relatively modernized eastern parts of the country.

The fifth type was the military press. This press was organized according to the structure of military garrison districts and to the internal organization of the armed forces. In each garrison district and military unit, a paper was published and controlled by the Political Department of the respective unit. At the national level, the military press was headed by the *Liberation Army Daily,* organ of the General Political Department of the Ministry of Defense.

When we view the press structure as a whole, we see two almost independent press systems that were equally penetrative from national to lower organizational levels: the Party and the military presses. The Party press supervised and controlled the papers of mass organizations, public institutions, and the bourgeoisie. None of these three extended to all operational levels: national, regional, and lower. As Chart 3 shows, the non-military press was heavily concentrated in urban areas; only the Party press had rural editions. The penetration by the press into the rural areas of China was less impressive than that by the radio network.

There was only one news agency, the New China News Agency; it provided foreign news to all Chinese newspapers and national news to the regional and lower-level newspapers. The agency itself was operated on territorial levels corresponding to the organization of the state and the Party.[2]

The Propaganda Department of the Party Committee at each territorial level supervised and controlled all the non-military papers within its jurisdiction. Before 1958, the control pattern was mainly in the form of "external control"; regional Party Committees served as advisors more than as policy-makers. But the general shift to a leftist ideology and policy in 1958 changed the pattern to "internal control."[3] The regional Party Committees, headed by the first Party secretary, took over the actual policy-making in individual newspapers. This was part of the overall change in the Party's relationship to all public institutions at that time. In general, the Party expressed more concern over control of the press than of radio.

The growth pattern of the press was not much different from that of radio. The impetus came from above rather than from below. The exact number of newspapers at each operational level (especially at the lower level) cannot be ascertained. According to Wang Mu, former Deputy Director of the Newspaper and Journal Section of the Propaganda Department of the Party Central Committee, in 1959 there were "28 central newspapers and 1,427 local newspapers, not including those issued by the factories, mines, institutions, and schools."[4] At least a thousand of these were county newspapers published during the heat of the Great Leap Forward in 1958.

CHART 3:

Structure of the Chinese Press

	Type of Ownership (Functional Division)				
	Party	Mass Organizations	Institutions	Bourgeoisie	Military
National	*People's Daily*	Organ of the Group's Central Committee			*The Liberation Army Daily*
Regional	1. Provincial Party Newspapers 2. Autonomous Region Party Newspapers 3. Municipal Party Newspapers	Newspapers of the Regional Branches		Circulating in a few Cities	1. First-level Military District Newspapers 2. Provincial Military District Newspapers
Lower	Rural Editions of Provincial Newspapers in County, Commune, Production Brigade, and Team		Operationally classified as Lower Press; Circulating Mainly in Urban Areas		Newspapers and wall newspapers in every unit

Operational Levels

As Table 2 indicates, the number of newspapers in China grew very little between 1950 and 1956, though circulation quadrupled. Yet within a year, from 1956 to 1957, the number of newspapers suddenly increased by almost four times. From 1957 to 1958, the number of newspapers again jumped upward. It is quite implausible that such a sudden growth could be due to a spontaneous rise of newspaper reading by the public. It was probably due to the Party's deliberate actions to increase propaganda in rural areas in the two radical collectivization campaigns, the 1955–56 campaign for agricultural producers' cooperatives and the 1958 campaign for people's communes. Each campaign increased mass agitation in the rural areas of China. On the whole, it seems that the growth of newspaper circulation before 1956 occurred mainly in urban areas and was of a spontaneous kind, while the growth between 1956 and 1959 represented the Party's efforts to mobilize the rural population.

TABLE 2

Number and Circulation of Newspapers
in Communist China

Year	Number of Newspapers	Combined Circulation of Single Issue
1950	382	3,010,000
—	—	—
1955 (May)	(265)*	(9,360,000)*
1956	392	12,000,000
1957	1,429	15,000,000
1958	1,884	30,000,000
1959 (September)	1,455	20,932,177

* The number of newspapers and the circulation figure include only those published at the national, provincial, and municipal level; they do not include newspapers published at county level or by institutions.

SOURCES: The figures for 1950 and 1959 are from Wang Mu, "Some Experiences in Newspaper Work Since the Great Leap Forward," in *Extracts from China Mainland Magazines* (ECMM), no. 196, p. 14; those for 1955 are from *Kuangming Jih-pao,* May 20, 1955; those for 1956 are from Yuan Chang-chao *Chung-kuo Pao-yi Shaw-shih* (A Concise History of Chinese Newspapers) (Hong Kong, 1957); and those for 1957 and 1958 are from an unpublished *Research Report* (1958 and 1959 edition) of U.S.I.S. (Hong Kong).

The failure of the Great Leap affected the press structure as well as all other aspects of the political system. In both the number and circulation of newspapers, the year 1959 was a step down from 1958. The mushroom of rural newspapers in 1958 disappeared. By 1963, according to both eyewitness accounts and press reports in China, there were no more county or commune newspapers. Instead, provincial newspapers published special rural editions for distribution to all the counties and communes within each province.

Before the Cultural Revolution of 1966, the structure of the Chinese press at and above the municipal level had stabilized. The regime, however, had not been able to establish a viable press at the county level. During the Cultural Revolution, almost all the newspapers at and above the municipal level were either reorganized or suspended. Of the seven leading national newspapers, only three continue publishing: *People's Daily, Liberation Army Daily,* and *Kuang-ming Daily.* After severe purges and possibly the dissolution of the Young Communist League and the All-China Labor Union Federation, the *China Youth Daily* and *Workers' Daily* were suspended. The exact situation of the newspapers in provincial capitals and other cities is unknown; from sketchy data, it seems that no criterion by which papers were suspended or reorganized can be detected.

Despite the Cultural Revolution, the basic principle of integrating the press with the Party structure is not likely to be abandoned in the future. In fact, judging from the emphasis on ideology and politics in the Cultural Revolution, the integration between the press and the political structure will only be increased after the Maoist faction has completed its reconstruction of the Party.

INTEGRATION BETWEEN CONTENT AND POLITICS *

The content of the Chinese press, even more than that of radio, reflected the changes in the Party's integration strategy, though always within the basic Leninist conception that the functions of the press were propaganda, agitation, organization, and self-criticism. Mao Tse-tung told the staff of a Communist news-

---

* For a statistical content analysis of the *People's Daily*, see Appendix 4.

paper in 1948: "Your job is to educate the masses, to enable the masses to know their own interests, their tasks, and the Party's general and specific policies." [5]

From 1949 to 1952, since the Party was mainly concerned with building its authority, two functions of the press were emphasized: criticism and self-criticism, and organization. For example, in 1950, the Party Central Committee initiated a campaign of criticism and self-criticism in the newspapers. This was designed to create a favorable image of the Party among the people. The *People's Daily* editorialized: "A newspaper must face the broad masses and reality. It must keep close contact with all types of readers, listen to their opinions, and strengthen the organization and education of worker-peasant correspondents." [6] Whenever the Party followed a leftist policy, the worker-peasant correspondents were emphasized. Apparently this was part of the populist appeal that the left-wing Party leaders like to exploit. The first three years of the regime, as I have mentioned, were the heyday of leftism.

The Communist Party was also building up its organization rapidly during this period. Because of the press ability to print documents and instructions, the Party wanted to use it to transmit and instruct regional cadres on organizational matters. This was the "organization function" of the press. Furthermore, the press was expected to strengthen the organization by initiating concrete criticisms of local Party activities.

The shift of integration strategy and the beginning of the first Five-Year Plan in 1953 called for a new emphasis in newspaper content. The press was now required to concentrate on two functions: industrial propaganda and mass ideologizing. The Party directed the Chinese press to learn from the performance of the Soviet press in the first and second Five-Year Plans of the Soviet Union. Domestically, the press was told to emulate the newspapers in Manchuria, the center of China's heavy industry. The Party also called on the press to "educate the masses in the Communist spirit." [7] The masses must be taught the Communist world outlook.

The two functions, industrial propaganda and mass ideologizing, were to be combined in practice. According to the

Party, this meant that the press must put reports about production into the proper context:

The economic propaganda in the newspapers should not just report few concrete facts. Through reporting these facts, they must elucidate a policy.

This is the ideological character of our Party press. We do not report facts uncritically and purely objectively. We select those facts to report according to policy requirements so that the reporting of these facts becomes an effective propaganda for our policy.[8]

Then, in late 1956 and the first half of 1957, in a brief period of loosened political control, the Party's guidelines to the press underwent another change. The *People's Daily*, as usual, signaled the change. On July 1, 1956, the paper enlarged its format from six to eight pages. It published a special announcement explaining the reasons for enlarging the paper and it conducted a self-criticism. The paper criticized itself for not presenting a wide range of news in the past, for not promoting public discussions of governmental policies, and for publishing long and stereotyped political writings in which readers had no interest. Most interesting of all, the paper now stated that a newspaper was an organ of public opinion. It made the statement that both the Party and the non-Party newspapers had the responsibility for "leading the views of society into the right channels."[9] From now on, according to the announcement, the *People's Daily* would not only publish those views approved by its editors but also those that were not. The paper pledged that it would now extend the scope of news, promote free discussion of policies, and improve the quality of its style.

The impact of the Great Leap on the press was a continuation of the Party's reactions to the Hundred Flowers campaign, with an intensified emphasis on propaganda brought about by the ascendancy of the left-wing Party leadership. The Party tightened its control over the press and initiated an anti-professionalism drive in journalistic circles. In the meantime, the press was directed to emphasize mass political agitation. All reports about domestic events must be on the people's communes and the Great Leap. No criticism was allowed. The catch phrase at that time was "filling the spirit up, but never deflecting it."

In this period, the press, like the radio, was directed to propagandize on behalf of the military. The Party maintained that propaganda about soldiers could help educate the younger generation about patriotism, internationalism, and the revolutionary tradition of the Communist Party in a lively way. In military propaganda, newspapers were to emphasize three qualities of the Chinese Red Army: selflessness, perseverance in the face of hardship, and firm ideological faith.[10] Undoubtedly this propaganda about the military was part of the left-wing leadership's desire to create the new Communist man and society, which was the goal of the Great Leap Forward. We can also view it as partly expressing the Party's concern over the ideological faith of the nation's youth.

The economic crisis that followed the failure of the Great Leap caused the Party to retreat from its militant mass mobilization. The immediate task for the regime was to insure public quiescence. Militant and agitational reports disappeared from the newspapers. Meanwhile, a subtle diversion of public attention was undertaken by the press. The models singled out for praise in the *People's Daily* were not production heroes but people representing traditional types of authority, such as teachers and parents. Some sample stories included a report on a primary school teacher who had persisted in diligent teaching for forty years, and a story about the home town of Confucius which quoted the sage's praise of his disciple Yen Hui for perseverance in study while leading a wretched life.

The content of the papers from 1963 to the breakout of the Cultural Revolution in 1966 showed no dominant themes. On the whole, their content resembled closely that in the period of 1953 through 1956—a balance of industrial propaganda and mass ideologizing. The two most prominent features in the Chinese press in this period were the nationwide campaign for emulating army heroes and the polemics with the Communist Parties of the Soviet Union and other Communist nations. The latter often occupied all the space in national and regional newspapers. It was also during this period that some major Party newspapers carried essays containing veiled attacks on

Mao Tse-tung. If so, the lack of a predominant function of the press in this period may have reflected dissension within the top Party leadership.

At all periods within the Party press, the territorial level of a paper determined the scope of its news, though the front page of all regional papers had to carry important national events. For the other three types of non-military press, the specific social group that each paper served determined the nature of its news. The *Kuang-ming Daily*, for example, was to serve the intellectuals in literature and the social sciences, and the *Impartial Daily*, professionals in finance and commerce. But these papers were also required to report important national news on their front page. The national news that every paper was required to carry unified all the papers. And it was the national news that followed the shifts and turns of the Party's strategy of integration and national construction.

In sum, the total integration of the Chinese press with the Communist organizational structure enabled the Party to mobilize public attention. Unity of theme, however, was not achieved at the expense of diversity; each type of paper addressed a specific group and related it to the national task.

The Cultural Revolution, with its across-the-board attacks on the press and particularly with the dissolution of mass organizations, has destroyed the unity-in-diversity principle. Though a formerly specialized paper like the *Kuang-ming Daily* has survived so far, its content is now little different from the other Party newspapers. It is likely that the new press under the Maoist and left-wing leadership will be more uniform in content than the old press.

NEWSPAPERS AND FACE-TO-FACE COMMUNICATION

The instrument that the Communists used to link newspapers with face-to-face communication among the masses was collective newspaper reading.

From 1949 to 1952, in coordination with the Party's strategy of building authority by linking the masses with the new regime in a series of mass campaigns, collective newspaper reading became both intensive and extensive. At this time, there were few regional differences; a wave of collective reading swept the nation. For example, the *People's Daily* on February 6, 1952, reported that in October 1951, in southern Kiangsu, there were 11,207 newspaper reading groups with 203,700 members, including workers, peasants, soldiers, cadres, students, monks, and nuns. Of these, 65 percent were workers and peasants. There were apparently both political and practical reasons for emphasizing collective reading among workers and peasants. First, most of them were illiterate, and second, the Party was anxious to establish a degree of genuine identity of interest between itself and these two social groups.

After the beginning of the first Five-Year Plan in 1953, collective newspaper reading in urban areas fell off and became a routine part of the weekly study sessions in various institutions. Yet, starting in 1954, collective reading was intensified in rural areas, as the Party began to set up agricultural producers' cooperatives. The Party claimed that, now that the villages had been organized into cooperatives, a natural organizational foundation for collective newspaper reading had been laid. The cooperatives would, first of all, solve the problem of subscription fees. It was easier for the cooperative treasury to pay the newspaper's bill than to ask individuals to pay. Furthermore, since every cooperative had a treasurer or accountant who was necessarily literate, he could be assigned to read newspapers for the cooperative members. Lastly, with production collectivized, newspaper reading could be easily integrated with concrete tasks of production.[12] That was the Party's line of reasoning; in reality, whether the cooperatives provided a viable base for instituting collective reading is much in doubt.

The Great Leap in 1958 gave another impetus to collective reading in the countryside. The movement subsided after the failure of the Great Leap. The Socialist Education campaign in 1963 again started collective newspaper reading in rural areas, in coordination with the gradual assertion of Mao's leadership and his strategy of intensifying political indoctrination among the people.

The combination of newspaper reading with oral agitation can be illustrated with an account of an experience in Hsinhsing county, Kwangtung province, which was based on an interview with a former resident of this county. In 1965 and 1966, Hsinhsing had 3,000 production teams, which were originally village units before the communes were organized in 1958. Each production team had two or three newspaper reading groups with at least one "newspaper reader" for each group.

Newspaper readers usually conducted their work at three sites: in the field, in peasants' homes, and in the production team's meeting place. Because readers also worked as common peasants in the fields, they often used rest periods to do newspaper reading. The Communists called this "position warfare." Every evening, peasants had to go to the production team meeting place to receive their assignments for the next day. Readers would read and talk about newspapers with those who came to the meeting place. This was called "mobile warfare." Not all peasants came to the meeting place at the same time, so readers had to repeat their reading or talking from group to group as they came. The two methods described above reached only those who worked in the fields. To reach housewives and older people, newspaper readers paid for house-to-house visits to "talk," not "read," news from newspapers. This was called "guerrilla warfare."

The newspaper reading groups in Hsinhsing county used four types of reading materials: the *People's Daily,* the *Southern Daily* and its rural editions, Mao Tse-tung's works, and important political documents of current relevance.

Oral agitation was combined with newspaper reading. Except in "position warfare," readers were supposed to reinforce their reading with ad-lib oral agitation. A unique advantage of oral agitation is its flexible approach; an agitator can adjust his content and style quickly according to the reactions of his audience. This was illustrated in newspaper readers' handling of anti-American propaganda, focusing on the war in South Vietnam. While in the field, they read from the international pages of the *People's Daily* about the American air force bombing North Vietnam, American battleships visiting Hong Kong, the soldiers of the Liberation Front attacking Saigon, anti-Vietnam war demonstrations in America, and the "resurgence of militarism in Japan." During the evenings, when peasants came to production team meeting places, newspaper readers began to talk, instead of reading the news, about "America helping Taiwan to invade the Chinese mainland" and about how "we must intensify our militia training and production and save food to prepare for war." When they visited peasants' homes, they talked about the "criminal acts of the American imperialists: "Americans used poisonous gas in Vietnam; American soldiers raped Vietnamese women; and American soldiers massacred Vietnamese children."

This eyewitness account of the combination of newspaper reading with oral agitation in a single county should be projected to the whole nation only with care. Given the time period of the account—1966, it seems likely that the intensified use of collective newspaper reading was a combined result of the Cultural Revolution and a general war scare in China, caused by America's increased involvement in the Vietnam War. I do not believe that in normal times collective newspaper reading was a self-sustaining action in rural areas. Unless the Party exerted pressure on rural cadres, as in mass campaigns, the cadres did not usually organize collective newspaper reading on their own initiative. Like collective radio listening, collective newspaper reading is essentially coercive and not something spontaneously desired by peasants. Peasant enthusiasm for the regime has waned over the years. If the reader was not skillful, uneducated peasants were often unable to understand the prevailing expository style of news writing. When these factors are considered, it is not surprising that the Communist regime did not succeed in making collective newspaper reading a self-sustaining activity in rural areas.

LIMITATIONS ON THE EFFECTIVENESS OF NEWSPAPERS

I have already shown that the press in China was urban centered and that the regime was unable to establish a viable county press. The difficulty of integrating collective newspaper reading into the daily routine of rural life has also been noted. The fact is that rural China was too illiterate and too economically underdeveloped to generate sustained interest in a printed medium like the press, which requires intellectual sophistication.

The close correlation between rural underdevelopment and the difficulty of reaching the peasantry by newspapers in Communist China is further indicated by a report about the distribution of the rural press in Kwangtung province. In consonance with the Socialist Education campaign of 1963, a drive to disseminate rural newspapers in Kwangtung province was initiated. A report revealed that of eleven counties that were regarded as model *hsien* because eighty to ninety percent of their production brigades subscribed to the rural edition of the *Southern Daily*, seven were near Canton. The highways and railways that focus on Canton have made it possible for the counties and villages in the immediate area not only to have but also to *want* to have newspapers.[13]

Although ideology and organization enabled the Communist Party to control and manipulate the press for political and social purposes, they were not sufficient to insure that the press could reach and communicate effectively with the illiterate and underdeveloped rural society.

NEWSPAPERS AND NATIONAL INTEGRATION

The newspapers in China, as I have noted, are concentrated mainly in urban areas. They are essentially a medium for the middle and upper class, that is, the literate and urban. As such, the press in Communist China has the advantage of reaching those groups that are likely to seek an active career in the Communist system. They consist of cadres, bureaucrats, students, and professionals. The integrative effect of the press is thus strengthened by the predisposition of its readers.

Though the Chinese Communist press imparts little of what is considered "factual information" in non-Communist nations, it still performs the news function. For, it provides information about what utterances and actions are considered "loyal" and "disloyal," respectively, for those who seek a career in the Communist system. In other words, the press in China performs actively the function of political socialization. Because the Party line changes from time to time and because the press is an authoritative public record, reading newspapers is one of the few keys for students and professionals in China who have to adjust to the changes in Party policy. According to a young former diplomat who defected to the West from one of Communist China's missions in Africa: "Reading the domestic newspapers had been helpful—they had kept me posted on the various shifts in official policy, and this more than any other factor had earned my admission to a university." [14]

Like the press in the Soviet Union, newspapers in China encouraged people to criticize "bureaucratism" in the Party and state. Letters of this nature from readers were sometimes given front-page prominence. At times the Party press undertook on its own initiative "anti-bureaucratic" campaigns in newspapers. To some, these campaigns function as a means of political participation, though of a very limited nature. A more subtle function is to divert the aggression of the public away from top leaders and the Communist Party to a few individuals. The monolithic information structure and the uniformity of its message inevitably make people suspicious of the truthfulness of public information, so the anti-bureaucratic campaigns were also designed to reduce this type of suspicion and to increase the credibility of the press.[15]

Newspapers in China were also a sounding board for testing policies that the Party was unsure of. For instance, newspaper articles on birth control appeared before the Party formally announced it as a public policy in 1956. The Party could thus sound out the opinions of interested groups, while at the same time preparing the public psychologically for such new policies. Another example is the language reform initiated by the Chinese Communists. As mentioned before, the Communist Party was sensitive to the charge that by tampering with the Chinese language, the Party was trying to destroy Chinese culture. Thus, before the Party formally announced the specific methods of language reform, the press undertook an extensive publicity campaign to rationalize the need for reform.

The press in Communist China, more than any other mass medium, teaches people a new and uniform political language. Such a language is taught in the press with a good deal of sophistication. Every event reported is contextualized according to the Party line. Franz Schurmann, for example, has analyzed the newspaper content in Communist China in terms of six categories: (1) policy decisions; (2) concrete experiences in policy implementation; (3) general principles; (4) criticisms; (5) propaganda; and (6) public information.[16] Functionally, the substance of the press in China can be categorized according to its dominant values.[17] Some items in the Chinese press, for example, are for attention value. Major policy decisions are always printed in full on the front page. Because most working people in China will be informed in great detail of such policies in group discussions at their working places, the value of the press is simply to arouse public attention. Some items are for explanation value, editorials being the primary example. Unlike editorials in non-Communist newspapers, which have a feedback function, those in the Chinese press are intended to rationalize Party policies. Stories about model workers and martyrs are for appeal and participation value. These stories not only serve to increase conformism; they are also designed to appeal to people's motives and expectations, particularly those who want to carve a career in the Communist system. All these examples of news management are achieved through a new political language that organizes a varied reality into a single perspective. In a society where social relations and culture are in flux, such a single perspective and a new uniform language both serve an integrative function.

The Cultural Revolution landed hard on the pre-1966 intellectual orientation of the Chinese press. The left-wing, which now controls the Party, wants to turn the press into a medium of mass agitation. The press before 1966 was accused of emphasizing too much knowledge and variety at the expense of "Party spirit, class struggle, and militancy."[18] The new orientation is to present a simple, direct, and uniform type of newspaper content. The leftists have not changed the integrative function of the press, but they want to accelerate it by feeding the public with unsophisticated and undisguised political agitation. By trying to make the press more penetrative, the leftists may actually have isolated the press. Though the press was concentrated in urban areas in the past, it was at least able to provide a link between the urban-literate group and Communist politics. The countryside, as mentioned before, was largely dominated by oral communication; repeated efforts to institutionalize a county press had failed. The Cultural Revolution has not changed this situation. The "de-intellectualization" of the press by the leftists thus has grossly weakened the press' link with the literate and professional groups in urban areas, without appreciably strengthening its link with the rural masses.

8

Book Publishing

As a written medium, book publishing shares many characteristics with the press. Books are even better able to put things
into context than is the press. To read a book requires more
intellectual sophistication and motivation than to read a newspaper. Even in a highly literate society, books have the smallest
audience of all the mass media.

Other studies have described the structure and production of
Chinese publishing in detail; the emphasis here is on interpretation.[1]

INTEGRATION BETWEEN PUBLISHING STRUCTURE AND POLITICS

The Chinese regime used the same methods to integrate publishing with political organization as were used with the press.
The principles of centralization and functional specialization
run through the organization of the publishing industry too.

Two centralizing structures that served to knit the publishing
enterprise into the political organization were the People's Publishing Houses and the distribution chain of New China (*Hsin-
hua*) Bookstores. The former system paralleled the territorial
organization of the Party and the government. The People's
Publishing House in Peking was the national headquarters for
publishing books on "political theories, policies, and current
events" that were intended for the whole Chinese population.
At regional levels, every province and autonomous region had

its People's Publishing House, turning out books about ideology, current events, and Party programs particularly relevant to the region. The chief function of the People's Publishing House at every operational level was political.

The New China Bookstore had a monopoly on book distribution. From its national headquarters in Peking, its regional divisions corresponded exactly to that of the organization of the government: province, municipality, and county. The arms of this book company reached down to villages. Barnett describes the branch of the New China Bookstore in a county in Kwangtung province as follows:

The bookstore had overall responsibility for sales and distribution of all published material put out by the many state publishing companies in China, as well as for distribution of stationery. It ran one central bookstore in the county seat. In the countryside it distributed through the larger supply and marketing cooperatives. Subscriptions to magazines and journals were also handled by its staff. It had a total of six state cadres, including a manager . . ., an accountant. . ., and four salesmen. . . .

The bookstore was expected to do more than simply make materials available. Following Party instructions, it was also active in promoting the sale of publications considered especially important in relation to current policies and programs. Periodically, it dispatched agricultural extension workers . . . to survey and push priority items.[2]

Complementing these two centralized systems were the publishing companies that the Party designated to produce specialized books, such as the Workers' Publishing House, Youth Publishing House, Commercial Press (science and technology), Science Publishing House, and so forth. By 1956, China had a publishing enterprise consisting of 40 national and 101 regional publishing houses.[3]

Besides its monopoly on distribution through the New China Bookstore, another of the Party's controls over publishing was the requirement that every publishing house must submit long-term plans to the propaganda department of its respective Party Committee, which in turn transmitted the plans upward to the propaganda department at the next higher level of the

Party hierarchy.[4] There were indications that, as occurred with the press, the control that regional Party Committees had over publishing houses was changed from "external" to "internal" in 1958. Before that year, the regional Party Committees controlled the policy-making of individual publishing houses within their respective areas indirectly, through the Party fraction; the editorial staff of each publishing company retained a substantial degree of independence in deciding yearly plans. After 1958, however, Party Committees took over the decision-making power in each publishing house. In the meantime, a campaign of anti-professionalism was initiated by the Party; each publishing house purged a substantial number of experienced and professional editorial personnel.[5] This was a combined result of the anti-rightist campaign after the conclusion of the Hundred Flowers campaign and the ascendancy of the left-wing leaders in 1958.

The Cultural Revolution dealt a severe blow to the publishing industry. Early in 1967, the *People's Daily* began to report that "revolutionary workers" in one publishing house after another had seized control of their company and its production plant. A revolutionary committee was formed in each company and soon resolved to concentrate on publishing only Mao's works. For example, in Peking, a printing plant that used to specialize in literature and art was taken over in early 1967 by "revolutionary workers" who decided to publish only Mao's works from then on; the first production target was two million copies of Mao's "Combat Liberalism." [6] The principle of functional division was eliminated almost totally. The new publishing enterprise, like the new press structure, is highly uniform and political and will be so long as the left-wing Party leadership is in ascendance.

INTEGRATION BETWEEN PUBLISHING CONTENT AND POLITICS

Politically, the function of publishing as defined by the Communist Party was to propagandize ideology and the policy of the Party. Economically, publishing was to assist production in industry and agriculture and promote the long-term scientific and technological development of China. Culturally, publishing was to create a new set of values conforming with Marxism-Leninism-Maoism. Even a medium like book publishing, which had primarily a long-term function of creating a new cultural identity for China, was subject to the radical policy changes of the Communist regime. In the subsequent discussion, though all types of books will be dealt with in general, attention will be focused on books about politics and ideology, for these were manifestly intended for national integration.*

To determine the coordination between publishing and Party strategy, I analyzed the *Chinese National Bibliography* (*Chuan-kuo Tsung-shu-mu*). This bibliography was first published in 1950 as a quarterly. At that time, it was divided into eleven categories: social sciences, philosophy, history and geography, language, art and literature, natural sciences, applied technology, popular readers, juvenile readers, textbooks, and reference books. Social science books included those on ideology, the Communist movement in the world, and mass campaigns in China. In 1950 this category of books was the largest. During the first three years of the regime, when the Party was mainly concerned with the establishment of its authority, publishing a large number of books about the Party's programs and ideology served several useful purposes. It familiarized those who had little knowledge about the Communist political system with the ideology and programs of the new regime. It also served to sustain and strengthen the faith of the activists, especially the younger ones. Publishing in this period complemented the action programs of mass campaigns in a joint effort to link the masses with the new Communist authority.

The period from 1953 to 1957 was characterized in my analysis as that of building legitimacy. Diversification of publishing was emphasized. In a major review article on the nation's publishing enterprises in 1954, the *People's Daily* explained the new policy:

The demands for scientific and cultural books by the state and the people are varied. Publishers must meet this demand. In order to develop scholarship and culture and uplift the ideological and cultural standards of the people, all types of books that are basically not

* For a statistical analysis of Chinese publishing, see Appendix 5.

in conflict with the main principles of Marxism-Leninism and are of value to us should be published. There are certain types of books that do not seem to be relevant to our present political struggle. But, so long as they can enlighten the people, increase their knowledge, and cultivate their virtue, then we ought to consider them for publication.[7]

To put the new policy in terms of the Communist categories, the emphasis was to shift from "political" to "knowledge" types of books. As a result, a large number of books on technology and science were published, mostly translated versions of foreign books. It was reported that from 1949 to 1955, 3,400 foreign books on science and technology were published in Chinese, and of these 2,400 were Soviet works.[8]

During the period of the first Five-Year Plan (1953–1957), the Communist regime appealed to the Chinese people's patriotism and nationalism to push forward the industrialization program. Publishing fit into this strategy through the reprinting of a large amount of classical Chinese literature. Previously, the regime had largely ignored these works, partly because the whole publishing enterprise was still in the process of being integrated into the political system and partly because of the Party's strategy of militant social revolution. At the Second National Conference of Literary and Art Workers in 1953, the Party declared that publishing classical works was one of the most important current tasks of the publishing enterprises. In the next year, the nation's chief newspaper for intellectuals, the *Kuang-ming Daily,* started a special series called "Literary Heritage," which formally legitimized and encouraged research on and publishing of classical works. In 1955, the Classical Works Publishing House began to turn out reprints of classical literature and modern volumes containing selections from the classics. The publishing of classical works in this period was apparently designed to appeal to nationalism and to promote a more conservative type of social stability in contrast to the militantly anti-tradition era of 1949 to 1952. Industrialization called for social stability and genuine popular enthusiasm.[9]

The Great Leap Forward in 1958 brought back the predominance of politics and ideology. From 1958 to 1960, a new category, "Special Subjects," was added to the *National Bibli-*

ography. Books published under this category dealt with subjects like Socialism and Communist Education; Theory, System, and Experience of People's Communes; Education for Service to the Politics of the Proletariat; and Combination of Education and Labor. In general, publishing in this period resembled that in 1950; a large number of pamphlet-like books on current economic and political campaigns were published. In the first two months of 1959, for example, the publishing houses in Shanghai printed twenty-four million copies of the *General Line of Socialist Construction.*[10] Even the *Chinese National Bibliography* was published and released three times a month.

The rationale underlying this renewed emphasis on mass printing of political books was the leftist ideology of precipitating mass ideological awakening. It was an action parallel to the establishment of rural radio stations and the distribution of rural newspapers. Mass printing of simple political tracts reached the masses better and faster than books on sophisticated subjects.

The frenzy of publishing subsided after 1961, when the Party felt the pinch of the failure of the Great Leap. The *Chinese National Bibliography* was changed to a biweekly and the category "Special Subjects" disappeared from it. In the meantime, the new international and domestic situation required a new heading, "The Movement of International Communism and Building of the Communist Party." Two kinds of books were published under this category. One dealt with China's relationship with Communist nations other than the Soviet Union —which, in hindsight, represented the Party's attempt to prepare the Chinese people psychologically for the eventual break with the Soviets. But more important than this was the second type, books which dealt with organizational matters of the Chinese Communist Party itself.

The new emphasis on the internal organization of the Party was in line with political developments immediately after the disaster of the Great Leap. The Maoist strategy of the Great Leap had been based on a faith in the revolutionary militancy of the base-level cadres; organizational discipline was considered a hindrance to the expression of the revolutionary enthusiasm of the lower-level cadres. Consequently, Party discipline was brushed aside by the left-wing leaders during 1958 and 1959. But the assumption of power of a non-left-wing leadership after the Great Leap resulted in a general strengthening of organizational discipline. This group of leaders had no illusions about the abilities and sentiments of the lower-level cadres. The emphasis on organizational discipline was designed to prevent the cadres from interfering with production excessively.[11] The increase in the literature on Party organization from 1961 to 1963 reflected the change of leadership and strategy of integration in this period.

After 1963, Mao Tse-tung sought to reassert his authority and prepare for a new Great Leap Forward. To make sure that this new Leap would not fail, Mao decided to indoctrinate the masses thoroughly before he really embarked upon the new program. The series of "emulation of the army" campaigns was for this purpose. In publishing, this was accomplished through mass printing of three abridged editions of Mao's *Selected Works,* formally entitled *Selected Readings of Mao Tse-tung.*

Thus, as with other media, the changes in the Communist regime's integration strategy resulted in corresponding changes in book publishing. The publishing industry, which deals with many long-term tasks of national integration—scientific and technological development, cultural identity—and which normally should follow a coherent strategy of its own, was not immune to the radical changes in Chinese politics.

BOOKS AND FACE-TO-FACE COMMUNICATION

To link book reading with face-to-face communication confronted the Chinese Communist with a dilemma. Of all the media, books require of their readers the most genuine motivation. The dilemma facing the Communists was that precisely because few people were regular book readers, collective reading was needed to insure that books about the Party's programs and ideology were not ignored. Yet because of people's natural reluctance, collective book reading was more coercive and less effective than collective radio listening or newspaper reading.

Nevertheless, the regime still made efforts to promote collective book reading in rural areas. In the Socialist Education Campaign of 1963, "revolutionary novels" were read in mass meetings in the countryside.[12] Just before the Cultural Revolution broke out, the *People's Daily* reported that the distribution personnel of the New China Bookstore had the responsibility to organize rural residents for reading Mao's works or to assist rural cadres to do it. One article stated that in a county in Shensi province, the distribution personnel of the bookstore "helped village Party branches reorganize many small teams for learning Chairman Mao's works and reading them to 264 illiterate and semi-literate peasants." [13]

On the whole, however, collective book reading was a haphazard and, at best, intermittent affair in rural China. It was even more rare in urban areas.

LIMITS ON THE EFFECTIVENESS OF BOOKS

In discussing the limits on the effectiveness of newspapers, I noted the problem of the wide gap between urban and rural areas. The problem is even greater for book publishing. Rural China is still too illiterate and economically underdeveloped to sustain any continuous interest in or demand for books. There are specific examples of this. First, it was revealed during the Hundred Flowers campaign of 1957 that the distribution plans of the New China Bookstore were usually fulfilled in urban areas and not in rural areas. Of the great number of unsaleable books that accumulated in the bookstores all over China, the majority were originally intended for rural distribution.[14] Perhaps the strongest evidence of the lack of rural demand for books was the dissolution of two publishing houses sometime in 1961, the Popular Readers Publishing House and the Publishing House for Popularization of Science. Both companies were originally assigned to publish simple texts for rural residents. In the Cultural Revolution, Maoist leaders accused the former deputy director of the Propaganda Department, Chou Yang, of closing down these publishing companies arbitrarily.[15] But the real cause seems to have been absence of demand for these books.

Book publishing also suffered from the lack of cultural integration between the dominant Chinese (Han) race and other minority nationalities in China. In 1958, for example, an important Party official in charge of minority nationality affairs charged that some nationality publishing houses turned out books advocating separatism and disseminating religious thought:

The regional nationalists did their utmost to try to split the unification of our motherland and the unity among regional nationalities. In publishing, they sold books with separatist ideas under the cloak of "nationality cultural heritage," "nationality literature," or "nationality history." Some disseminated the idea of "Uighurstan" in their textbooks. Some publications depicted our motherland and their regions as two independent nations. Some works distorted history by describing nationalities' anti-Chinese battles in the past as "righteous rebellions" and the leaders of these battles as "nationality heroes," regardless of facts. Some publishing houses printed seventy percent of their textbooks for elementary and secondary schools in one foreign language. This kind of textbooks naturally diluted students' motherland consciousness. In creating new vocabularies, the regional nationalists used the excuse of preserving the "purity" of nationality languages to coin new words or even borrow foreign languages but refuse to use Chinese.[16]

The publishing houses in Tibet were accused of turning out more than twenty percent of their literary publications on religious matters. It was also reported that some nationality publishing houses used excessively "foreign" language in their publications. This most likely refers to the Russian language used in Inner Mongolia and Sinkiang.

As a consequence, a seminar jointly sponsored by the Ministry of Culture and the Nationality Affairs Commission decided in 1962 that, from then on, if an equivalent expression was lacking in a minority race language when translating Chinese books into minority language, Chinese should be used.[17]

PUBLISHING AND NATIONAL INTEGRATION

Generally speaking, the integrative effects of book publishing are similar to those of the other printed media—dissemination of the Communist ideology and providing a coherent ideological framework for the varied actions of the government. But these effects are mostly felt through political publications.

Publishing in Communist China also included books on science, technology, art, and literature, which have not been discussed in this chapter. The integrative effects of these books are organically linked with the growth or decay of what Edward Shils calls "the intellectual system" of a nation.[18] The main body of such a system consists of schools and research institutes. This, however, is not the place to discuss the development of the intellectual system in Communist China. But we can speculate that, given the strong anti-intellectual strain in Mao's thought, which has been either supported or acquiesced in by a large number of illiterate and rural Chinese, the integrative effects of the intellectual system and its publishing enterprise in China are likely to be limited.

9

The Film Industry

Movies are perhaps the most effective of all the mass media for communicating with illiterate and intellectually unsophisticated people.[1] Movies not only transmit oral messages but also illustrate them with vivid images. Through these vivid images, illiterate and traditional-minded peasants acquire some basic notions of nationhood, often through the image of a national leader.[2] Lenin recognized the political effects of motion pictures when he stated that "when the masses take possession of the film and it comes into the hands of true supporters of socialist culture, it will become one of the most powerful means of educating the masses."[3] In the course of analyzing the integrative effects of the film industry in Communist China, it is not necessary to present detailed descriptions of the structure of the Chinese film enterprise;[4] emphasis will be on analysis and interpretation.

INTEGRATION BETWEEN FILM INDUSTRY STRUCTURE
AND POLITICS

For the Chinese film industry, the years from 1949 to 1952 were a period of revolutionary destruction. The Communists were then preoccupied with destroying the foundations of the pre-Communist industry. With the beginning of the first Five-Year Plan in 1953, and the change of the Party's strategy to building legitimacy and institutions, the Communist regime began seriously to construct a new type of film enterprise. Film making requires not only complex technology but also artistic sophistication. It is, therefore, not as well adapted as other mass media to integration with the territorial structure of the Party and the state. Consequently from 1953 to 1957, the Chinese film industry was organized according to specialization. Film making was concentrated in three cities: Changchun in the Northeast, Peking in the North, and Shanghai in Central China. In a rough way, these three centers divided their labor. The Changchun film studio specialized in dubbing Chinese sound-tracks onto Soviet films. The studios in Peking specialized in feature films and newsreels. The studios in Shanghai specialized in education and science films, cartoons, and occasionally dubbing the Chinese soundtracks onto some "progressive" European films. The usefulness of Shanghai as the center of Western influence was thus exploited in this film structure. The system of film making seems to have been based on the Party's need to use the small number of professionals available and the facilities built in these cities in the pre-Communist era.

If the structure exploited existing facilities and professional skills, however, it also increased the cultural gap between the modernized eastern areas of China and the underdeveloped interior. Peking and Shanghai were the most modernized regions of the country. The films produced there reflected the culture of their regions. To redress this imbalance, two new studios were built in 1957; one in Sian, in the depths of Northwest China, and one in Canton, in the deep South, a region where language diversity is most serious and a region that was historically the last to be integrated into the mainstream of Chinese culture.

A territorial organization for the film industry emerged only in 1958, in the heat of the Party's effort to reach the peasant masses directly. Now, every province was to build its own newsreel and documentary studio. It was also anticipated at that time that eventually each of the major geographical regions of China would create a semi-independent film enterprise to meet regional needs.[5] The rationale behind these organizational changes was both ideological and social. Ideologically, it represented the leftist leaders' desire to reach the masses directly and intensively in order to awaken their ideological conscious-ness. Socially, cultural diversity in China was such that only regionally based film production could meet local require-ments. In the end, the goal of comprehensive regional film enterprises was never realized, but a system of provincial news-reel and documentary studios was built. These studios were the functional equivalent of the rural radio stations and rural news-papers also installed during this period.

INTEGRATION BETWEEN FILM CONTENT AND POLITICS

In general, the function of films was no different from that of newspapers or radio. As the *People's Daily* commented in 1954: "Our film is a tool to educate the people in patriotism and so-cialism; it is also a major means to lift people's cultural stan-dards." [6] Among the three types of films—features, newsreels, and scientific and educational films—there was a division of function. Moreover, the changing emphasis on the three from one period to another reflected the Communist regime's shifts in integration strategy.*

During the period of revolutionary destruction from 1949 to 1952, feature films of the Communist type were mainly trans-lated Soviet films. The main emphasis was on newsreels and documentaries depicting major mass campaigns. Their function was similar to that of the radio or press—to establish an image of authority for the Party.

The change in the Party's strategy in 1953 resulted in a corresponding change in the film industry. The new policy gave equal emphasis to newsreels, feature films, and scientific and educational films. Newsreels were required to promote in-dustrial propaganda and patriotism, as were the newspapers in this period. Documentaries were to show beautiful scenery, resorts, ancient monuments, and art works from classical China. Like the republishing of classical literature in this period, these documentaries on China's ancient relics and beauty were de-signed to arouse popular nationalism as a spiritual force to push forward the first Five-Year Plan.

* For a statistical analysis of the types of film produced in Communist China, see Appendix 6.

By 1953, the terrorist campaign "Thought Reform of Chinese Intellectuals" had effectively suspended all feature film production. But the Party deliberately loosened political control over professional film workers after that year. The result was a substantial increase in feature films. They were supposed to transform the world outlook of the Chinese people, much as the mass ideologizing function was given to the press in the same period. The *People's Daily* commented that feature films "must reflect from all aspects the excitement and liveliness of our motherland, the true contradictions in life, and growing new forces in it, and must deal merciless blows to those dying things that obstruct our progress." [7]

Before 1953, there was no plan for producing scientific and educational films. But a major decision on film production published in 1954 set an annual target for these films equal to that for feature films. The Shanghai studios were mainly responsible for producing them.[8] This decision was appropriate to the central task of that time—industrialization.

The Great Leap in 1958 affected film making as it did all the mass media in China. Newsreels and documentaries about the communes and other political campaigns then dominated film making. Even feature films became semi-newsreels, then called "feature-documentaries." The new policy on film making was spelled out in a directive from the Ministry of Culture:

newsreels, documentaries, and scientific and educational films must be made to play a greater role under the present situation. In the face of the Great Leap Forward, more films that meet the taste of the masses of the people must be produced rapidly. Motion pictures that depict the leap forward in industry and agriculture must take up a higher proportion of films. Reporting and publicity on the technological and cultural revolutions must be strengthened. Advanced experiences and technical innovations created by the masses of the people must be popularized.[9]

This directive reflected the leftist view on mass persuasion. Mao emphasized simple and direct political agitation. Feature films, as a sophisticated art form, do not deal with politics as directly and bluntly as newsreels and documentaries do. Furthermore, Mao had an ingrained contempt for intellectually sophisticated works. The Great Leap, after all, was based on anti-intellectual and anti-professional appeals. It is no wonder, then, that newsreels and documentaries received predominant emphasis in this period.

Even the scientific and educational films of 1958 and 1959, were permeated with politics. For example one so-called educational film entitled *People's Communes Fight Drought* showed how the commune system enabled peasants to overcome drought, while in the past, such collective action was not possible.[10]

The failure of the Great Leap and the assumption of power by a non-leftist leadership after 1960 affected the film industry in two ways. First, there was a general liberalization of the restrictions on feature films. Second, there was a new emphasis on producing scientific and educational films for rural consumption.

The most dramatic example of the liberalization in the post-Leap period was the Party-sanctioned policy of "writing about middle-position characters." Writers should not write only about heroes or villains, but were to write more about characters between the poles. This was a marked departure from the Party's former stand, when writers were allowed only to praise Communist heroes and condemn villains. Announcing the new policy, Shao Chuan-lin reportedly told Chinese writers: "Heroic and backward characters are two poles. But most people are in the middle. We ought to write about these people's complicated state of mind. The main objective of art and literature is to educate the middle-position people."[11] The liberalized policy had two effects on feature films in China from 1961 to 1963. First of all, there was a general tendency to make films more entertaining than those in the past, which were heavily laden with politics. Also, many films appeared with non-proletarian characters, such as teachers, merchants, or artists.

At the same time, a national conference was called on the production of scientific and educational films. The importance that the Party leadership saw in this conference is indicated by the attendance of famous scientists like the rocket expert Chien Hsueh-shen. The main topic was how to make scientific and educational films popular and effective in the countryside. One commentary on the conference summarized the problems of communicating with peasants:

The responsibility of producing more and better scientific and educational films to meet the needs of peasants is on the shoulders of scientific and educational film workers. Aside from ideological problems, there are also involved the problems of understanding peasants, getting familiar with their life, and improving techniques [of film production]. It is not an easy task to make peasants interested in and completely accept a scientific-educational film. If a film is too sophisticated, the peasant cannot comprehend it. If it is too simple, the peasant loses interest. If a film has too many subsidiary facts then the main subject does not stand out. . . . To make the peasant like to see the scientific-educational films, we must find new techniques and adjust the content to the peasant's need.[12]

The liberalization in feature films and the emphasis on distribution of scientific and educational films in rural areas represented the ideology of the non-leftist leaders in the Party, who took a long-range and gradual view of transforming the ideology of the Chinese people. Their emphasis was on education, and they did not share Mao's belief in the effectiveness of simple and direct political agitation accompanied by mass campaigns.

Mao's time came in late 1963, when he revived the appeal for class struggle. Immediately, in 1964, Shao Chuan-lin's statements on "middle-position characters" came under attack. The authoritative *Literary Gazette* (*Wen-yi Pao*) called the policy of writing on middle-position characters "the literary principle of the bourgeoisie." Soon, purging of the feature films made in 1962 and 1963 began. All were attacked for committing one variant or another of the sin of not emphasizing class hatred.

The Cultural Revolution brought newsreels and documentaries back into prominence, as in the original Great Leap of 1958. Under the slogan "Masses of Workers and Peasants Grasp Theory Directly," newsreels and documentaries about Red Guard activities and the receptions Mao held for the Red Guards in Peking were supposed to inspire the masses. The seemingly non-political feature films of 1962 and 1963 were seen as blocks to a direct political identification between the

Party and the masses; worse still, they were also regarded as "sugar-coated bullets" to dull the class consciousness of the masses. Newsreels and documentaries depicting Red Guards and the army shown in China today are, like the mass distribution of Mao's quotations, designed to arouse mass emotion and establish a direct link between Mao and the people so that when a new Great Leap is launched in the future, the masses will be ideologically prepared.

In conclusion, film making in Communist China, like the other mass media, was closely coordinated with the shifts in the Communist regime's integration strategy. The changes in the themes of film propaganda were in complete harmony with the changes in other media.

FILMS AND FACE-TO-FACE COMMUNICATION

To insure that film propaganda succeeded in reaching the people, the Communists greatly broadened access to film showings. There are two types of access to movies in China, the regular cinema and the mobile film projection teams. The cinema is predominantly an urban facility. Outside the county towns, access to movies is through the mobile film projection teams.* Through these mobile teams, which numbered twelve thousand in 1964, the Communist regime linked film showing with oral propaganda and agitation. Again, the technique of linking movies with face-to-face communication was used mainly in rural areas. The oral messages in films that were produced in urban centers were often beyond the comprehension of rural residents. Consequently, a personal intermediary was required to "translate" the cosmopolitan culture to peasants. Language diversity and cultural particularism in rural China also required oral communication to explain motion pictures that used the "common speech." Let me now briefly describe how the mobile film-showing teams worked in rural areas.

A mobile film projection team was made up of two or three persons, often young girls. A team was typically equipped with a generator, a 16 mm. projector, a gramophone, and slide-

* For a statistical portrayal of the development of the film showing units in Communist China, see Appendix 7.

making facilities. Because trucks were not available to them, they traveled on foot with their equipment on the back of a horse or donkey.

In order to facilitate peasants' comprehension of films, the projection teams were required to use oral explanations, which in some cases had to be in local dialects. A single show involved three steps: pre-show propaganda, impromptu explanation during the show, and after-show collection of opinions.

Pre-show propaganda was designed to mobilize peasants to attend the film and was followed by a pre-show speech to ensure that the peasants interpreted the film properly and to introduce them to its characters and themes. Mobilization for attending the film involved propaganda sheets distributed by local cadres, school teachers, and activists, and wall newspapers, oral agitation, and broadcasting over loudspeakers. Introduction of the main characters was usually done orally, sometimes assisted by slide shows.

The impromptu explanation during the show was designed to help introduce the characters and to explain the meaning of scenes that used special film techniques.

The after-show collection of audience opinion meant either calling a film review conference, or requiring the local cadres to go to the shows and take down any spontaneous comments made by the peasants while they watched. This, at least, was the required procedure. In reality, perhaps not many of the teams adhered to it strictly.

After the gradual recovery of the economy from the Great Leap in 1962–1963, the Party concentrated almost all its attention on increasing the frequency of film viewing by peasants. Given the impact that movies had on illiterate peasants, the Party's tactics seem to have been realistic. One measure of the Party's attention to rural film showing was that after 1960, no nationwide figure for film attendance was reported, but that of rural film attendance was reported several times in the press. It was reported, for example, that in 1962, peasants attended an average of three movies a year. A 1965 report gave the rural film audience in 1964 as two billion and stated that this was one-quarter more than that in 1963. The same report stated that this was one-quarter more than that in 1963. The same report stated that a Chinese peasant attended an average of five movies a year.[13] In Manchuria in 1964, the rural film audience reached 210,000,000.[14]

In normal conditions, the county seat was the dispatch center of the mobile projection teams in each county. The distance between natural villages and the county seat was considerable. The poor roads and lack of motorized vehicles tended to confine the teams to the villages near the county seat. Barnett, for example, described the situation in a production brigade in Kwangtung:

Motion pictures played a role in the propaganda system in Brigade B, but even though they were very popular they were less important in the system as a whole than some other media were. Neither Brigade B nor Commune C owned a motion picture projector. When the brigade wished to show films, it had to rely, therefore, on the county's one roving Movie Team. It had to pay a remarkably high fee for each showing (Y60 each), and each team had to contribute its share to pay the bill. Consequently, Brigade B was able to arrange only occasional showing, perhaps two to four times a year. When films were shown, attendance was good, and reportedly the local peasants thoroughly enjoyed most of them, viewing them as a major entertainment despite their high political content.[15]

After 1963, the Party was determined to achieve a breakthrough in this situation. Not only was the number of teams increased greatly, a new system of establishing permanent film showing sites was created to increase accessibility for village residents. On January 12, 1965, the *People's Daily* published the cases of Chekiang and Shantung as models for other provinces to emulate. In Chekiang, every mobile team established film showing sites according to the population of the settlement, the distribution of natural villages, and the state of transportation, economic development, and educational level of the area. In Shantung, 34,182 villages were designated as optimal film showing sites. In the plains, every three natural villages now had an easily accessible film showing site; in the mountainous regions, the area that each site covered was smaller.

The fact that projection teams were mobile and that the film audience consisted of members of a single production unit enabled the Party to integrate film showing with other organizational and propaganda activities. The two main purposes of rural film showing were to aid in increasing production and to disseminate the Communist ideology. A Heilungkiang mobile projection team leader, a young girl, reported:

Movie projection teams in the villages are the vanguards of propaganda for supporting agriculture and constructing new socialist farms. In order to maximize our function, we should not only let more peasants see more movies but also select appropriate films according to the Party's policy and the demands of the masses. Thus, the peasants can have deeper socialist education and scientific knowledge and can better fulfill their production plan. . . . For example, when we learned about the Ching Lin Commune's repairing a dam, we showed them "The Young Men in Our Village." After viewing it several times, some young men in that commune said: "Since they can bring water into the mountains, we can surely dig a reservoir in the ground."

In order to do a good job in village movie showings, the film team must keep in close contact with the local Party members and the commune members and understand their work, thoughts, and demands. Then we can select the appropriate film according to the current political situation and the struggles and demands of the masses. To better serve agricultural production, it is essential that we do a good job in the selection and scheduling of the films.[16]

Technically, the greatest advantage of the mobile team was its ability to overcome language diversity. In each county, the teams could be staffed by local youths who could explain the films in dialect. A language problem occurred mostly in the regions where the minority races resided; there the mobile teams were usually Chinese who did not speak the minority people's languages. An intensified language training program was carried out for them; in 1965, the teams in thirty minority race regions—almost all the minority races in China—were trained in minority languages. At the same time, the teams in Fukien, a province with a great number of different dialects, devised the use of a tape-recorder as a substitute for the live translation during a show.[17]

In all likelihood, the Communists were successful in their linking of film propaganda with face-to-face communication. Film showing in rural areas was infrequent because of the great shortage of projection facilities and consequently did not constitute an excessive intrusion into people's privacy. Mobile film projection teams by nature operated in a collective setting, which enabled the Party to merge films with oral propaganda smoothly. There was no need to coerce people to gather around a film showing team.

The penetration of movies into the countryside is a most remarkable achievement. Despite the fact that the number of film projection teams at present is still not adequate to meet the Communist goal of equipping every commune with a mobile film projection team, a network of twelve thousand such teams is an unprecedented penetration by the national authority and culture into the traditionally isolated villages. Compared with the development of film projection in the Soviet Union, the Chinese Communists achieved greater success in enlarging the rural residents' accessibility to movies.[18]

It is conceivable that films have enhanced the Chinese peasants' awareness of being an integral part of the whole nation. Perhaps the effect of films on the promotion of economic development in rural areas has been limited, because of the still low frequency of film viewing and the low educational standard among the rural residents.

On the other hand, as Barnett's description shows, peasants still regarded movies as their major entertainment. Movies therefore provided the Communists with an attractive and efficient way to "package" their ideology. A peasant's world outlook may be gradually changed. The intensified efforts after 1965 to increase rural film showing showed that the Party seriously intended to exploit this function of the films for the long-range purpose of national integration.

The Cultural Revolution undoubtedly disrupted the whole film enterprise, but it could not obliterate the nationalizing effect that films had already created in the countryside. However, the strong anti-intellectualism of Mao's ideology of mass persuasion may prove to be an obstacle to the full exploitation of the non-political functions of films, especially education in science and technology in the countryside.

10

Patterns of Reception

In previous chapters, I have concentrated on the "top to bottom" process, describing how the Chinese Communists utilized various media of communication to politicize the Chinese people. National integration, however, is based ultimately on the "bottom to top" process, i.e., popular identification with the political system. In this chapter, I shall make a brief attempt to explore the "bottom to top" process by examining some suggestive data on the Chinese people's reception of various mass media. This discussion is based on a survey of some four hundred former residents of mainland China conducted by Professor Paul J. Hiniker in Hong Kong in 1964 and 1965.[1] The statistical data presented in this chapter are part of Hiniker's preliminary findings and, further, the figures are not a cross-tabulation of actual survey results. They are national projections based on survey data.

First, let us examine the projected rate of Chinese people's reception of four major media: meetings, newspaper, radio, and film. The result is as follows:

Meeting: 96%   Film: 70   Radio: 58   Newspaper: 40

The most striking thing about this set of data is the primacy of oral media: meetings and films. The press, an urban and literate medium, has the lowest reception rate. The reality of China's underdevelopment can not be made clearer. A no less significant idea suggested by this set of data is the effectiveness of the Communist Party's mass politicization through mass campaigns. For campaigns were carried out mainly in meetings and group discussions and even routine meetings were increased during any campaign period. Undoubtedly, this is the most impressive achievement of the Chinese Communists. By relying on skills in mass organization, the Communists had brought a semblance of integration to a land as diverse and bisected by particularism as China was before 1949.

To explore the interaction of multiple factors in Chinese people's reception of political propaganda, I have divided Hiniker's projections into four groups, each presenting the interactions between a single medium and three background factors: residence, literacy, and sex. They are presented in Table 3.

The data in Table 3 again suggest the power of mass oral agitation in the form of political meetings. Except for the single group of female-urban-illiterate, the background factors exercised little impact on the rate of reception. Almost every social group was equally highly exposed to meetings. This is the one propaganda medium that has indeed brought the entire nation together. Before the Cultural Revolution, the arms of the Party enabled the leaders to accomplish this deed. Though the Party was paralyzed by the turmoils of the Cultural Revolution, the equally penetrative military machinery kept up this medium of mass politicization.

Moving on to the other three media, the impact of background factors become clear. Except for the single group of male-urban-illiterate under the category of film reception, literacy and urban residence are found to consistently produce a higher rate of reception. This is most conspicuous in newspaper reading. The impact of sex is not clear from this set of data. In every medium, as we move from urban to rural categories, a drop in reception occurs, though less so in radio and film than in newspaper reading. Thus, media reception in China seems to be "patterned" as it is in the Soviet Union and United States; "that is to say a person who is frequently exposed to one medium is likely to be frequently exposed to certain other media." [2]

Hiniker further surveyed, and then projected to the entire nation, the reception patterns of some specific social groups

TABLE 3

Percentage of Reception by Residence, Literacy, and Sex

	Urban		Rural	
	Literate	*Illiterate*	*Literate*	*Illiterate*
Meeting				
Male	97*	97	94	97
Female	92*	81	97	95
Newspaper				
Male	92*	32	74	13
Female	88*	19	57	13
Radio				
Male	87*	87	60	47
Female	95*	78	70	43
Film				
Male	72*	90	84	57
Female	74*	50	83	57

* The percentages for all male-urban literates are averages of Hiniker's data on three groups: students, professionals, and others. The percentages for all female-urban-literates are averages of two groups: housewives and others.

and found that the reception rate of cadres, students, and professionals are extremely high, cadres being the highest. The rate of these groups' exposure to mass media is presented in Table 4. The high rate of reception by these three groups suggests the correlation between use of media and what Rossi and Bauer called "involvement" in the Communist system. "Involvement" in this sense means

the tendency of the individual actively to relate himself to the system. It does not mean that he favors the system: he might, in fact, be quite opposed to it, or, as is more likely, be relatively indifferent to it politically. What is essential is that he intended to carve out for himself a role in the system, and that he regards himself as an participant. He does not, as the typical peasant, regard it as something external to himself.[3]

The opposite of the cadres, students, and professionals in China in terms of media consumption is the peasantry that is represented by the category of "rural illiterate" in Table 3. Despite the tremendous efforts of the Communist Party to

TABLE 4

Percentage of Reception by Cadres, Students, and Professionals

	Meeting	*Newspaper*	*Radio*	*Film*
Cadre	100%	94	92	92
Student	100	94	91	85
Professional	97	97	90	68

politicize the countryside with incessant propaganda, the peasants in China today remain least involved in the media system. The same is true in the Soviet Union, where the collective farmer "is a person almost isolated from the communications network." [4]

Hiniker's survey data and his national projection support the results of the preceding structural analysis. I have shown that of all the media in China, it is the oral ones—campaigns, radio, and film—that have penetrated down to the countryside. I have discussed the difficulty that the Party encountered in attempting to institutionalize a rural press and a reading public. But even oral agitation and propaganda in rural areas have their limitations, in the difficulty of stabilizing newspaper reading groups and the failure of the Great Leap Forward campaign to involve the rural masses in intensive propaganda activities. The Cultural Revolution and the current massive propaganda campaign in rural China further support these empirical findings. The Chinese intellectuals and Party propagandists who were cast out by the leftists in the Cultural Revolution were invariably accused of refusing to "go near the worker and peasant masses." The leftists thus implicitly acknowledged a gap between peasants and the Party. The massive study campaign in rural China at present is designed to close this gap.

But the prospect of closing the gap between the peasantry and the Party by sheer political indoctrination is not bright, as evidenced in the futility of mass involvement of the Great Leap campaign in 1958. Ever since the Communist takeover of mainland China in 1949, the Communist Party has relied mainly on manipulation of political structure and propaganda to change the countryside. Compared with industry in urban centers, rural areas have received little in resource allocations. It is a strange phenomenon that a group of political leaders who regard themselves as true Marxists have been so preoccupied with what Marx called the "superstructure" of society at the expense of its material foundation. The history of rural collectivization in China has shown that Mao Tse-tung was caught in a continuous process of misunderstanding with regard to peasantry. He tended to regard his abstract ideas as materially workable, when in fact they were not. Whenever the Party encountered difficulty and resistance by peasants in its drive to collectivize, Mao's typical solution was to legislate "an upsurge" or "a high tide" in the countryside and then storm through Party policies by organizational manipulation.[5]

Although the Communist Party has undoubtedly enhanced greatly peasants' political awareness and though the rural areas were brought into national coordination, little has changed with respect to the attitudes and values of peasants. Traditional modes of thought were hidden behind behavioral compliance brought forth by massive doses of political penetration. Thus when, at times, political control had to be reduced, the Party faced what it branded as a "resurgence of capitalism and feudalism." To counter this resurgence, the Socialist Education campaign was initiated in 1962. The revival of various traditional customs such as conspicuous consumption, marriage by sale, superstition, and petty trade is well documented in the confidential files of the Party branch in Lien-chiang county, Fukien province.[6]

Seen against this background, the Cultural Revolution dealt mainly with the symptoms but not the cause of lack of identification between peasants and the Party leadership. The left-wing faction has now apparently resorted to the old method of political penetration to change peasants' outlook. A new instrument of penetration used in and after the Cultural Revolution is the forced migration of urban youth and bureaucrats to the countryside. An estimate made in 1969 reported that "25 million people—or 15 per cent of China's urban population—have been or soon will be 'sent down,' . . ."[7] This mass movement was ostensibly intended to bridge the gap between urban and rural areas. But physical contact between groups with sharp social and economic differences is more likely to generate conflict in the short run. Clashes between peasants and workers occurred in some places during the Cultural Revolution.[8] In the long run, the effect of large numbers of frustrated urban refugees in the countryside may be an acceleration of the "revolution of rising expectations" among peasants. Unless the leftist faction that now controls the Party makes a major change in its long-term plan of resource allocation, to couple political penetration with a change in the material conditions of peasants' life, the prospect that the Chinese peasantry will be fully integrated with the rest of the nation is quite dim.

11

National Integration
in Communist China:
Problems and Prospects

Ever since the first Western intrusions into China in the mid-nineteenth century, Chinese political leaders have sought "wealth and power" for their country in order to resist the West. But the Chinese Communists were the first to build a political machine that could make a start on that ambitious goal. In this study, I have concentrated on one important part of the Communist political machinery, its political communications network. Because this study is based on documentary sources, I have focused on structural development and attempted to gauge integrative impact from the patterns of such development. In other words, we have looked mainly at the "top to bottom" process rather than the "bottom to top." Though a complete study of national integration in terms of political communication requires one to examine both directions of the communication process, much can be learned by studying structural development.

In what sense, then, is China in 1970 a more integrated nation than China in 1949, in terms of political communication?

Structurally, different parts of China are more closely connected with the national government than they were under the

Nationalists. Central planning under the Chinese Communist Party has had, by and large, uniform consequences all over the nation, both constructive and destructive ones. No longer can any region in China be unaffected by developments in other regions; gone are the days when provinces under powerful warlords could issue their own currency and maintain a separate administrative structure. A single political structure now penetrates into every region of China. Mass media are an important part of this enhanced structural integration under the Communist rule. The hierarchical structure of the broadcasting network, newspapers, publishing, and the film industry is a vital instrument of policy implementation by the Communist government.

Before 1949, China did not have such a penetrative network of political communication. The Chinese Nationalist government had endeavored to build a system of mass media to extend its authority. But the Nationalists never had total control of the nation, as the Communists have now. In areas controlled by the Nationalist government, the media were isolated in few urban centers as they are in many developing nations in the world. Before 1949, no wired radio stations had been extended from the central broadcasting system to natural villages. Neither was there a system of oral agitation connecting media with face-to-face communication before 1949. In fact, before 1949 the countryside of China was penetrated by the Communists, who built a face-to-face network of communication to undermine the Nationalist authority. Though today localism may be resilient in certain parts of China and an informal oral network of rumor and traditional beliefs is still alive, a qualitative change has occurred in terms of the interactions between the center and the region. The center now conspicuously dominates the region, and in two-way communication flow, the center talks much more to region than region does to center.

Because the Communists have laid such a penetrative political communication infrastructure, substantive integration has also been greatly enhanced. Under the Chinese Nationalist rule, the symbol of national authority was progressively weakened and, indeed, opposed as it was diffused from the center to the region. In the vast interior and numerous rural communities, the image of the Nationalist authority was all but overwhelmed by tradition and, worse, the symbol of a counter-elite. This is not true today. To be sure, tradition dies hard and still counters the message from the center to a certain extent. But the modern media erected by the Communist Party have dominated the stage. Through radio, wall posters, and newspaper reading groups, the personal images of national leaders such as Mao and, before his purge in the Cultural Revolution, Liu Shao-chi, have been spread far and wide. The Party, as the supreme national institution, has reached every corner of the nation.

Through the media, other integrative symbols have been disseminated among the populace. Above all, the media have played upon the symbol of a threatening foreign enemy—"U.S. imperialism." The mass media in China have kept the foreign threat alive through continuous anti-America campaigns and the propaganda for "liberation of Taiwan." The media in China have also focused popular attention on the excitement of developing China industrially into a modern state. The media have portrayed regional developments in the context of national progress and unity. Just as televisions have enabled Americans across the country to laugh at same jokes, the media in China have greatly increased the number of terms, news items, stories, and personalities that the Chinese people now can share. The end result is inevitably a much enhanced national awareness.

This enhanced national awareness has mobilized the Chinese people, mobilized them in the sense that they are now more ready, psychologically and physically, to be integrated into new institutions. An important side effect is political legitimation. Socialism as the "right" way to organize China has been accepted, even by the regime's most vociferous critics.[1] Political legitimacy is also achieved by direct propagandizing of socialism in the news media.

But, as I noted at the outset of this study, mass media are a necessary but not a sufficient cause of national integration. The media are a tool. In Communist China, the media are a tool of the Communist leadership. Thus, the nature of the media's impact depends to a large extent on the activities of the Communist leadership. The Cultural Revolution has wrecked the Party, and in this process the media can hardly perform any integrative function. The media reflected the turmoils and faction struggles within and without the Party and thus presented a negative image of the Party during this period. The legitimacy of the Party has been greatly damaged and the media, as a tool, contributed to this.

However, once national identity and consciousness have been built up, they are relatively independent of the rise and fall of any particular political regime. A political regime can contribute greatly to the enhancement of national identity but can not, so to speak, turn it on or off at will. National identity, once activated, has its own momentum and inertia. The Chinese Nationalist government had contributed to the increase of national identity in China, though it was toppled by the Communists on the mainland. John Fairbank states it well: "In some ways (but not others) the Kuomintang period may now be viewed, at the peril of distortion, as a part-way stage toward the present regime. At least in respect of party government, the creation of a party army, the mobilization of youth, and the modernization of the economy, the Kuomintang took faltering steps down the road which the Communists have since traveled." [2] The strength of national identity and experience in national mobilization in both Germany and Japan survived the destruction of the fascist political machine and enabled these two nations to recover so quickly after the war. The Cultural Revolution has by no means dealt such a crushing blow to the Communist Party as the war did to the political regime in fascist Japan or Germany. The Cultural Revolution cannot cancel the rising Chinese nationalism that the Party propaganda apparatus has worked so hard and long to build.

SOME PROBLEMS IN CHINA'S INTEGRATION

In the foregoing, I have cast the discussion of China's integration in a historical context, and my conclusion is a positive one. China in 1970 is, in terms of national identity, a more integrated nation than China before 1949. But, if we look further and consider perspective of modernization, then China's national integration is still fraught with problems.

A national language is yet to be institutionalized. Dialects are still much used in China. It is interesting to read an account by the official New China News Agency on the Red Guards. Describing the gathering of Red Guards from various localities in Peking railway station, this account says: "The young people speak different local dialects, but the red armband of their organizations and a red-covered little book 'Quotations from Chairman Mao Tse-tung,' bring them very close to each other." [3] The Red Guards were mostly high school and college students who were supposed to have been taught in the official common speech in schools. It is understandable that Red Guards from the same locality might speak to each other in dialects, despite knowing the common speech. But the news account suggested that Red Guards from different places had difficulty in verbal communication with each other. The preference of dialects to common speech undoubtedly reinforced regionalism. Factional conflicts in the Cultural Revolution must have been greatly aggravated by such regional identities and difficulty in communication.

Another problem in China's national integration is the continuous lack of involvement of the peasantry in the Communist media system, except the oral ones. The transformation that is needed to make peasants more participatory in mass media warrants a separate study. I have already mentioned that a major cause of peasants' lack of involvement was the Communist Party's unwillingness to improve the material conditions of peasant's life. What is important is the immediate impact of peasant's non-involvement on China's politics. As we have seen, the lack of identification between the Party and the peasantry as shown in the Great Leap campaign has been a continuous source of frustration to the Party, Mao and the left-wing faction in particular. The impassivity of peasants has been a temptation to the left-wing faction to use populist slogans and embark on mass campaigns like the Great Leap and the Cultural Revolution, hoping to storm through with their programs.

In the meantime, because of the Party's unwillingness to improve conditions in the countryside, because of Mao's penchant for group manipulation and because of his left-wing disciples' populist slogans, antagonism between peasants and the urban workers was intensified. Even before the Cultural Revolution, the Party, at times, had to initiate campaigns of promoting "alliance between workers and peasants" to deal with peasants' antagonism toward workers and the latters' contempt for peasants. In the Cultural Revolution, peasants openly clashed with workers and students in some places. In Shanghai, bands of peasants entered the city "creating a situation wherein peasants, workers, and students oppose each other." [4]

A no less important problem in China's integration is the Party leaders', especially Mao's, virulent anti-intellectualism. It may be true as Marshal Lin Piao stated: "Our nation is a great socialist country under the dictatorship of the proletariat with 700 million people. We need a unified, revolutionary and correct thought. This is Mao Tse-tung's thought." [5] But national identity needs more than just a single political doctrine. As Edward Shils puts it: "The very establishment of a society on a national scale, coterminous with the scope of sovereignty, requires a sense of national identity which, at least in part, focuses on a cultural activity concerned with the past, the present, and the future of its society." [6] Intellectuals, especially literary intellectuals, perform such a function. They were the ones who were suffered severely during the Cultural Revolution. Even before that, Chinese intellectuals in artistic and literary work had been under Mao's continuous attack. The oppression of literary intellectuals and their works in China has resulted in increased tensions and insecurity among the Chinese people which were aggravated by political leaders' further exploitation of such tension for political maneuver.

I have selected these three problems to discuss because they stand out from a study of the communication system in Communist China. A complete study of national integration in China requires a much more comprehensive list of factors than have been included in our study.

PROSPECTS

China is a country where the process of institutionalization in a modern context is intermittent and, sometimes, erratic. In such a situation, political leaders like Mao and Lin Piao have

an extraordinary degree of freedom in manipulating the course
of national development. The early work of the Party propaganda apparatus had greatly extended and accelerated the
growth of Chinese nationalism. The danger is that political
leaders in China, during the Cultural Revolution especially,
have been hardening such an enhanced nationalism into "national will." As described by Deutsch, "in practice this meant
the closing of inconvenient channels of communication in
society, and the attempted closing of the mind of individuals." [7]
The massive campaign of learning Mao's works and the destruction of the publishing enterprise to make way for exclusive
printing of Mao's works are certainly intended to close the
mind of individuals and indeed the entire nation. The hardening of nationalism into will, as manifested in mass movement,
is characterized by the worship of the dead. "The ultimate symbol of will power is the dead man returned from the grave to
complete a mission left unfinished." [8] From the Learn from Lei
Feng campaign in 1963 to the present, the left-wing Party faction has paraded a series of dead heroes in front of the Chinese
youth and the general public. A news account in December
1969 reported:

The Chinese Communists have stepped up their campaign urging
the young to "fear neither hardship nor death" and have publicized
a new group of modern folk heroes to serve as exemplary models,
including a child of 10 who died in a forest fire.

Peking apparently hopes to imbue China's youth with a spirit of
total selflessness and a willingness to "die for the people" so that
they will more readily accept resettlement in remote rural areas,
where living conditions are rigorous and can be dangerous.[9]

Now, with an emasculated intellectual group, with a Party
machine dominated at the top by a corps of parochially oriented
ideologues, and with the military dominating the middle and
lower strata of the Party and state apparatus, the probability is
increased that Chinese nationalism may be directed outward.
Nationalism hardened into will is likely to spill over the border.
In this connection, it is interesting to quote conversations between a Japanese youth and two Red Guards:

A Japanese youth asked: "Have you ever thought of traveling abroad? Where would you like to go?"

A Tientsin middle school Red Guard answered: "I have not thought about it; we do not think of sightseeing, but if I had the chance I would like to go to Vietnam and fight at the side of the fraternal Vietnamese people to wipe out the U.S. invading gangsters."

When the Japanese friends asked about their aim in life, a Red Guard from the Peking Aeronautical Engineering Institute said: "We are young people in the era of Mao Tse-tung. Chairman Mao has taught us 'The world is yours as well as ours, but in the last analysis it is yours. You young people, full of vigor and vitality, are in the bloom of life, like the sun at eight or nine in the morning. Our hope is placed on you. . . .' The fact that two-thirds of the oppressed people in the world are not liberated comes to our mind.[10]

We can not dismiss this lightly as ritualistic responses by two Chinese students. As noted, the Chinese Communist propaganda apparatus had been building up this virulent sense of nationalism for two decades. The violence that the Red Guards committed against foreign diplomats in Peking during the Cultural Revolution was a logical result of years' of nationalistic propaganda and education. To consolidate its power, the left-wing faction may want to direct the attention of the nation outward, and the force of national will is there for it to exploit.

Plausible as this development is, it is not inevitable. As I mentioned previously, the leaders in Communist China have a great deal of freedom in manipulating the course of China's development. It remains to be seen whether the present signs of hardening into nationalism are a temporary tactic or a long-term strategy.

Reference Matter

Appendix 1

A Functional Categorization of Mass Campaigns, 1949-1966

A. Functionally diffuse and with a target group
  1. Suppression of Counterrevolutionaries (1950)
  2. Suppression of Counterrevolutionaries (1956)
  3. Anti-rightists (1957)
  4. Socialist Education (1962)
  5. Cultural Revolution (1966)

B. Functionally diffuse and without a target group
  1. Anti-America Aid-Korea (1950)
  2. Signing of Peace Movement Documents (1950)
  3. Hundred Flowers Movement (1956)
  4. Army Love People Movement (1960)
  5. Police Love People Movement (1960)
  6. Cadres and People Get-Together Movement (1960)
  7. Learn from Lei Feng (1963)

  8. Send Culture to Village (1963)
  9. All Nation Learn from Army (1964)
  10. All Nation Learn from the "Four-Good" Spirit of the Army (1964)
  11. Raising Revolutionary Successors Movement (1964)
  12. Mass Singing of Revolutionary Songs (1964)
  13. Learn from Ta Sai Brigade (1965)
  14. Learn from Ta Chin Oil-field (1965)
  15. Learn from Wang Chieh (1965)

C. Functionally specific and with a target group
  1. Land Reform (1950)
  2. New Marriage Law (1950)
  3. Thought Reform of Chinese Intellectuals (1950)
  4. Three-anti Movement (1951)
  5. Five-anti Movement (1952)

6. All People Rectification Movement (1957)

D. Functionally specific and without a target group
   1. Labor Emulation Drive (1951)
   2. Study of Election Law (1953)

3. Study the General Line of Socialist Transition (1953)
4. Discussion of Draft National Constitution (1954)
5. Socialist Education among Peasants (1957)
6. Great Leap Forward (1958–1959)

Appendix 2

*Growth of Provincial and Municipal "People's Broadcasting Stations" in China**

Year	Number of Stations
1951	54
1952	71
1953	73
1958	97
1959	122
1961	138
1962	141
1963	141

Distribution of Radio Stations, 1962

Province	Number of Stations
Kiangsu	11
Hopeh	11
Inner Mongolia	10
Liaoning	10
Heilunkiang	9
Kirin	8
Kansu	8
Honan	7
Hunan	7
Anhwei	5
Chekiang	5
Kiangsi	5
Shansi	5
Kwangsi	5
Hupeh	4
Fukien	4
Shensi	4
Shantung	4
Kwangtung	4
Szechwan	4
Kweichow	3
Tsinghai	3
Sinkiang	2
Yunnan	2
Tibet	1

* Rural wired stations are excluded.

Source: Chao Tse-jen, "A Study of Chinese Communist Broadcasting," *Ta-lu Fei-chin Chi-pao* (Taipei, 1962).

Appendix 3

A Statistical Analysis of Radio Programs in Communist China, 1963 and 1967

Before the Cultural Revolution, the Central People's Broadcasting Station broadcast three sets of programs. Table 5 shows the station's programs of September 2, 1963.

TABLE 5

Distribution of Broadcasting Time

Nature of Program	First Program		Second Program		Third Program	
	Time (minutes)	%	Time (minutes)	%	Time (minutes)	%
News	235	21	300	31	5	1.5
Politics	115	10	0	0	0	0
Music	365	33	340	35	45	14.0
Education	30	3	15	2	0	0
Literature	60	5	60	6	60	19.0
Theater	160	14	75	8	205	64.0
Total Broadcasting Time (in minutes)	1,110		980		320	

The "news" is defined here as the regular national and international news programs of the station. "Politics" refers to commentaries and special reports. "Education" programs were those that popularized science and technology. "Literature" included readings of poetry and novels. "Music" included Chinese and Western music. "Theater" refers to both modern and traditional Chinese opera and stage shows.

With 97 percent of its time on theatrical, musical, and literary programs, the third program seems to have been predominantly designed for recreation. Judging from its hours on the air, 5:40 a.m. to 11:00 a.m., and the predominance of theatrical programs, the most likely audience for this program would be housewives without outside jobs, whose educational background would be, on the average, poor.

The second program seems to have been not very different from the first. News programs occupied 31 percent of the time, 10 percent more than in the first program, but half of this time was reading at dictation speed for local stations and monitoring teams and was not of direct interest to ordinary audiences. Seen in this light, the second program had less political matter than the first.

On the whole Chinese broadcasting resembled closely the domestic programs of Radio Moscow. According to Inkeles, the central stations in Moscow sent out two sets of programs before 1947. The first was intended for general consumption. The second program was "directed to a more restricted audience, and might be regarded as highbrow." *

THE IMPACT OF THE CULTURAL REVOLUTION
ON RADIO PROGRAMS

The Cultural Revolution brought on overall increase in political broadcasting. In the following table, Table 6, the first and second programs of the Central People's Broadcasting Station on September 2, 1963 are compared with those on January 3, 1967.

As far as the first program is concerned, there was less news presented in 1967 than in 1963, but more political programs. Both musical and educational programs took a dip in 1967, while literary reading and theatrical programs increased.

With respect to the second program, there was an increase in "dictation news" in 1967 from 150 minutes (50 percent of total news time) in 1963 to 225 minutes (65 percent) in 1967. The most significant development was the addition of political material to the second program in 1967, where there had been none in 1963. The overall

* Alex Inkeles, *Public Opinion in Soviet Russia* (Cambridge, 1958), pp. 255–256.

political radicalism in the nation in 1967 is shown in this change. There was a sharp cut in musical programs in 1967, in both the first and second programs.

TABLE 6

Comparison of Radio Programming

Nature of Program	Sept. 2, 1963		Jan. 3, 1967		Sept. 2, 1963		Jan. 3, 1967	
	First Program				Second Program			
	Time	%	Time	%	Time	%	Time	%
News	235	21	185	16	300	31	345	43
Politics	115	10	225	20	0	0	50	6
Music	365	33	195	17	340	35	55	7
Education	30	3	15	1	15	2	15	2
Literature	60	5	120	11	60	6	150	19
Theater	160	14	245	21	75	8	30	4
Total Broadcasting Time (in minutes)	1,110		1,140		980		800	

Appendix 4

A Statistical Content Analysis of the "People's Daily"

To see how the content of the *People's Daily* reflected political trends, I took a random sampling from the paper for four different years, 1950, 1955, 1960, and 1965. I had planned to use the papers from April 1 through April 7 for each year so as to have a common basis for comparison; but this was not possible for 1960 because a party congress started on April 5 and news coverage became distorted by lengthy speeches until April 24. So, for 1960, I selected papers from April 1 through April 4, and April 24, 25, and 28. Domestic news was classified into economic, political, social, literary, and diplomatic. It is not easy to distinguish between economic and political news in the Communist Chinese press. My rule was to classify any report about political campaigns, organizational matters, or political speeches as political news. Thus, if a report on production described the organization of production, it was classified as political. But if it was about production per se, then it was classified as economic. The social news refers to public health, recreational activities, and other such items; the literary news to publications, reviews, and research notes; the diplomatic news to activities of foreign diplomats in China.

The result of this first analysis is presented in Table 7. It shows a sharp decline in economic news from 1950 to 1965; the total proportion of domestic news, as opposed to international news, also declined, from 83 percent in 1950 to 54 percent in 1965.

For a second analysis, I took a random sample of the content of the *People's Daily* for eleven years, from 1956 to 1966. For each year, fifteen issues of the paper were selected at random, their contents analyzed in terms of six categories. However, for 1966, the sam-

TABLE 7
Comparison of News Coverage in *People's Daily*

	1950		1955		1960		1965	
	Column Inches	%	Column Inches	%	Column Inches	%	Column Inches	%
I. Domestic News								
1. Economic	2,429	63	1,353	43	3,106	50	875	19
2. Political	322	8	300	10	890	14	254	6
3. Social	43	1	34	1	76	1	24	0
4. Literary	429	11	85	3	256	4	376	8
5. Diplomatic	0	0	311	10	100	2	955	21
Total Domestic News:	3,233	83	2,083	67	4,428	71	2,484	54
II. International News								
1. Asia	117	3	415	13	547	8	1,586	35
a. Australia	3		0		0		0	
b. Burma	0		6		7		0	
c. Cambodia	0		0		12		10	
d. India	4		40		12		0	
e. Indonesia	3		9		18		70	
f. Japan	34		84		83		118	
g. North Korea	3		16		114		219	
h. South Korea	0		25		171		9	
i. Laos	0		24		13		86	
j. Malaya	8		0		0		32	
k. Nepal	0		0		19		0	

l. Pakistan	0		2		10		72	
m. Philippines	24		0		0		0	
n. Taiwan	5		20		0		5	
o. Thailand	9		0		0		20	
p. North Vietnam	24		14		39		0	
q. South Vietnam	0		7		18		909	
r. General	0		168		4		45	
2. West	238	6	157	5	296	5	331	7
a. United States	140		54		109		275	
b. United Kingdom	7		56		0		11	
c. France	41		24		1		0	
d. Canada	4		0		0		0	
e. Western Europe	46		14		134		45	
f. South America	0		9		52		0	
3. Soviet Bloc	269	7	424	13	601	9	47	1
a. U.S.S.R.	143		266		198		36	
b. East Europe	126		158		366		11	
c. Cuba	0		0		37		0	
4. Africa & Middle East								
a. Africa	1		6		231		106	
b. Middle East	0		27		7		0	
Total International News:	650	16	1,062	32	1,756	26	2,070	45
III. Other	25	1*	33	1	74	3	0	1
Total News:	3,883	100	3,145	100	6,184	100	4,554	100

* The percentage figures for news other than that categorized are not very exact.

Table 8
News Content of the *People's Daily*

	1956 Column Inches	%	1957 Column Inches	%	1958 Column Inches	%	1959 Column Inches	%	1960 Column Inches	%	1961 Column Inches	%
I. National News												
1. Economic	4,751	37	4,916	35	5,155	40	7,061	46	7,066	39	3,398	31
2. Political	2,117	16	3,295	23	2,125	16	1,875	12	3,868	21	2,675	24
3. Social	187	2	376	3	285	2	359	2	825	5	330	3
4. Literary	869	7	969	7	1,700	13	1,431	10	1,959	11	723	6
Total National News:	7,924	62	9,556	68	9,265	71	10,726	70	13,718	76	7,126	64
II. International News												
1. Communist Nations	2,307	18	2,431	17	1,654	13	2,285	15	1,976	11	2,164	20
2. Non-Communist Nations	2,474	20	2,156	15	2,036	16	2,303	15	2,316	13	1,762	16
Total International News:	4,781	38	4,587	32	3,690	29	4,588	30	4,292	24	3,926	36
Total	12,705	100	14,143	100	12,955	100	15,314	100	18,010	100	11,052	100

TABLE 8 (Cont'd.)

	1962		1963		1964		1965		1966	
	Column Inches	%	Column Inches	%	Column Inches	%	Column Inches	%	Column Inches	%
I. National News										
1. Economic	2,249	25	1,150	12	925	9	1,337	13	1,364	14
2. Political	2,314	25	4,709	50	4,230	39	3,599	36	4,031	41
3. Social	444	5	207	2	774	7	371	4	69	1
4. Literary	339	4	147	2	900	8	511	5	161	2
Total National News:	5,346	59	6,213	66	6,829	63	5,828	58	5,625	58
II. International News										
1. Communist Nations	1,412	16	1,751	19	2,021	19	1,747	18	570	6
2. Non-Communist Nations	2,247	25	1,436	15	1,986	18	2,447	24	3,572	36
Total International News:	3,659	41	3,187	34	3,998	37	4,194	42	4,142	42
Total	9,005	100	9,400	100	10,827	100	10,022	100	9,767	100

ple covers only the period from January to April, for only these issues were available. The result of this analysis is presented in Table 8.

Again in this table, we can see a sharp decline in economic news, along with a rise in political news. Foreign news, though with fluctuations, has been rising, especially after 1963. The rise in foreign news is largely accounted for by the increase in news about Asia at the expense of the Soviet bloc. Another analysis of the same paper for 1959 and 1960 found the same result:

Statistics recently made available in Hong Kong reveal some interesting trends in the foreign news now being published in the press of Red China.

The total amount of space devoted by the Chinese Communist press to foreign news is not great, but it appears to be on the increase. Moreover, an intensified interest is being shown in news from those countries which are in the course of development, even at the expense of stories from other countries in the Eastern bloc. One analysis recently made of the newspaper of the Central Committee of the Communist Party, *Jen-min Jih-pao* (People's Daily), shows that in 1959 news from the Soviet Union and other countries of the Eastern bloc amounted to 40.9%, namely U.S.S.R. 11.7%, other eastern countries 29.2%. Noticeable in these figures is the large share of the news devoted to other countries as compared with the Communist fatherland Russia. In the year 1960 the share of the Eastern bloc shrank to 28.4% with the Soviet Union obtaining only 8.6% of foreign news. Countries which gained increased attention, at the expense of the Eastern bloc, were: Japan (1959, 5.1%; 1960, 10.5%) and in particular the developing countries. The latter raised their proportion of news in China from 15.5% in the year 1959 to 34.8% in 1960. Thus news from Southeast Asia went up from 4.4% in 1959 to 12.1% in 1960; Latin America from 3.5% to 9.1%; and Africa from 2.5% to 9.0%.

Southeast Asia, Africa and Latin America have thus claimed the attention of newspaper readers in China in recent months to a far greater extent than the Soviet Union with its 8.6% share.*

Due to the differences in sample periods and units of counting, the specific statistics of distribution reported by the International Press Institute do not precisely match mine for 1960, but the distributions are basically similar.

In hindsight, the decline of economic and the rise of political news over these years seems quite significant in the light of the Cultural Revolution, which erupted in late 1966. It shows that long before the appearance of the Red Guard and the purges of middle-rank Party cadres, the *People's Daily* indicated the emerging orientation of the regime.

* *International Press Institute Report,* vol. X, no. 5 (September 1961), p. 3.

Appendix 5

Types of Books Published in Communist China, 1949-1958

The following table, Table 9, is based on *Chinese Publishing: Statistics, 1949–1959,* a study done by the Committee on American Library Resources on the Far East of the Association for Asian Studies. As stated in the text, publishing was not immune from the shifts in the Communist regime's integration strategy. The table here shows that publishing had two spurts, one in 1953 and one in 1958. The beginning of industrialization in 1953 is shown in the percentage of increase in new titles on various subjects: new books on technology increased by 83 per cent; on natural sciences, by 151 percent; on art and literature, 94 percent; and on social sciences, 75 percent. The overall increase in publishing in 1958 is clear. However, in view of the general inflation of statistical information in 1958–1959, we must reserve judgment on the actual growth from 1957 to 1958. Undoubtedly, a majority of the so-called books on technology were short pamphlets about farming techniques, and a majority of the literature published during this period were "worker and peasant creative works."

TABLE 9

Types of Books Published in Communist China

Year	Books on Technology*		Natural Sciences*		Art and Literature*		Social Sciences*		Others*		Total*	
	No.	%	No.	%	No.	%	No.	%	No.	%	No.	%
1949	20	7	18	6	86	31	103	37	53	19	280	100
1950	156	15	38	4	434	42	228	22	119	17	966	100
1951	471	24	76	4	617	32	478	25	296	15	1,938	100
1952	576	27	114	5	594	28	712	33	161	7	2,157	100
1953	1,058	25	287	5	1,152	27	1,245	29	561	14	4,303	100
1954	1,545	24	356	6	1,646	26	1,946	30	909	14	6,402	100
1955	2,002	21	415	4	2,686	29	2,825	30	2,218	16	9,146	100
1956	3,426	24	494	4	3,440	24	4,088	29	2,622	19	14,070	100
1957	3,501	27	801	6	3,409	26	3,204	24	1,219	17	12,134	100
1958	7,391	34	1,029	5	5,883	27	5,167	24	2,406	10	21,876	100

* Titles of new books only.

Appendix 6

Film Production in Communist China, 1951-1961

The analysis of types of films produced between 1951 and 1961 given demonstrates in Table 10 that film production reflected the changes in the Party's strategy of integration. Feature films were the most sensitive to the changes, i.e., the cycles of tightening and loosening of political control over art and literature. That there was only one feature film produced in 1951 testified to the debilitating effect of the campaign of Thought Reform of Intellectuals in process then. The marked increase of feature films after 1953 was a result of the Party's loosening of control over artists and film professionals. The sudden rise of feature films in 1958 is largely explained by the mass production of semi-documentaries. The sharp increase in newsreels, documentaries, and scientific and educational films in 1958 was also a reflection of the leftist ideology prevailing during 1958 and 1959.

TABLE 10

Types of Films Released in Communist China

Year	Types of Film				
	Feature	Newsreel & Documentary	Scientific-Educational	Cartoon	Foreign Dubbed
1951	1	36	3	—*	58
1952	5	38	12	—	59
1953	15	50	9	—	56
1954	26	65	15	4	80
1955	18	65	18	—	105
1956	42	79	37	—	72
1957	38	155	40	—	—
1958	103	255	154	54	151
1959	77	155	86	—	—
1960–61	62	—	—	17	—

* No information.

SOURCES: The figures for 1951 to 1954 and 1956 are from *Ta-tsung Tien-ying* (no. 18, 1956); 1955 is from *Wen-Yi Pao* (no. 24, 1955), p. 22; 1957 is from "Development of Communist China Film Industry in 1959," (Hong Kong, U.S.I.S., 1960); 1958 is from *Wen-Yi Pao* (nos. 19–20, 1959), p. 50; 1959 is from *Ta-tsung Tien-ying* (no. 6, 1960), p. 26; and 1960–1961 are from *Current Background* (no. 690, 1962), p. 2, and *SCMP* (no. 2730), p. 19.

Appendix 7

Growth of Film Showing Units in Communist China, 1949-1964

When the Chinese Communist regime first decided to expand its film showing network in 1953, priority was given to factories and industrial areas. Mobile film projection teams were first operated by labor unions, which reflected the spirit of industrialization from 1953 to 1957. After the first wave of agricultural collectivization in 1955 and 1956, the regime began to expand the mobile film projection teams to the countryside. The failure of the Great Leap did not diminish the Party's efforts to penetrate the countryside with mobile teams. Table 11 shows the growth of film showing units and of cinema houses.

TABLE 11

Film Projection Teams in Communist China

Year	Cinemas	Mobile Film Projection Teams
1949	596	100
1950	641	522
1951	724	734
1952	746	1,110
1953	779	2,154
1954	815	2,723
1955	868	3,742
1956	938	4,400
1957	1,030	6,692
1958	1,386	8,384
1959	1,758	9,212
1960	—*	—
1961	—	—
1962	—	9,000
1963	—	9,000
1964	2,000	12,000

* No information.

SOURCES: The 1949–1956 data are from *Ta-tsung Tien-ying,* 18 (1956); the 1957 and 1958 data are respectively from *Ten Great Years* (Peking, 1960), p. 207, and "Development of Communist China Film Industry in 1959," (Hong Kong, U.S.I.S., 1960), p. 90; the 1959 data are from *Tien-ying Yu Fang-yien,* 12 (1959), p. 1; the 1960 data are from *Communist China Digest,* 20 (July 26, 1960), p. 8; the 1962 data are from *Ta-kung Pao,* December 14, 1962; the 1963 data are from *Evergreen,* no. 2 (April 1963), pp. 46–47; and the 1964 data are from *SCMP,* no. 3204, pp. 19–20.

Notes

FOREWORD

1. Cf. also a companion study of Alan Liu's at the Massachusetts Insitute of Technology Center for International Studies by John Kramer, "A Computer Simulation of Audience Exposure in a Mass Media System: The United Nations Information Campaign in Cincinnati, 1947–1948," Ph.D. diss., M.I.T., 1970.

2. Carl I. Hovland, "Reconciling Conflicting Results Derived from Experimental and Survey Studies of Attitude Change," *American Psychologist*, vol. 14, 1959, pp. 8–17.

3. Paul F. Lazarsfeld, Bernard Berelson, Hazel Gaudet, *The People's Choice* (New York: Columbia University Press, 1948), and Bernard Berelson, Paul Lazarsfeld, William McPhee, *Voting: A Study of Opinion Formation in a Presidential Campaign* (Chicago: University of Chicago Press, 1954). Claire Zimmerman and Raymond A. Bauer show that the audience selects what will make it most comfortable, not necessarily that with which it already agrees ("The Effect of an Audience Upon What Is Remembered," *Public Opinion Quarterly*, XX, 1 [Spring 1956], pp. 239–248).

4. Lucian W. Pye, *The Spirit of Chinese Politics: A Psychocultural Study of the Authority Crisis in Political Development* (Cambridge: Massachusetts Institute of Technology Press, 1968), and Richard Solomon, "The Chinese Revolution and the Politics of Dependency" (Ph.D. diss., Massachusetts Institute of Technology, 1966).

5. Karl Marx, *The Communist Manifesto* (Chicago: Henry Regnery Co., Gateway Edition, 1954), pp. 39–41.

CHAPTER 1

1. Alex Inkeles, *Public Opinion in Soviet Russia* (Cambridge, 1958).

2. See, for example, Daniel Lerner, *The Passing of Traditional Society* (Glencoe, 1958), and Lucian W. Pye, ed., *Communication and Political Development* (Princeton, 1963).

3. Two major works on the mass media in Communist China that are descriptive in nature are: Franklin Houn, *To Change a Nation* (Glencoe, 1961) and Frederick T. C. Yu, *Mass Persuasion in Communist China* (New York and London, 1964).

4. For a classification of integrative powers, see Amitai Etzioni, *Political Unification* (New York, 1965), pp. 37–40.

5. For more discussions on the integrative process, see Karl W. Deutsch, "Nation Building and National Development: Some Issues for Political Research," in *Nation Building* ed. by Karl W. Deutsch and William J. Foltz (New York, 1963).

6. Richard Pipes, "Communism and Russian History," in *Soviet and Chinese Communism: Similarities and Differences* ed. by Donald W. Treadgold (Seattle and London, 1967), p. 6.

7. For discussions on the general effects of the Soviet media, see Alex Inkeles and Raymond A. Bauer, *The Soviet Citizen* (Cambridge, 1959).

8. Ithiel de Sola Pool, "The Mass Media and Politics in the Modernization Process," in Lucian W. Pye, *op. cit.*

CHAPTER 2

1. A. Doak Barnett, *China on the Eve of Communist Takeover* (New York, 1963), p. 105.
2. W. W. Rostow, *The Prospects for Communist China* (New York and London, 1954), p. 262.
3. T. R. Tregear, *A Geography of China* (Chicago, 1965). The second highway and railroad bridge over the Yangtze was completed in January 1969, at Nanking. *The New York Times,* January 5, 1969.
4. *Jen-min Jih-pao* (referred to in the text as *People's Daily*), December 24, 1957.
5. Chou En-lai, "Current Tasks of Reforming the Written Language" in *Reform of the Chinese Written Language* (Peking, 1965), pp. 8–9.
6. Paul L. M. Serruys, *Survey of the Chinese Language Reform and the Anti-illiteracy Movement in Communist China* (Berkeley, 1962), p. 8.
7. *Jen-min Jih-pao,* June 19, 1952.
8. Wu Yu-chang, "Report on the Current Tasks of Reforming the Written Language and the Draft Scheme for a Chinese Phonetic Alphabet," *in Reform of the Chinese Written Language* (Peking, 1965), p. 31.
9. *Jen-min Jih-pao,* November 9, 1955.
10. Chou En-lai, *op. cit.,* pp. 1–2.
11. *Jen-min Jih-pao,* December 11, 1957.
12. Chou En-lai, *op. cit.,* p. 11.
13. *Jen-min Jih-pao,* December 11, 1957, and Chou En-lai, *op. cit.,* p. 7.
14. *Jen-min Jih-pao,* December 11, 1957.
15. *Jen-min Jih-pao,* December 11, 1957.
16. Chou En-lai, *op. cit.,* p. 9.
17. Wu Yu-chang, *op. cit.,* p. 35.
18. Chou En-lai, *op. cit.,* p. 4.
19. Paul Serruys, *op. cit.,* p. 102.
20. *Ibid.,* pp. 101–109.
21. A. Doak Barnett, *Cadres, Bureaucracy, and Political Power in Communist China* (New York, 1967), p. xvi; and Franz Schurmann, *Ideology and Organization in Communist China* (Berkeley and Los Angeles, 1966), p. 48.
22. *Jen-min Jih-pao,* April 28, 1952.
23. *Jen-min Jih-pao,* June 25, 1952.
24. *Jen-min Jih-pao,* May 25, 1954.
25. *Jen-min Jih-pao,* September 23, 1954.
26. *Jen-min Jih-pao,* November 27, 1955.
27. *Jen-min Jih-pao,* February 6, 1957.
28. *Jen-min Jih-pao,* May 4, 1955.
29. *Jen-min Jih-pao,* November 19, 1957.
30. *Jen-min Jih-pao,* March 7, 1958.
31. *Jen-min Jih-pao,* December 24, 1958.
32. *Jen-min Jih-pao,* May 3, 1964.

CHAPTER 3

1. Edgar Snow, *Red Star Over China* (New York, 1961), p. 150.
2. *Selected Works of Mao Tse-tung,* vol. I (Peking, 1965), p. 47.
3. Stuart R. Schram, *The Political Thought of Mao Tse-tung* (New York, 1963), p. 29.
4. *Selected Works of Mao Tse-tung,* vol. IV (Peking, 1967), p. 72.
5. Stuart Schram, *op. cit.,* p. 52.
6. For changes in Soviet ideology on the role of "consciousness," see Raymond A. Bauer, *The New Man in Soviet Psychology* (Cambridge, 1952).

7. Alex Inkeles and Raymond Bauer, *The Soviet Citizen* (Cambridge, 1959), p. 161.

8. *Selected Works of Mao Tse-tung*, vol. III (Peking, 1965).

9. *Jen-min Jih-pao*, June 12, 1960.

10. For some illuminating statements on this attitude, see Chou Yang's speech in the Fifth National Conference on Broadcasting Work in *Hsin-wen Chan-hsien* (News Front), no. 5 (1958).

11. Alex Inkeles, *Public Opinion in Soviet Russia* (Cambridge, 1958), Chapters 5 and 17.

CHAPTER 4

1. *The New York Times,* April 26, 1968.

2. Gayle Durham Hollander, *Soviet Newspapers and Magazines* (Cambridge, 1967), p. 3.

3. Alex Inkeles, *Public Opinion in Soviet Russia* (Cambridge, 1958), p. 36.

4. "The Propaganda Department of the Chinese Communist Party Has Become an Anti-Communist Agency," *Mainland Today* (Taipei), July 16, 1966.

5. Alex Inkeles, *op. cit.*, p. 35.

6. Stuart R. Schram, *The Political Thought of Mao Tse-tung* (New York, 1963), p. 94.

7. Allen S. Whiting, "Political Dynamics: The Communist Party of China," in *Modern Political Systems: Asia,* ed. by Robert E. Ward and Roy C. Macridis (Englewood Cliffs, 1963), p. 160.

8. *Ibid.*, p. 180.

9. *Jen-min Jih-pao,* April 12, 1967, and *Hungchi* (Red Flag), no. 10 (1967), as cited in Chao Tsung, "A Brief Account of the 'Great Proletarian Cultural Revolution,'" *Tsukuo* (China Monthly), no. 41 (August 1, 1967), p. 18.

10. Charles Neuhauser, "The Chinese Communist Party in the 1960's: Prelude to the Cultural Revolution," *The China Quarterly,* no. 32 (October–December 1967), p. 35, and also, *The New York Times,* December 27, 1966.

11. *Ibid.*, p. 28.

12. Charles Neuhauser, *op. cit.*, p. 28, and Chao Tsung "A Brief Account of the 'Great Proletarian Cultural Revolution,'" *Tsukuo,* no. 45 (December 1967), p. 25.

13. Chao Tsung, "A Brief Account of the 'Great Proletarian Cultural Revolution,'" *Tsukuo,* no. 44 (November 1, 1967), p. 28.

14. Carl J .Friedrich and Zbigniew K. Brzezinski, *Totalitarian Dictatorship and Autocracy* (New York, 1965), p. 109.

15. *Mainichi* (Tokyo), January 5, 1961.

16. See Alexander Eckstein, *Communist China's Economic Growth and Foreign Trade* (New York, 1966).

17. Alex Inkeles, "The Totalitarian Mystique: Some Impressions of the Dynamics of Totalitarian Society," in *Totalitarianism,* ed. by Carl J. Friedrich (New York, 1964), pp. 96–97.

18. Lately, a new regional propaganda organization seems to be emerging. A radio broadcast from Shantung province mentioned "the propaganda section of the political departments of Shantung provincial and Tsinan municipal revolutionary committees."

19. Chin Tak-kai, *A Study on Chinese Communist Propaganda, Its Policy and Operations* (Hong Kong, 1954), p. 32.

20. Karl W. Deutsch, *The Nerves of Government* (New York, 1966), p. 154.

21. Alex Inkeles, "The Totalitarian Mystique," p. 93.

22. Franz Schurmann, *Ideology and Organization in Communist China* (Berkeley and Los Angeles, 1966), p. 115.

23. For an example of these organizations at brigade level, see A. Doak Barnett, *Cadres, Bureaucracy, and Political Power in Communist China* (New York, 1967), p. 366.

24. Chao Tsung, "Communist China's Art and Literature in 1964," *Tsukuo*, no. 5 (May 1, 1965), p. 37.

25. Robert Loh and Humphrey Evans, *Escape from Red China* (New York, 1962), p. 123.

26. The definition of mobilization used here is based on Karl W. Deutsch, "Social Mobilization and Political Development," *The American Political Science Review*, LV: 3 (September 1961), pp. 493–514.

27. So far as I can determine, "Cultural Revolution" was first used in the phrase "The Great Socialist Cultural Revolution" in a speech by Mme. Mao at a conference on literary work in the army which was held in Shanghai in February 1966. See Chao Chung, "An Account of the 'Great Proletarian Cultural Revolution' (Part 9)," *Tsukuo*, no. 54 (September 1968), p. 28.

28. *Hsin-wen Chan-hsien* (News Front), no. 5 (1958).

29. For Mao's own statements on the change of leadership, see *Mainichi* (Tokyo), January 5, 1967, and "Speech of Mao Tse-tung at the Central Work Conference (October 25, 1966)," *Tsukuo* no. 48 (March 1, 1968). As Mao revealed in 1966, he was compelled to resign as the state chairman but initiated the division of leadership responsibility into "front and rear line" himself; Mao was to be in the "rear line."

30. "Full Text of the 'Ten Articles on Literature and Art,'" *Tsukuo*, no. 67 (October 1, 1969). Italics added.

31. Stephen Uhalley, Jr., "The Cultural Revolution and the Attack on the 'Three Family Village,'" *The China Quarterly*, no. 27 (July–September 1966). Also see Ezra F. Vogel, *Canton Under Communism: Programs and Politics in a Provincial Capital, 1949–1968* (Cambridge, 1969), pp. 289–290.

32. See the onetime confidential military journal of the Chinese army in J. Chester Cheng, ed., *The Politics of the Chinese Red Army* (Stanford, 1966), pp. 11–19.

33. On political work in the army, see Chiang I-san, "Communist Political Work in the Army Units," *Tsukuo*, no. 9 (September 1, 1965), and "The Art and Literary Work in the People's Liberation Army," *Tsukuo*, no. 31 (October 1, 1966).

34. For a general description of the military district system in Communist China, see *Ti-Chin Yen-Chiu Lun-wen-chi* (An Anthology of Studies on Enemy Situation), vol. 3 (Taipei, 1962).

35. Philip Bridgham, "Mao's 'Cultural Revolution': Origin and Development," *The China Quarterly* (January–March 1967).

36. *Ibid.*

37. In J. Chester Cheng, *op. cit.*, pp. 593–597.

38. Chiang I-shan, "Communist Political Work in the Army Units," *Tsukuo*, no. 9 (September 1, 1965).

39. See Teng To's statement on the play *Hai Jui* in *Jen-min Jih-pao*, May 12, 1966 as quoted in Chao Chung, "An Account of the 'Great Proletarian Cultural Revolution' (Part 8)," *Tsukuo*, no. 53 (August 1, 1968), p. 12.

40. Chao Tsung, "A Brief Account of the 'Great Proletarian Cultural Revolution' (Part 2)," *Tsukuo*, no. 41 (August 1, 1967), p. 16.

41. *Ibid.*

42. Cheng Feng, "Communist China's Cultural Work in 1963," *Tsukuo*, no. 6 (June 1964).

43. Ezra F. Vogel, *op. cit.*, pp. 303–304.

44. Ezra F. Vogel, *op. cit.*, p. 305, and see also Vincent V. S. King, *Propaganda Campaigns in Communist China* (Cambridge, 1966).

45. Chao Tsung, "A Brief Account of the 'Great Proletarian Cultural Revolution' (Part 3)," *Tsukuo*, no. 42 (September 1, 1967).

46. Chao Tsung, "A Brief Account of the 'Great Proletarian Cultural Revolution' (Part 4)," *Tsukuo*, no. 43 (October 1, 1967).

47. Ezra F. Vogel, *op. cit.*, p. 311.

48. Chao Tsung, *op. cit.* (Part 4).

49. For some speculations on Mao's use of Peng Chen, see Charles Neuhauser, *op. cit.*, pp. 31–33.

50. Chao Tsung, "A Brief Account of the 'Great Proletarian Cultural Revolution' (Part 5)," *Tsukuo*, no. 45 (December 1967).

51. For discussions on the critique of historiography, see Harold Kahn and Albert Feuerwerker, "The Ideology of Scholarship: China's New Historiography," in *History in Communist China*, ed. by Albert Feuerwerker (Cambridge, 1969); and for critique on art and literature, see Merle Goldman, "The Fall of Chou Yang," *The China Quarterly*, no. 27 (July–September 1966); and for discussion on ideological education, see Donald J. Munro, "Chinese Communist Treatment of the Thinkers of the Hundred Schools Period," in Albert Feuerwerker, ed., *op. cit.*, and Munro's "The Yang Hsien-chen Affair," *The China Quarterly*, no. 22 (April–June 1965).

52. "Speech of Mao Tse-tung at the Central Work Conference (October 25, 1966)," *Tsukuo*, no. 48 (March 1, 1968).

53. Chao Chung, "An Account of the 'Great Proletarian Cultural Revolution' (Part 7)," *Tsukuo*, no. 52 (July 1, 1968).

54. *Wen-hui Pao*, August 25, 1967, as translated in *New China News Agency* (hereafter NCNA), August 25, 1967.

55. Chao Chung, "An Account of the 'Great Proletarian Cultural Revolution' (Part 8)," *Tsukuo*, no. 53 (August 1, 1968).

56. *Ibid.*

57. Chao Chung, "An Account of the 'Great Proletarian Cultural Revolution' (Part 9)," *Tsukuo*, no. 54 (September 1, 1968).

58. *Ibid.*

59. Chao Chung, "An Account of the 'Great Proletarian Cultural Revolution' (Part 11)," *Tsukuo*, no. 56 (November 1, 1968).

60. *Ibid.*

61. Chao Chung, "An Account of the 'Great Proletarian Cultural Revolution' (Part 13)," *Tsukuo*, no. 58 (January 1, 1969).

62. *Ibid.*

63. *Nihon Keizai Shimbun* (Tokyo), June 22, 1966.

64. *NCNA*, July 30, 1966.

65. Merle Goldman, *op. cit.*, p. 32.

66. Alex Inkeles, "The Totalitarian Mystique," p. 97.

67. "Collection of Mao Tse-tung's Directives during the Cultural Revolution (Part 2)," *Tsukuo*, no. 67 (October 1, 1969), p. 38. From several records of Mao's impromptu talks during the Cultural Revolution, Mao had repeatedly rebuked Teng for ignoring Mao after 1958 in policy making, including the charge that Teng deliberately sat a distance from Mao in meetings. But Mao's comments on Liu were always ambivalent; he said more than once that Liu could not be blamed for everything. For sources, see the article cited above and also Part 1 of the same collection in *Tsukuo*, no. 66 (September 1, 1969).

68. Ezra F. Vogel, *op. cit.*, pp. 300–308.

69. Ting Wang, ed., *Chung-kun Wen-hwa Ta-ke-ming Tzi-liao Hwei-pien* (A Collection of Materials on the Great Proletarian Revolution in Communist China), vol. 1 (Hong Kong, 1967), pp. 502–505.

70. See two articles by Philip Bridgham, "Mao's Cultural Revolution in 1967: The Struggle to Seize Power," *The China Quarterly*, no. 34 (April–June 1968),

and "Mao's Cultural Revolution: The Struggle to Seize Power," *The China Quarterly*, no. 41 (January–March 1970).

71. Chao Tsung, "An Account of the 'Great Proletarian Cultural Revolution' (Part 21)," *Tsukuo*, no. 67 (October 1, 1969).

72. Reuter news from Tokyo, January 21, 1967, cited in Chao Tsung, "Cultural Affairs of Communist China in 1967," *Tsukuo*, no. 49 (April 1, 1968), pp. 15–16.

73. Chao Tsung, *op. cit.*

74. *NCNA*, June 10, 1967.

75. *The New York Times*, April 19, 1968.

76. "Lin Piao and the Cultural Revolution," *Current Scene*, VIII: 14 (August 1, 1970).

77. See, for example, the editorial in *Wen-hui Pao*, February 22, 1967, on the antagonism between Red Guards and soldiers.

78. See, for example, *Shensi Jih-pao*, July 24, 1969, as cited in Chung Hua-min, "Cultural Affairs of Communist China in 1969," *Tsukuo*, no. 73 (April 1, 1970) and as broadcast from Provincial Heilungkiang People's Broadcasting Station on September 17, 1968.

79. See *Survey of China Mainland Press*, no. 1567, pp. 14–16; for a sketchy report on Yao's career, see Yu Heng, "The 'Big Stick' of Cultural Revolution— Yao Wen-yuan," *Tsukuo*, no. 55 (October 1, 1968).

80. Yu Heng, "Chang Chun-chiao—the 'Roly-Poly' That Cannot Be Pushed Over in the Cultural Revolution," *Tsukuo*, no. 56 (November 1, 1968).

81. For a brief look on Chiang Ching's career, see Ting Wang, *Chiang Ching Chien-chuang* (A Short Biography of Chiang Ching) (Hong Kong, 1967).

82. *The New York Times*, August 6, 1970.

83. *Ibid.*, September 8, 1970.

84. *Ibid.*, August 6, 1970.

CHAPTER 5

1. For some examples of these organizations, see Li Meng-chaun, "The Leading Organs of Political Movements in the Past," *Tsukuo*, no. 31 (October 1, 1966), pp. 34–35.

2. *Jen-min Jih-pao*, February 15, 1952.

3. *Jen-min Jih-pao*, April 3, 1952.

4. These interview data are from a report by Frederick T. C. Yu, submitted to Dr. Ithiel de Sola Pool of the Center for International Studies, M.I.T.

5. For a general discussion on social mobilization and integration, see Karl W. Deutsch, "Social Mobilization and Political Development," *The American Political Science Review*, LV: 3 (September 1961).

6. Allen S. Whiting, *China Crosses the Yalu* (New York, 1960).

7. For more on this subject, see James R. Townsend, *Political Participation in Communist China* (Berkeley and Los Angeles, 1967).

8. *Jen-min Jih-pao*, March 4, 1953.

9. Karl Deutsch, in a general discussion on the building of national strength in new nations, also mentions the dilemma of increasing versus decreasing political control over society. See Karl W. Deutsch, *Nationalism and Social Communication* (Cambridge, 1966), pp. 83–84.

10. Charles Neuhauser, "The Chinese Communist Party in the 1960's: Prelude to the Cultural Revolution," *The China Quarterly*, no. 32 (October–December 1967), p. 20.

11. Tung Chi-ping and Humphrey Evans, *The Thought Revolution* (New York, 1966), p. 160.

12. H. C. Chuang, *The Little Red Book and Current Chinese Language* (Berkeley, 1968), pp. 33–41.

13. See Dennis J. Doolin, trans. *Communist China; the Politics of Student Op-*

position (Stanford, 1964), especially pp. 60–67; and J. Chester Cheng, ed., *The Politics of the Chinese Red Army* (Stanford, 1966), p. 13.

14. *Jen-min Jih-pao,* July 25, 1966.

15. Chao Tsung, "An Account of the 'Great Proletarian Cultural Revolution' (Part 14)," *Tsukuo,* no. 60 (March 1, 1969).

16. Charles Neuhauser, "The Chinese Communist Party in the 1960's: Prelude to the Cultural Revolution," *The China Quarterly,* no. 32 (October–December 1967), p. 35.

17. From a booklet published in Communist China to clarify the key terms used in official documents on the Cultural Revolution; see *Current Background,* no. 904 (April 20, 1970).

18. Chao Tsung, "An Account of the 'Great Proletarian Cultural Revolution' (Part 14)," *Tsukuo,* no. 60 (March 1, 1969), pp. 40–41.

19. "Speech of Mao Tse-tung at the Central Work Conference (October 25, 1966)," *Tsukuo,* no. 48 (March 1, 1968), p. 41.

20. "Collection of Mao Tse-tung's Directives during the Cultural Revolution (Part 1)," *Tsukuo,* no. 66 (September 1, 1969), p. 44.

21. "Collection of Mao Tse-tung's Directives during the Cultural Revolution (Part 2)," *Tsukuo,* no. 67 (October 1, 1969).

22. *Mainichi* (Tokyo), November 8, 1966.

23. *The New York Times,* July 27, 1968.

24. *NCNA,* June 20, 1966.

25. *Mainichi* (Tokyo), January 5, 1967.

26. *Tokyo Shimbun,* March 30, 1967.

27. Philip Bridgham, "Mao's 'Cultural Revolution': Origin and Development," *The China Quarterly,* no. 29 (January–March 1967), pp. 30–31.

28. *Asahi* (Tokyo), September 25, 1967.

29. *The New York Times,* July 27, 1968.

30. *NCNA,* June 20, 1966.

31. For this aspect of the reconstruction effort, see Philip Bridgham, "Mao's Cultural Revolution: The Struggle to Seize Power," *The China Quarterly,* no. 41 (January–March 1970).

32. See the table in Tsai Tan-yeh, "Cultural and Educational Work," *Studies on Chinese Communism,* vol. 4, no. 1 (January 10, 1970).

33. *SCMP,* no. 4569–4573, p. 15.

34. *SCMP,* no. 4597–4601, p. 205.

35. *SCMP,* no. 4569–4573, p. 18.

36. *Wen-hui Pao,* October 5, 1969.

37. See, for example, *Hsin Anhwei Jih-pao,* February 5, 1969.

38. *SCMP,* no. 4584–4588, p. 31.

39. *SCMP,* no. 4634–4638, p. 1.

40. For the concept of communalization of communication, see Alex Inkeles, "The Totalitarian Mystique: Some Impressions of the Dynamics of Totalitarian Society," in *Totalitarianism,* ed. by Carl J. Friedrich (New York, 1964), pp. 101–102.

41. *SCMP,* no. 4584–4588, p. 31.

42. *SCMP,* no. 4569–4573, p. 19.

43. *Selected Works of Mao Tse-tung,* vol. II (Peking, 1965), pp. 337–338 and vol. III (Peking, 1965), pp. 227–228 and 321–324.

44. *NCNA,* February 8, 1966.

45. *SCMP,* no. 4569–4573, p. 21.

46. From R. H. Tawney's Foreward to *The Protestant Ethic and the Spirit of Capitalism,* by Max Weber, trans. by Talcott Parsons (New York, 1958), p. 2.

47. *SCMP,* no. 4584–4588, p. 31.

48. A. Doak Barnett, *Cadres, Bureaucracy, and Political Power in Communist China* (New York, 1967), p. 33.

49. Chou En-lai, "A Great Decade," *Ten Glorious Years* (Peking, 1960), p. 60.

50. Ko Ching-shih, "Mass Movements on the Industrial Front," *Ten Glorious Years* (Peking, 1960), p. 192.

51. T. A. Hsia, "A Terminological Study of the Hsia-Fang Movement," Studies in Chinese Communist Terminology (Berkeley, 1963), p. 2.

52. Hsia, *op. cit.*, p. 3.

53. T. A. Hsia, "Metaphor, Myth, Ritual, and the People's Commune," Studies in Chinese Communist Terminology (Berkeley, 1961), p. 12. The campaign of exterminating sparrows was called a "great battle" and the participants "brave warriors."

54. Karl W. Deutsch, "Social Mobilization and Political Development," *op. cit.*

55. See Alex Inkeles, *Public Opinion in Soviet Russia* (Cambridge, 1958), pp. 67–93; and see Frederick C. Barghoorn, *Politics in the USSR* (Boston, 1966), pp. 164–172.

56. For a comprehensive description of this system, see Frederick T. C. Yu, *Mass Persuasion in Communist China* (New York, 1964), pp. 78–89.

57. *Jen-min Jih-pao*, January 12, 1955.

58. See, for example, the organization of 3,000 "reporters" and "temporary reporters" in Shanghai in November 1953, *Jen-min Jih-pao*, November 21, 1953.

59. See Chen Feng, "Communist China's Cultural Work in 1964," *Tsukuo*, no. 5 (May 1, 1965).

60. Alex Inkeles, *Public Opinion in Soviet Russia* (Cambridge, 1958), p. 87.

61. *Ibid.*, p. 90.

62. *Ibid.*, p. 85.

CHAPTER 6

1. *The New York Times*, December 4, 1964.

2. *Union Research Service*, 55: 1 (April 1, 1969).

3. Yeh Knang Chien, "The Confusion of the Provincial Radio Broadcasting Stations," *Tsukuo*, no. 35 (February 1, 1967).

4. For a description of a county radio station in Communist China, see A. Doak Barnett, *Cadres, Bureaucracy, and Political Power in Communist China* (New York, 1967), pp. 270–271; for a more factual description of the radio in China, see Alan P. L. Liu, "Radio Broadcasting in Communist China," mimeographed (Center for International Studies, M.I.T., June 1, 1964).

5. *Hsin-wen Chan-hsien*, no. 5 (1958).

6. *Hsin-hua Yueh-pao* (New China Monthly) (May 1951), p. 81.

7. *Jen-min Jih-pao*, February 6, 1954.

8. Alex Inkeles, *Public Opinion in Soviet Russia* (Cambridge, 1958), p. 256.

9. *Hsin-wen Chan-hsien*, no. 5 (1958).

10. *Ibid.*

11. For more on this, see Alice Langeley Hsieh, *Communist China's Strategy in the Nuclear Era* (Englewood Cliffs, 1962); and John Gittings, *The Role of the Chinese Army* (London, 1967).

12. "A Day with Radio Peking," *Current Scene*, II: 37 (July 15, 1964).

13. Hadley Cantril and Gordon W. Allport, *The Psychology of Radio* (New York, 1941), pp. 19–21.

14. *Hsin-wen Chan-hsien*, no. 6 (1959).

15. A. Doak Barnett, *op. cit.*, p. 271.

16. *Jen-min Jih-pao*, August 10, 1966.

17. Ting I-feng, "Some Suggestions on the Problem of the Standardization of the Chinese Language," in *Hsien-tai Han-yu Kwei-fang Wen-ti Hsueh-shu Hwei-yi Wen-chien Hwei-pien* (A Collection of Materials Presented at the Conference on Standardization of Modern Chinese Language) (Peking, 1956), p. 143.

18. *Jen-min Jih-pao*, February 6, 1954.

19. *Hsin-wen Chan-hsien*, 5 (1958).

20. Yu Yu-hsiu, "Radio in the Villages," *China Reconstructs* (April 1963), p. 12.

21. For an example of the historic peasant's image of central authority, see C. K. Yang, *Chinese Communist Society: The Family and the Village* (Cambridge, 1965), p. 108.

22. For some examples of the peasants using official terms to describe their experiences, see Jan Myrdal, *Report from a Chinese Village* (New York, 1966).

CHAPTER 7

1. For general discussion on the relationship between the press, literacy, and modernization, see Daniel Lerner, *The Passing of Traditional Society* (Glencoe, 1958).

2. Ignatius Peng Yao, "The New China News Agency: How It Serves the Party," *Journalism Quarterly* (Winter 1963), p. 84.

3. For a general analysis of the pattern of control, see Franz Schurmann, *Ideology and Organization in Communist China* (Berkeley and Los Angeles, 1966), p. 313.

4. *Communist China Digest*, no. 25 (November 1960), p. 94.

5. *Selected Works of Mao Tse-tung*, vol. IV (Peking, 1967), p. 241.

6. *Jen-min Jih-pao*, April 23, 1950.

7. *Jen-min Jih-pao*, May 26, 1954.

8. *Jen-min Jih-pao*, March 24, 1954.

9. *SCMP*, no. 1328, p. 3.

10. For some examples of these criticisms, see the section on the press in Roderick MacFarquhar, *The Hundred Flowers Campaign and the Chinese Intellectuals* (New York, 1960).

11. *Extracts from Chinese Mainland Magazines*, no. 151, pp. 23–24.

12. *Jen-min Jih-pao*, October 19, 1954.

13. *SCMP*, no. 2980, p. 4.

14. Tung Chi-ping and Humphrey Evans, *The Thought Revolution* (New York, 1966), p. 71.

15. For a general discussion of bureaucracy and mass communication in totalitarian countries, see Paul Kecskemeti, "Totalitarian Communications as a Means of Control," *Public Opinion Quarterly*, vol. XIV (Summer 1950).

16. Franz Schurmann, *op. cit.*, pp. 62–68.

17. This functional categorization is inspired by Hans Speier's classification of the radio news in Nazi Germany: see Hans Speier, *Social Order and the Risks of War* (New York, 1952), pp. 343–356.

18. Radio Canton, January 11, 1967.

CHAPTER 8

1. Raymond Nunn, *Publishing in Mainland China* (Cambridge, 1966); and Alan P. L. Liu, "Book Publishing in Communist China," mimeographed (Center for International Studies, M.I.T., October 1965).

2. A. Doak Barnett, *Cadres, Bureaucracy, and Political Power in Communist China* (New York, 1967), p. 270.

3. *Jen-min Jih-pao*, July 23, 1957 and *Kuang-ming Jih-pao*, February 18, 1957.

4. The plans submitted by the Chinese publishing houses to the Party were similar to the "thematic plan" that Soviet publishing houses were required to submit to their Party authority; see Boris I. Gorokhoff, *Publishing in the U.S.S.R.* (Washington, D.C., 1959).

5. *Jen-min Jih-pao*, March 19, 1958.

6. *Jen-min Jih-pao*, February 16, 1967.

7. *Jen-min Jih-pao*, June 12, 1954.

8. *Jen-min Jih-pao,* August 30, 1955.

9. The Soviet Union used exactly the same tactics in its era of industrialization; see Adam B. Ulam, "The Russian Political System" in *Patterns of Government,* ed. by Samuel H. Beer and Adam B. Ulam (New York, 1965), p. 641.

10. *Wen-hui Pao,* February 2, 1959.

11. The issue of the "revolutionary enthusiasm" of base-level cadres was again revived in the Cultural Revolution; see Charles Neuhauser, "The Chinese Communist Party in the 1960's," *The China Quarterly,* no. 32 (October–December 1967), pp. 7–14.

12. *Jen-min Jih-pao,* March 25, 1963.

13. *Jen-min Jih-pao,* August 1, 1965.

14. *Wen-hui Pao,* February 17, 1957.

15. *Jen-min Jih-pao,* July 20, 1966.

16. *Jen-min Jih-pao,* December 23, 1958.

17. *SCMP,* no. 2671, p. 21.

18. Edward A. Shils, "Toward a Modern Intellectual Community in the New States," *Education and Political Development,* ed. by James S. Coleman (Princeton, N.J., 1965), p. 498.

CHAPTER 9

1. Joseph T. Klapper, "The Comparative Effects of Various Media," *The Process and Effects of Mass Communications,* ed. by Wilbur Schramm (Urbana, 1954), pp. 91–105.

2. For some empirical findings on this, see Frederick W. Frey, "Socialization to National Identification: Turkish Peasants" (Paper delivered at the 1966 Annual Meeting of the American Political Science Association, New York).

3. Quoted in Alex Inkeles, *Public Opinion in Soviet Russia* (Cambridge, 1958), p. 280.

4. For detailed study of the structure and operation of the Chinese Communist film industry, see Alan P. L. Liu, *The Film Industry in Communist China* (Cambridge, 1965).

5. See the speech by Hsia Yen, former deputy Minister of Culture, in *SCMP,* no. 1867.

6. *Jen-min Jih-pao,* January 12, 1954.

7. *Jen-min Jih-pao,* January 12, 1954.

8. *Ibid.*

9. *SCMP,* no. 1787, p. 33.

10. *Ta-tsung Tien-ying* (Popular Cinema), no. 22 (1959), p. 25.

11. Chao Tsung, "Communist China's Art and Literature in 1964," *Tsukuo,* no. 5 (May 1, 1965), p. 37.

12. *Ta-tsung Tien-ying,* no. 11 (1962).

13. *Ta-kung Pao,* December 14, 1962, and *Jen-min Jih-pao,* January 25, 1965.

14. *Ta-tsung Tien-ying,* no. 10 (1965), p. 21.

15. A. Doak Barnett, *Cadres, Bureaucracy, and Political Power in Communist China* (New York, 1967), p. 383.

16. *Kwang-ming Jih-pao,* May 1, 1963.

17. Chen Feng, "Communist China's Cultural Affairs in 1965," *Tsukuo,* no. 4 (April 1, 1966).

18. According to Inkeles (*op. cit.,* p. 305), even as late as 1947, rural film projection in the Soviet Union remained a weak link. A major reason for this was, of course, the destruction of the war.

CHAPTER 10

1. Professor Hiniker's research and the research for this book were both part of the same research project sponsored by the Advanced Research Projects

Agency of the Department of Defense (ARPA) under contract 920F–9717 and monitored by the Air Force Office of Scientific Research under contract AF 49(638)–1237. The data used in this chapter are from Paul J. Hiniker, "The Effect of Mass Communication in Communist China" (Ph.D. diss. M.I.T., 1966).

2. Peter H. Rossi and Raymond A. Bauer, "Some Patterns of Soviet Communications Behavior," *Public Opinion Quarterly*, XVI: 4 (Winter 1952–1953), p. 654.

3. *Ibid.*, p. 663.

4. *Ibid.*, p. 658.

5. Kenneth R. Walker, "Collectivization in Retrospect: The 'Socialist High Tide,' of Autumn 1955—Spring 1956," *The China Quarterly*, no. 26 (April–June 1966).

6. C. S. Chen, ed., *Rural People's Communes in Lien-chiang*, trans. by Charles Price Ridley (Stanford, 1969), pp. 44–49.

7. *The New York Times*, April 6, 1969.

8. One such place is Shanghai; see *Wen-hui Pao*, October 19, 1967.

CHAPTER 11

1. Dennis J. Doolin, trans., *Communist China: The Politics of Student Opposition* (Stanford, 1964), pp. 13–14.

2. John King Fairbank, *The United States and China* (New York, 1958), p. 313.

3. *NCNA*, October 20, 1966.

4. *Wen-hui Pao*, October 19, 1967.

5. *Jen-min Jih-pao*, June 19, 1966.

6. Edward A. Shils, "Toward A Modern Intellectual Community In The New States," in *Education and Political Development*, ed. by James S. Coleman (Princeton, 1965), p. 502.

7. Karl W. Deutsch, *Nationalism and Social Communication*, (Cambridge, 1966), p. 181.

8. *Ibid.*

9. *The New York Times*, December 17, 1969.

10. *NCNA*, October 16, 1966.

Bibliography

BOOKS

Barghoorn, Frederick C. *Politics in the U.S.S.R.* Boston: Little, Brown and Co., 1966.

Barnett, A. Doak. *China On the Eve of Communist Takeover.* New York: Frederick A. Praeger, 1963.

———. *Cadres, Bureaucracy, and Political Power in Communist China.* New York: Columbia University Press, 1967.

Bauer, Raymond A. *The New Man in Soviet Psychology.* Cambridge, Mass.: Harvard University Press, 1952.

Cantril, Hadley and Gordon W. Allport. *The Psychology of Radio.* New York: Peter Smith, 1941.

Chen, C. S., ed. *Rural People's Communes in Lien-chiang.* Translated by Charles Price Ridley. Stanford: The Hoover Institution on War, Revolution, and Peace, 1969.

Cheng, J. Chester, ed. *The Politics of the Chinese Red Army.* Stanford: The Hoover Institution on War, Revolution and Peace, 1966.

Chin, Tak-kai. *A study on Chinese Communist Propaganda, Its Policy and Operations.* Hong Kong, 1954.

Chou, En-lai. "A Great Decade." In *Ten Glorious Years.* Peking: Foreign Language Press, 1960.

———. "Current Tasks of Reforming the Written Language." In *Reform of the Chinese Written Language.* Peking: Foreign Language Press, 1965.

Deutsch, Karl W. "Nation Building and National Development: Some issues for Political Research." *Nation Building,* edited by Karl W. Deutsch and William J. Foltz. New York: Atherton Press, 1963.

———. *Nationalism and Social Communication.* Cambridge, Mass.: M.I.T. Press, 1966.

———. *The Nerves of Government.* New York: Free Press, 1966.

Doolin, Dennis J., trans. *Communist China: The Politics of Student Opposition.* Stanford: The Hoover Institution on War, Revolution, and Peace, 1964.

Eckstein, Alexander. *Communist China's Economic Growth and Foreign Trade.* New York: McGraw-Hill Co., 1966.

Etzioni, Amitai. *Political Unification.* New York: Holt, Rinehart and Winston, 1965.

Fairbank, John King. *The United States and China.* New York: Viking Press, 1958.

Feuerwerker, Albert. ed. *History in Communist China.* Cambridge, Mass.: M.I.T. Press, 1969.

Friedrich, Carl J. and Zbigniew K. Brzezinski. *Totalitarian Dictatorship and Autocracy.* New York: Frederick A. Praeger, 1965.

Gittings, John. *The Role of the Chinese Army.* London: Oxford University Press, 1967.

Gorokhoff, Boris I. *Publishing in the U.S.S.R.* Washington, D.C.: Council on Library Resources, 1959.

Houn, Franklin. *To Change A Nation.* New York: Free Press of Glencoe, Ill., 1961.

Hsieh, Alice Langeley. *Communist China's Strategy in the Nuclear Era.* Englewod Cliffs, N.J.: Prentice-Hall, 1962.

Inkeles, Alex. *Public Opinion in Soviet Russia.* Cambridge, Mass.: Harvard University Press, 1958.

—— and Raymond A. Bauer. *The Soviet Citizen.* Cambridge, Mass.: Harvard University Press, 1959.

——. "The Totalitarian Mystique: Some Impressions of the Dynamics of Totalitarian Society." In *Totaliarianism,* edited by Carl J. Friedrich. New York: Grosset and Dunlap, 1964.

Kahn, Harold and Albert Feuerwerker. "The Ideology of Scholarship: China's New Historiography," In *History in Communist China,* edited by Albert Feuerwerker. Cambridge, Mass.: M.I.T. Press, 1969.

Klapper, Joseph T. "The Comparative Effects of Various Media." *The Process and Effects of Mass Communications,* edited by Wilbur Schramm. Urbana, Ill.: University of Illinois Press, 1954.

Ko, Ching-shih. "Mass Movement on the Industrial Front." In *Ten Glorious Years.* Peking: Foreign Lanugage Press, 1960.

Lerner, Daniel. *The Passing of Traditional Society.* Glencoe, Ill.: Free Press of Glencoe, Ill., 1964.

Loh, Robert and Humphrey Evans. *Escape from Red China.* New York: Coward-McCann, 1962.

MacFarquhar, Roderick. *The Hundred Flowers Campaign and the Chinese Intellectuals.* New York: Frederick A. Praeger, 1960.

Mao, Tse-tung. *Selected Works of Mao Tse-tung.* Volumes I, III, and IV. Peking: Foreign Language Press, 1965 and 1967.

Munro, Donald J. "Chinese Communist Treatment of the Thinkers of the Hundred Schools Period." In *History in Communist China,* edited by Albert Feuerwerker. Cambridge, Mass.: M.I.T. Press, 1969.

Myrdal, Jan. *Report from a Chinese Village.* New York: Pantheon Books, 1966.

Nunn, Raymond. *Publishing in Communist China*. Cambridge, Mass.: M.I.T. Press, 1966.

Pipes, Richard. "Communism and Russian History." In *Soviet and Chinese Communism: Similarities and Differences,* edited by Donald W. Treadgold. Seattle and London: University of Washington Press, 1967.

Pool, Ithiel de Sola. "The Mass Media and Politics in Modernization Process." In *Communication and Political Development,* edited by Lucian W. Pye. Princeton, N.J.: Princeton University Press, 1963.

Pye, Lucian W. *Communication and Political Development*. Princeton, N.J.: Princeton University Press, 1963.

Rostow, W. W. *The Prospects for Communist China*. New York: John Wiley & Sons, 1954.

Schram, Stuart R. *The Political Thought of Mao Tse-tung*. New York: Frederick A. Praeger, 1963.

Schurmann, Franz. *Ideology and Organization in Communist China*. Berkeley and Los Angeles: University of California Press, 1966.

Shils, Edward A. "Toward a Modern Intellectual Community in the New States." In *Education and Political Development,* edited by James S. Coleman. Princeton, N.J.: Princeton University Press, 1965.

Snow, Edgar. *Red Star Over China*. New York: Grove Press, 1961.

Speier, Hans. *Social Order and the Risks of War*. New York: George W. Stewart, Publisher, 1952.

Tawney, R. H. Foreword to *The Protestant Ethic and the Spirit of Capitalism,* by Max Weber. Translated by Talcott Parsons. New York: Charles Scribner's Sons, 1958.

Ting, I-feng. "Some Suggestions on the Problems of the Standardization of the Chinese Language." In *Hsien-tai Han-yu Kwei-fang Wen-ti Hsueh-shu Hwei-yi Wen-chien Hwei-pien*. Peking: Science Publishing House, 1956.

Ting, Wang. *Chiang Ching Chien-chuang* (A Short Biography of Chiang Ching). Hong Kong: Tang-tai Chung-kuo Yen-chiu Sou, 1967.

––––––. *Chung-kun Wen-hua Ta-ke-ming Tze-liao Hwei-pien* (A Collection of Materials on the Great Proletarian Revolution in Communist China). Hong Kong: Ming Pao Yueh Kan Chu Pan, 1967.

Townsend, James R. *Political Participation in Communist China*. Berkeley and Los Angeles: University of California Press, 1967.

Tregear, T. R. *A Geography of China*. Chicago: Aldine Publishing Co., 1965.

Tung, Chi-ping and Humphrey Evans. *The Thought Revolution*. New York: Coward-McCann, 1966.

Ulam, Adam B. "The Russian Political System." In *Patterns of Gov-*

ernment, edited by Samuel H. Beer and Adam B. Ulam. New York: Random House, 1965.

Vogel, Ezra F. *Canton Under Communism: Programs and Politics in a Provincial Capital, 1949–1968.* Cambridge, Mass.: Harvard University Press, 1969.

Whiting, Allen S. *China Crosses the Yalu.* New York: Macmillan and Co., 1960.

————. "Political Dynamics: The Communist Party of China." In *Modern Political Systems: Asia,* edited by Robert E. Ward and Roy C. Macridis. Englewood Cliffs, N.J.: Prentice-Hall, 1963.

Wu, Yu-chang. "Report on the Current Tasks of Reforming the Written Language and the Draft Scheme for a Chinese Phonetic Alphabet." In *Reform of the Chinese Written Language.* Peking: Foreign Language Press, 1965.

Yang, C. K. *Chinese Communist Society: The Family and the Village.* Cambridge, Mass.: M.I.T. Press, 1965.

Yu, Frederick T. C. *Mass Persuasion in Communist China.* New York: Frederick A. Praeger, 1964.

Anonymous. *Ti-chin Yen-chiu Lun-wen-chi* (An Anthology of Studies on Enemy Situation). Vol. 3. Taipei: Kuo-fan Yen-chiu Yuan, 1962.

JOURNAL ARTICLES

Bridgham, Philip. "Mao's Cultural Revolution: Origin and Development." *The China Quarterly* 29 (January–March 1967).

————. "Mao's Cultural Revolution in 1967: The Struggle to Seize Power." *The China Quarterly* 34 (April–June 1968).

————. "Mao's Cultural Revolution: The Struggle to Seize Power." *The China Quarterly* 41 (January–March 1970).

Chao, Chung. "Cultural Affairs of Communist China in 1967." *Tsukuo* 49 (April 1, 1968).

————. "An Account of the 'Great Proletarian Cultural Revolution' (Part 7)." *Tsukuo* 52 (July 1, 1968).

————. "An Account of the 'Great Proletarian Cultural Revolution' (Part 8)." *Tsukuo* 53 (August 1, 1968).

————. "An Account of the 'Great Proletarian Cultural Revolution' (Part 9)." *Tsukuo* 54 (September 1968).

————. "An Account of the 'Great Proletarian Cultural Revolution' (Part 11)." *Tsukuo* 56 (November 1, 1968).

————. "An Account of the 'Great Proletarian Cultural Revolution' (Part 13)." *Tsukuo* 58 (January 1, 1969).

Chao, Tse-jen. "A Study of Chinese Communist Broadcasting." *Ta-lu Fei-chin Chi-pao* (July–September 1962).

Chao, Tsung. "Communist China's Art and Literature." *Tsukuo* 5 (May 1, 1965).

———. "A Brief Account of the 'Great Proletarian Cultural Revolution' (Part 2)." *Tsukuo* 41 (August 1967).

———. "A Brief Account of the 'Great Proletarian Cultural Revolution' (Part 5)." *Tsukuo* 44 (November 1967).

———. "A Brief Account of the 'Great Proletarian Cultural Revolution' (Part 6)." *Tsukuo* 45 (December 1967).

———. "An Account of the 'Great Proletarian Cultural Revolution' (Part 14)." *Tsukuo* 60 (March 1, 1969).

———. "A Brief Account of the 'Great Proletarian Cultural Revolution' (Part 3)." *Tsukuo* 42 (September 1, 1967).

———. "A Brief Account of the 'Great Proletarian Cultural Revo lution' (Part 4)." *Tsukuo* 43 (October 1, 1967).

———. "An Account of the 'Great Proletarian Cultural Revolution' (Part 21)." *Tsukuo* 67 (October 1, 1969).

Chen, Feng. "Communist China's Cultural Work in 1964." *Tsukuo* 5 (May 1, 1965).

Chen, Feng. "Communist China's Cultural Work in 1965." *Tsukuo* 4 (April 1, 1966).

Cheng, Fen. "Communist China's Cultural Work in 1963." *Tsukuo* 6 (June 1964).

Chiang, I-san. "Communist Political Work in the Army Units." *Tsukuo* 9 (September 1965).

———. "The Art and Literary Work in the People's Liberation Army." *Tsukuo* 31 (October 1, 1966).

Chin, Ssu-kai. "The 'Cultural Revolution' and the Internal Struggle for Power." *Tsukuo* 29 (August 1, 1966).

Chung, Hua-min. "Cultural Affairs of Communist China in 1969." *Tsukuo* 73 (April 1, 1970).

Deutsch, Karl W. "Social Mobilization and Political Development." *The American Political Science Review* LV:3 (September 1961).

Goldman, Merle. "The Fall of Chou Yang." *The China Quarterly* 27 (July–September 1966).

Kecskemeti, Paul. "Totalitarian Communications as a Means of Control: A Note on the Sociology of Propaganda." *Public Opinion Quarterly* XIV (Summer 1950).

Li, Meng-chuan. "The Leading Organs of Political Movements in the Past." *Tsukuo* 31 (October 1, 1966).

Munro, Donald J. "The Yang Hsien-chen Affair." *The China Quarterly* 22 (April–June 1965).

Neuhauser, Charles. "The Chinese Communist Party in the 1960's: Prelude to the Cultural Revolution." *The China Quarterly* 32 (October–December 1967).

Rossi, Peter H. and Raymond A. Bauer. "Some Patterns of Soviet Communication Behavior." *Public Opinion Quarterly* XVI:4 (Winter 1952–1953).

Tsai, Tan-yeh. "Cultural and Educational Work." *Studies on Chinese Communism* IV:1 (January 10, 1970).

Uhalley Jr., Stephen. "The Cultural Revolution and the Attack on the 'Three Family Village.'" *The China Quarterly* 27 (July–September 1966).

Walker, Kenneth R. "Collectivization in Retrospect: The 'Socialist High Tide,' of Autumn 1955–Spring 1956." *The China Quarterly* 26 (April–June 1966).

Yao, Ignatius Peng. "The New China News Agency: How It Serves the Party." *Journalism Quarterly* (Winter 1963).

Yeh, Kang-chien. "The Confusion of the Provincial Radio Broadcasting Stations." *Tsukuo* 35 (February 1, 1967).

Yu, Heng. "The 'Big Stick' of Cultural Revolution—Yao Wen-yuan." *Tsukuo* 55 (October 1, 1968).

———. "Chang Chun-chiao—the 'Roly-Poly' That Cannot Be Pushed over in the Cultural Revolution." *Tsukuo* 56 (November 1, 1968).

Yu, Yu-hsiu. "Radio in the Villages." *China Reconstructs* (April 1963).

Anonymous. "Speech of Mao Tse-tung at the Central Work Conference (October 25, 1966)." *Tsukuo* 48 (March 1, 1968).

———. "Full Text of the 'Ten Articles on Literature and Art.'" *Tsukuo* 67 (October 1, 1969).

———. "Collection of Mao Tse-tung's Directives during the Cultural Revolution, (Part 1)," *Tsukuo* 66 (September 1, 1969).

———. "Collection of Mao Tse-tung's Directives during the Cultural Revolution." *Tsukuo* 67 (October 1, 1969).

———. "Lin Piao and the Cultural Revolution." *Current Scene* VIII:14 (August 1, 1970).

RESEARCH REPORTS

Chuang, H. C. "The Little Red Book and Current Chinese Language." Berkeley: Center for Chinese Studies, Institute for International Studies, University of California, 1968).

Frey, Frederick W. "Socialization to National Identification: Turkish Peasants." Paper presented at 1966 Annual Meeting of the American Political Science Association, New York.

Hiniker, Paul J. "The Effect of Mass Communication in Communist China." Ph.D. dissertation, M.I.T., 1966.

Hollander, Gayle D. "Soviet Newspapers and Magazines." Cambridge, Mass.: Center for International Studies, M.I.T., 1967.

Hsia, T. A. "A Terminological Study of the Hsia-Fang Movement." Berkeley: Center for Chinese Studies, Institute for International Studies, University of California, 1963.

King, Vincent V. S. "Propaganda Campaigns in Communist China." Cambridge, Mass.: Center for International Studies, M.I.T., 1966.

Liu, Alan P. L. "Radio Broadcasting in Communist China." Cambridge, Mass.: Center for International Studies, M.I.T., 1964.
———. "Book Publishing in Communist China." Cambridge, Mass.: Center for International Studies, M.I.T., 1965.
———. "The Film Industry in Communist China." Cambridge, Mass.: Center for International Studies, M.I.T., 1965.
———. "The Press and Journals in Communist China." Cambridge, Mass.: Center for International Studies, M.I.T., 1966.
Serruys, Paul L. M. "Survey of the Chinese Language Reform and the Anti-illiteracy Movement in Communist China." Berkeley: Center for Chinese Studies, Institute of International Studies, University of California, 1962.

NEWSPAPERS

Asahi, Tokyo.
Jen-min Jih-pao (People's Daily), Peking.
Kuang-ming Jih-pao (Kuang-ming Daily), Peking.
Mainichi, Tokyo.
Nihon Keizai Shimbun, Tokyo.
Ta-kung Pao (Impartial Daily), Peking.
Tokyo Shimbun, Tokyo.
Wen-hui Pao (Literary News), Shanghai.

PERIODICALS

Chin-jih Ta-lu (Mainland Today), Taipei.
Chung-kun Yen-chiu (Study on Chinese Communism), Taipei.
Hsin-hua Yueh-pao (New China Monthly), Peking.
Hsin-wen Chan-hsien (News Front), Peking.
Hungchi (Red Flag), Peking.
Ta-lu Fei-chin Chi-pao (Quarterly Report on Mainland China), Taipei.
Ta-tsung Tien-ying (Popular Cinema), Peking.
Tsukuo (China Monthly), Hong Kong.

Index

Anti-intellectualism: of peasants, 29; in Cultural Revolution, 53; in Great Leap Forward, 54. *See also* Mao Tse-tung

Barnett, A. Doak: 13, 148, 165
Bridgham, Philip: 59, 60
Brzezinski, Zbigniew K.: 43

Canton: 14, 67, 158
Changchung, Liaoning: 158
Chang Chung-chiao: 82
Chang Hsi-jo: 19
Changsha, Hunan: 16
Chekiang: 19, 127
Chen Huang-mei: 70
Chen Po-ta: deputy director of Propaganda Department, 37; member of Cultural Revolution Team, 41; heads Cultural Revolution Section, 76; in attack on Tao Chu, 77; controls propaganda work, 79
Chengchow, Honan: 16
Chengtu, Szechwan: 13, 14, 16
Chen, Tu-hsiu: 26
Chiang Ching: joins Cultural Revolution, 62; and drama reform, 63, 66; wins in Shanghai, 67; controls army literary work, 68, 73, 74, 78; deputy of Cultural Revolution Section, 76; conflicts with Tao Chu, 77; controls propaganda, 79, 82; followers of purged, 81; and Li Teh-sheng, 84; controls wall posters, 104
Chien Po-chan: 102
Chinghai: 16
Chi Pen-yu: 81
Chi Yen-min: 70
Chou En-lai: 17, 18, 19, 20
Chou Yang: deputy director of Propaganda Department, 37; allegedly revises Mao's policy, 42; has access to cadres, 43; on propaganda work, 54; and "culture to villages" movement, 65; purged in Cultural Revolution,

76; on propaganda about soldiers, 123; closes publishing companies, 154
Chungking, Szechwan: 13
Cultural Revolution: and integration strategy, 4; destroys mass media, 4, 8; purge of Propaganda Department, 37, 40; campaign techniques, 99

Deutsch, Karl W.: 47, 180
Dialects. *See* Language

Factions: left-wing, 4, 33, 62-64, 65, 81; among Red Guards, 80, 82
Film: structural transformation of industry, 157-159; themes change, 159-163; mobile projection, 163-167
Friedrick, Carl J.: 43
Fukien: 12, 14

Goldman, Merle: 76
Great Leap Forward: affects leadership, 44, 96; as forerunner of Cultural Revolution, 54-55
Group indoctrination: 31
Guerrilla war: affects techniques of persuasion, 28-30

Hanchow, Chekiang: 13
Harbin, Heilungkiang: 15
Hiniker, Paul J.: 168, 169
Honan: 22
Hong Kong: 42
Hsia, T. A.: 113, 114
Hsia, Yen: 70
Hsiamen, Fukien: 14
Hsining, Chinghai: 16
Hunan: 13, 26
Hupei: 19, 22

Identification: as second stage of integration, 2; in Soviet Union, 3
Ideology of mass persuasion: 6, 30-31
Inkeles, Alex: 33, 37, 39, 44, 47, 76, 117, 189

Inner Mongolia: 14
Izvestia: 35

Kiangsu: 19
Ko Ching-shih: 67, 71, 72, 113
Kuo Mo-jo: 23
Kwangsi: 19, 127
Kwangtung: 12, 65
Kweichou: 16

Laipin, Kwangsi: 14
Lanchow, Kansu: 13, 16
Language: national, 17; reform by government, 17-21; dialects, 127-128, 178
Lhasa, Tibet: 16
Liao Mu-sai: 74
Liaoning: 22
Lien-chiang county, Fukien: 172
Lin Mu-han: 42
Lin Piao: defense minister, 58; builds up Mao's prestige, 59-61, 99; purges cadres, 60; allies with Chiang Ching, 73, 74; conflicts with Chiang Ching, 81, 84; and Red Guards, 101
Li Teh-sheng: 84
Literacy: campaign for, 21, 22, 23; among youth, 22
Liu Shao-chi: chairman of republic, 44; and labor unions, 52; on art and literature, 55-57; first-line leader, 97; and work teams, 100; Mao attacks, 101; criticized in wall posters, 104; attacked in mass campaigns, 109
Lu Ting-i: director of Propaganda Department, 37; member of Cultural Revolution Section, 68; Minister of Culture, 70; purged in Cultural Revolution, 76

Mao Tse-tung: on mass persuasion, 8, 25-28, 53, 54; anti-intellectualism of, 25-27, 29; talks with Edgar Snow, 26; on Great Leap Forward, 27, 29; faith of in campaign, 32; on media, 33; on physical education, 39; needs intellectuals, 40; and propaganda policy, 41-42; and purge of propaganda apparatus, 44; speech of on contradiction, 50; criticized in media, 57; speech of at Tenth Plenum, 63-64; attacks journals, 69; statements of on Cultural Revolution, 75-76; as rear-line leader, 97; image of among masses, 100; writes wall posters, 101
Marxism-Leninism: affects persuasion, 30

Mass campaign: as instrument of persuasion, 31-32; defined, 87; classified, 87; organization of, 88-92; Three-anti, 89-92 *passim;* Five-anti, 89-92 *passim;* Anti-America Aid-Korea, 93; Study of Election Law, 94; for study of socialist transition, 94; for study of national constitution, 94; Suppression of Counterrevolutionaries, 95; Hundred Flowers, 95; Lei Feng, 98; for study of Mao's thought, 106-111; effects of, 111-115. *See also* Ideology of mass persuasion
Mass media: role of in nation-building, 1, 2; in penetration phase, 2, 3; in identification phase, 3; Lenin's concept of, 6; institutional characteristics of, 9-10; and oral propaganda, 10, 32-33; characteristics of individual, 10
Mass organization: 47-52
Ministry of Culture: 70

Nanking: 14
National identity, symbols of: 85-86
National will: 180-181
Neuhauser, Charles: 41
Newspapers. *See* Press
Ningching, Tibet: 16

Paochi, Shensi: 14, 16
Paotou, Inner Mongolia: 16
Party fraction: 49
Peasants: and workers, 179
Peking: 19, 21, 66, 67, 71, 78, 80, 158
Peking University: 26
Penetration: as first phase of integration, 2; in the Soviet Union, 3
Peng Chen: mayor of Peking, 68; in purge of Ministry of Culture, 70; conflicts with Mao, 72; struggles for survival, 73; conflicts with Chiang Ching, 74; Mao distrusts, 75
Peng Teh-hui: Minister of Defense, 57; challenges Mao, 58
Politburo: 40, 41, 43
Political consciousness, views on: 7-8
Political Departments, in army: 58-59
Po Yi-po: 89
Press: types of, 130-131; control of, 132; circulation, 134; political functions of, 136-137; in Great Leap Forward, 137-138; in Cultural Revolution, 139; collective reading of, 139-142; in Hsinhsing county, 140-142; and national integration, 143-146

Propaganda department: of Central Committee, 37-45; compared with Soviet, 39; in regions, 45-47; purged in Cultural Revolution, 52-86

Propaganda teams: 82, 106

Propagandists and reporters: 115

Publishing: structure, 147-148; control of, 149; in Cultural Revolution, 149; changing emphasis of, 150-153; collective book reading, 153-154; rural circulation, 154; and cultural gap, 155

Radio: wired broadcasting, 118-119; and mass campaigns, 121-122; propaganda function of, 122-123; in Great Leap Forward, 123; in Cultural Revolution, 124; collective listening, 125-127; and diversity of language, 127-128; affects national integration, 128; and cultural gap, 128

Reception: patterned, 169; "involvement" in politics, 170; isolation of peasants, 170-173

Red Guards: use new political terms, 20, 21; attack propaganda officials, 42; as substitute for youth league, 52; creation of, 78, 101; seize media, 79; functions of, 102-103; unity of, 178

Regionalism: and national integration, 12-13; in Cultural Revolution, 84

Reporters. *See* Propagandists and reporters

Schram, Stuart: 29

Serruys, Paul: 20

Shanghai: 13, 14, 66, 67, 71, 78, 82, 158

Shansi: 12, 22, 46

Shantung: 21

Shao Chuan-lin: 49, 69

Sheng Yen-pin: 70

Shensi: 12, 154

Shils, Edward: 156, 179

Sian, Shensi: 19, 158

Sinkiang: 14, 16

Snow, Edgar: 26

Soche, Sinkiang: 16

Social infrastructure: 4-6

Study class, on Mao's thought: 107

Szechwan: 12, 13, 16, 19

Tao Chu: 77, 78, 81, 103

Teng Hsiao-ping: 77, 78, 101

Teng To: 74, 75

Tibet: 16

Tienshui, Kansu: 13

Tihua, Sinkiang: 14

Transport: affects media, 5; affects integration, 13, 16; highway in Southwest, 16; railway, 13, 14, 16

Vogel, Ezra: 65, 66

Wall posters: 103-105

Wang Li: 81

Wang Mu: 132

Wenchou, Chekiang: 127

Whiting, Allen S.: 40

Wuhan, Hupei: 16

Wu Han: 70, 71, 72, 74

Wu Yu-chang: 19

Yaen, Kweichou: 16

Yangtze River: 14

Yao Wen-yuan: 71, 72, 82

Yingtan, Kiangsi: 14

Young Communist League: 48

Youth, forced to rural areas: 172-173

Yunnan: 16, 19